S,

Books

All Rights reserved

2014 Horses a Religion: By Stephen Place

No part of this book may be reproduced in any written, electronic or photocopying form without the written permission of the author Stephen Place

Although every precaution has been taken to verify the accuracy of the information contained herein, the author and publisher assume no responsibility for any errors or omissions. No liability is assumed for any damages that may result from the information contained therein

Printed and Bound by Createspace

Front cover designed by Stephen Place

Jacket designed by Stephen Place

Interior designed by Stephen Place

Foreword:

My first win at Badminton was in 2009 and the first person to hug me and share my joy in the press tent was Stephen Place.

Years before when I was ten he taught me at a pony club rally when I was a member of the Rockwood pony club.

He also taught my group at Pony club camp at Beverly racecourse and he would join in with us all playing cowboys and Indians on the Westwood. The camps at Beverly were great times and he ensured we had great fun on our days out at Bridlington on the fair ground.

More importantly he was one of my first sponsors when he gave me a training bursary of £500.

We all have our goals and ambitions, some are greater than others. Stephen achieved his by completing the International one star at Tweseldown and many other two and three day events throughout his career in eventing.

A real character and good friend I am delighted he has written his story. It's a funny, honest rollercoaster from the gypsies at Appleby horse fair to international three day eventing.

I hope you all enjoy it.

Oliver Townend.

Chapter One

'Get him off me Dad, get him off me!' I screamed out loud to my dad who was stood mesmerised at the edge of the field. He ran across the muddy grass and started hitting the pony I was sat on as hard as he could but it was not for moving. He had me trapped against a building wall and was rubbing my right leg against the concrete. It was not hurting me as such, but my new rubber riding boots which were my pride and joy were being scratched to bits.

We had gone to Wilsden in Bradford that Saturday morning to meet Judith Drake, she was the daughter of Alan Drake, a horse dealer who was well known in the area. We were looking at a pony that was for sale. He was 14.2 hands high and four years old. It was a gorgeous black pony and I sat on it straight away without seeing anyone else on him first. I got on by jumping onto him off the wall at the edge of the field. He was already tacked up and waiting for us. After I had got on he went away from the wall into the field and as I trotted him around in a circle he suddenly veered away straight towards the stable building in the middle of the field and began rubbing himself and me against the wall.

My dad just hit it and hit it to get it away from the wall. The pony was very calm, it was just determined to break my leg I think. I got off as soon as my leg was free and it ran off around the field. We didn't buy it.

My earliest recollection of the horses in my life was about three years earlier when I was eight. I was on a family holiday at Morecambe and my brother and I were allowed to go on a pony ride along the beach and right out to the sea. It was lovely and warm and I was riding a lovely Arab cross that was grey. We had a great time and that was it I was hooked. My dad had worked with hunting horses when he was sixteen and had technically been in service. That did not last long though and he returned to Bradford to be a wool sorter, the same as his dad and brother. His interest in horses though never waned and this was passed to me and my sister. My brother pursued fishing and motorbikes but has a horse now he is in his forties.

I had ridden quite a few different types of horses from being eight years old. All my school holidays were spent with horses wherever I could get to be in their company. I discovered about six miles from my home, a riding school at Lidget Green in Bradford called Birks Fold. This was owned by Mr and Mrs Robinson. Percy was a really nice bloke, he loved having the young people about and loved his horses.

My first ride, which we had at the end of the day by working hard all day, was a bay called Thunder. We would ride them bareback out to the field which was some way away from the actual stable yard and took about half an hour. We always found a wall or two to jump on the way to the field or somewhere to canter.

To earn this precious ride though, we had to catch the horses and ponies in the morning, groom them and tack them up. They spent most of the day in tack and did several rides. We had to walk alongside the horses whether or not it was in the field, round and round in a circle in a lesson, or walking with them out on a hack. We had two rides to walk alongside them, the half hour or full hour. After checking the diary first thing on a morning we all knew what time the rides were booked for and you could be sure that when the one hour hacks were on all the kids were nowhere to be found.

They had a tuck shop at the stables run by Mrs Robinson, she was Lithuanian and fearsome, everyone was scared of her. She was known as Mrs Rob and sold sweets and panda pop and crisps. She made a fortune out of that shop. They were clever really as they had free labour from loads of horse mad kids every weekend and also throughout all the school holidays and then made a small fortune out of us selling us food and drink. We did though, regularly, spend our lunch money on sweets and eat dog biscuits to keep us going!

I met a lot of people here from all walks of life. Some of them are still friends now. A lad called Mathew who lived in my street was a friend of mine and he too had the horse bug. We went everywhere together and we encouraged each other to keep running on the long jog home when we were very late leaving the stables, which was very frequent.

I had been coming to the school for ages before my dad turned up to watch me ride. My favourite horse there was a black gelding called Jubilee. I had though, when my dad came, to ride a horse called Lorenzo. He was about 16 hands high and was bright bay with a very thin poor tail. He was also a really grumpy horse.

I set off along the road out of the stables with my dad walking behind. We turned up a ginnel and my dad was too near the back of the horse and he got kicked. He was furious and I thought I had blown it. He was proper hobbling by the time we got back. I took Lorenzo out into the field and there were some jumps up which I jumped him around.

My dad was suitably impressed and I was told later that night that I could have a pony of my own when he could find one. That was it, I was so excited I couldn't sleep. I already had a riding hat with an elastic chin strap that left a red line around your jaw after a few minutes of riding, and a riding whip. I had been bought these for Xmas by my mum from the Grattan catalogue and she was paying for these weekly.

The first horse I tried I just fell in love with on first sight. He was a grey gelding, 14.2 hands high and seven years old. He rode beautifully and I wanted him. The problem was he had a really bad condition called sweet itch.

This is believed to be a parasitic condition that effects the horse particularly in the summer. It is a condition that makes the horses itch and they rub their tails and manes all the time to the point of bleeding. It is awful for the horse but also looks very unsightly and reduces considerably the value of the animal. We did not buy this horse after a great deal of discussion. He was already in a bit of a mess when I tried him.

A few weeks later we went to a house on the outskirts of Bradford and literally in the front garden there was a Palomino coloured horse. Golden coloured with a flaxen mane and tail I was very sold on this one too. He was lame though in is front leg. Not sure how or why, but he was lame. Disappointed, we were back on the lookout. Alan Drake knew my dad really well and told him in the pub about the black pony that tried to hurt me. It really did hurt my leg but the boots were my main concern.

My dad had been to the Pannal horse sales that were held every two weeks at Pannal auctions centre just outside Harrogate. The sales were a haven for dealers, gypsies and con men. You could buy virtually anything there from carrots to horse drawn vehicles. There were no suitable ponies but in the tack sales which ran alongside the horse sale he bought me a brand new pair of rubber riding boots. Full length, they were black and the total business. I had to wash them every Sunday afternoon and dry them off and put them away in the cardboard box they had come in.

The problem was though they were a size eleven and at that time I was in a size nine shoe. My dad though, being very enterprising, had bought me a pair of white big thick fisherman's wool socks to wear underneath. He said 'look after them boots lad you will grow into them'. They were fantastic, no one else had full length boots like this. In summer though it was a bit minging inside those boots with the big thick socks on! They also slopped about a lot as I walked.

We went back two weeks later to see Alan Drake at his stables in Wilsden. The stables were at the back of his house and he had a really small patch of grass in the front of them. A bay, 14.2 hand high pony, six years old was brought out. I got on him and trotted him around the grass area. I then rode him out up on to the main road and he was very well behaved. Perfect. £250 later and he was mine.

I wanted to call him Rex the Robber after the great Alwin Shockemohler's horse. Alwin was my hero in show jumping and Rex the Robber was a grey jumping stallion that was always on the TV. My dad was having none of this and he said he was to be called Romany Bay. My mum thought this was the best name too so that was it.

He came with a saddle and a bridle which were new. The colour though was a very light tan and the leather did not smell good. They were foreign made. A lot of cheap tack was being imported in those days from Pakistan and this saddle and bridle were a fabulous example. After a couple of months the saddle split all along the back and newspaper and ladies tights came out instead of the normal wool flocking that most English saddles were packed with.

The next day Romany was delivered in a cattle trailer to the farm at Thornton near where I lived. Edgar and Harriet Green had a small holding where they mainly produced pigs and cattle. They did DIY livery for a few ponies and this was the new home for my lovely new pony. He had quite a few acres of grassland to roam around in and would be very happy.

I had an old garden shed to keep my stuff in and I swept it out and cleaned it up making it into my 'tack room'. Edgar and Harriet were lovely to me and made me cups of tea when I got there. They were very old fashioned Yorkshire farmers and would not stand for any nonsense. Not that I caused them any problems because I would not dare.

The following Sunday and I got to the farm nice and early caught him and got ready to hack him to my first ever show at Bradshaw, which was about six miles away. We set off and it poured down. When I got there we were soaked. My mum and dad were there as well as my sister. I entered the clear round jumping and went in after two practice fences. He stopped dead at the third fence which was red and white poles with painted white tyres in front of it.

Not happy my dad paid for another clear round and we went in again. This time I was under orders to hit him if he slowed down to stop. I did hit him and he promptly bucked me off into the wet mud. Not the most auspicious of starts to our competing career. It was a long hack home in the rain with a wet muddy arse.

Undaunted, the following week we went for the first time to Aire Valley Riding Club at Cottingley just outside Bradford. It was miles to hack there but the weather was much better. A clear round was completed and I got my first ever rosette. In those days it was not about prizes it was all about rosettes. In the 14.2 hand high and under jumping I went clear again and in the jump off we went clear but did not go fast enough. I had a great day even though the hack back home took ages. Romany was very fit and took it all in his stride.

Aire Valley showground was a large field with a permanent wooden fenced arena jumping ring. It had a large round stone built tower in the middle of the field. This building was used as a café and entries secretary's office. There was a large wooden lean-to along one wall which we used to shelter under when it rained.

People from miles around used to come to compete and it would not be unusual to have over seventy horses in a jumping class. In charge of the warm up area was a fella called Bill. He used to shout at you to tell you to warm up as you were next but one in. He was brilliant at this job and did it for years. He ran that warm up arena with a rod of iron and military precision. Later, when all the lads had really long hair, he tried to tell us to wear hair nets, he thought we were all so scruffy.

I went for years to Aire Valley to compete and be part of the Pony Club and then the riding club itself. Both these movement are enormous with literally hundreds of thousands of members competing all over the country. The riding club was to play a big part of my equestrian life.

A couple of years later I attended the field on an evening to take my Pony Club D test. It was absolutely hammering down with rain. A very posh lady turned up in a Morris Minor motor car. She had a headscarf on and would not get out of the car because of the rain. We had to walk trot and canter around the car whilst she watched us from inside. We then went under the wooden shed to shelter.

One by one we were called to the car and she wound the window down. When I went to the car she showed me some bran in a jar and asked me what it was so I told her. She asked me about my pony and what type of bit he had in his mouth. I was soaked by the time I had finished. We were all awarded the D test certificate and yellow felt that you wore underneath your pony club badge to signify your level attained. I did not take any more tests with the Pony club.

The following week, after the first show at Aire Valley, on the Saturday morning I was booked into the farrier at his forge at Harecroft near Wilsden. I was told in no uncertain terms by my dad not to be late. I got there on time and the farrier was a man called Norman Ackroyd, safe to say he frightened me to death.

He had bright blonde hair and lots of it. He also had scary eyes. One eye catching a bus and one going to the shops. He was very strict and every time he used the anvil I had to brush it off with a small hand brush. If I missed I got a telling off. He would get two shoes on and then have a break. He made coffee with Carnation milk which was totally gross but I had to drink it. I dare not! He also did home-made nettle tea, my days, that was gross to drink

I was under strict instructions not to cheek him and be rude. I wouldn't anyway but it was a situation in those days that the farriers ruled and if you lost one they would close ranks and you could find yourself unable to get your horses shod. If you were a minute late though, he would refuse point blank to shoe your horse.

I went for years to Norman and as I got to know him I could relax more. He was a bit eccentric but very good at his job and I learned a lot from him. His brother John was also a farrier and he became the first mobile farrier working from a van that I can remember.

Over the next year I rode Romany Bay at various competitions. We eventually could borrow Edgar Green's cattle trailer and he travelled in it really well. This meant I could go further afield and compete much more. We went to Ella Ghyl which was a riding centre owned and run by the Everall family. It was very posh and the competitions were great. You had to ride into the arena through a big white archway and it made you feel very special going in.

Pool Court arena, at the bottom of Pool Bank near Harrogate, was owned by Andrew Fielder. He had been a competitor at the Olympics with a horse called Vibart. The place was super posh. It had an indoor arena and a large warm up outdoor arena which was covered in ash. If you fell off in this ash surface you bloody well knew about it! Inside there was a proper commentary box and a large bar called the 'foxhunters bar' and we got fish and chips or a large hotdog or sausage and chips in there and my dad always had a pint or two.

Romany would not canter in the indoor arena. I did not know why, but we all put it down to the surface and him not feeling safe. He was known there as 'trot on regardless'. I loved it because we were famous. He just would not canter and trotted to every jump. He was very fast though in the trot and I always did really well there and won a lot of nice prizes. At one championship event I was in the jump off and last to go as I was in the lead. I walked the course with my dad and decided on which way to go.

I went in and the commentator introduced me. The crowd were all cheering for me but were calling out 'come on trot on' 'trot on regardless.' A friend of mine was whistling really loudly. I did my round but finished in second place. I still got a sash and a small trophy which I have to this day. I was over the moon and my friends came out and chucked me up in the air a few times and I was elated. It was the best day up to that point in my life.

I had become friends with Anne and Mick Mortimer who had horses in Thornton, just up the road from where I kept Romany. Anne was a tall slim blond lady and a good rider. She had a big black mare called Midnight and she won a lot of classes. Mick was a rough diamond, he was a scrap metal dealer and his language was disgusting. He liked a pint or two and he and my dad got on very well.

Anne also bred a coloured gelding which she broke in to jump and did very well with him. They took me a few times in their wagon to different shows and I felt very privileged. I met Anne later in my life when she was getting married to an ambulance paramedic, it was a very good wedding. Mick sadly had type two diabetes and the drinking did not make him a well man, he sadly passed too early.

My ownership of my lovely pony and competing in those early days all ended though very suddenly. My dad had his own wagon and did haulage for a living, self- employed. The wagon was called Blue bird and it was an ERF make.

In the school holidays my brother and I would go with him. That was an education. One day we pulled into Liverpool docks and my dad reached for a massive spanner from his toolbox behind our seat. We pulled up and a bloke who was a stevedore on the docks came over. He opened the door and said to my dad 'Alright son, what have you got on?' meaning what goods was my dad carrying? My dad ignored this fella and just waved this big spanner up and down. He shut the door this man and walked off. My dad told us that if he had not done that they would have stolen loads of his stuff off the wagon and it would have cost him in penalties out of his wage.

He got caught though drinking and driving and eventually at court lost his licence for a year. It basically ruined us and in those days it was headlines in the bloody Bradford Telegraph and Argus newspaper. My mum was so upset.

Therefore the business went and his car was sold. He had to get a job as a mechanic nearby so he could get the bus to and from work. It also meant I had to lose my pony as my parents just could not afford to keep him and Romany Bay was sold back to Alan Drake, the dealer who I had got him from. I was quietly very heartbroken.

Chapter Two

I was hooked on horses and did not want to give up being around them. I had made a lot of friends and so began helping them. Rides were offered to me and I was very grateful. The people in the farm next door to where I had kept Romany invited me to the Great Yorkshire Show for the day with their horses. I was so excited. They had Anglo Arabs which they showed in hand. On the day, I was at their place well before they got up. I mucked out the three horses they had and was sat on the wall waiting for them when they came out.

They were very impressed with me for this and we set off. We had the best day. I watched all the top show jumpers competing and loved it. Harvey Smith, David Broom and Graham Fletcher were there. These were the David Beckhams of the day and household names, so were their horses. Matti Brown, San Salvadore, Sportsman and Tauna Dora.

That year, when I was thirteen, I also went to Appleby Horse Fair in Cumbria for the first time. My dad had a share in three ponies to sell there. We took them to the Foster Square railway station in the town centre. They were loaded with many others onto a cattle train. My dad had three matching neckerchiefs and he took these off and tied them firmly to the horse's tails. All the other dealers did this too so they could know which horse belonged to whom when they got to their destination.

The train went to Penrith in Cumbria and men met them there and herded them all to Appleby to the 'Fell End'. The fair is enormous. Thousands of Gypsies came from all over the country and across the water from Ireland too. Hundreds and hundreds of caravans and wagons were there. On the fair hill it was very noisy. People and horses were just everywhere. They rode bareback, or trotted them behind sulkies and flat carts. Horses were used to ferry people to and from the pubs, the shops and into the town.

There is a small road called "Flash Lane" where all the horses are shown in harness or being ridden. The owners would flash them up and down for people to see, try and hopefully buy. The dealing takes ages with people stood around watching the dealers slapping palms and negotiating.

We parked our caravan at a place near to a market town called Kirby Stephen called the Fell End. We had a camp fire and sat around it well into the evening drinking beer. I kept quiet and saw and learned a great deal. One evening there would be about ten maybe fifteen people sat around. One horse was sold to one man by another unseen. He sold it on to another man in the group and then he sold it on again later on. This horse which no one had even seen was sold about six times throughout the evening. They were all slapping hands in dealer style and much mirth and argument was going on.

These men were not true travelling gypsies. They all had jobs at home but dealt horses throughout their lives. There was a kind of uniform; they all wore flat caps, trilbies or pork pie type hats. They would all have neckerchiefs on, dirty looking jeans held up with braces, checked shirts under tweed jackets and of course brown leather dealer boots made by Loakes.

They were great characters and talked a very good story. Later on in the week I was taken to a bare knuckle fight. It was brutal and the winner was crowned king of the gypsies. In a flat cap on the floor, at the side of the fighting area, was ten thousand pounds which was the purse for the fight. Ten thousand pounds was an amazing amount of money in those days and today would be like a hundred thousand. It just lay there though and no one would have dreamed of touching it.

The fight did not last long but there was a great deal of blood. Everyone walked away and went to the pub. No recriminations and no trouble. It was an interesting education.

The following year I went to Appleby again with my dad and my uncle. We camped this time and it was boiling hot. I got involved washing the horses off in the river. People would bring their horses down to the river's edge to be washed ready for selling at the Fair Corner or on Flash Lane. I charged 50p per horse and covered the ponies in washing up liquid and soaped them all over. I then had to jump on them bareback and ride them into the river and swim with them until they were rinsed off.

I loved this and earned myself £9 on that day, although my dad took £4 as his share for arranging the horses for me to wash in the first place. He wanted this money for his beer. It was just the beginning sadly of a very complicated relationship I had with my dad throughout my life.

I was knackered at the end and a bit sickly with all the river water I had swallowed but it had been great fun. This was the infamous year when the Police from Glasgow were brought in and were very heavy handed. Also the townsfolk of Appleby decided that they did not want the Fair anymore, even though it has a Royal Charter and cannot be cancelled. The travellers just stampeded about four thousand horses through the town two or three times and they opened the pubs and shops again. It was a sight to see, all those horses running free through the town.

At the fair that year I saw something which I still cannot believe happened to this day. My dad was 6'2" tall and very skinny, he was not in any way a fighting man and always encouraged me and my brother to walk away but in the end, if we had to, we stood up for ourselves no matter what.

We were stood on a really narrow street in the town centre and this road had two pubs opposite each other. They were packed out and many people, including my dad, my uncle and me, were standing outside on the pavement. Two very big lads in their mid-twenties were throwing drinking pint glasses to each other across the road, like you would with eggs when you were a kid hoping they do not break.

They were regularly missing though and glasses were smashing on the floor. They were drunk and huge. A young couple walking up the road through the throng of people had a pushchair, a glass was missed and it shattered on the floor spraying glass onto the pushchair. It did not injure the child inside but the young lad remonstrated with the big lads and they threatened him and he walked away quickly.

My dad told me to hold his glass and he walked over to one of these lads who by now were upsetting everyone. Without warning he hit him really hard on the jaw and he went down like a sack of shit. His mate ran over and my dad turned on him and asked him if he wanted one too? He declined and my dad then told him to take his mate and fuck off. The whole road applauded him. I was stood there slack jawed and mouth open.

Back at home and a friend I went to school with lived just up the road from where I lived and he had two sisters who had a horse each. I used to go to this farm to play out, but really it was to see the horses. One of them was a cob type, 15.2 hands high. He was jet black and called Ebony.

He belonged to the older of the sisters and she was going off to college to train to be a nurse so he came up for sale. £500 was the asking price and it was a fortune. He was not worth this at all. I really wanted him and so I waited and waited until the last minute.

They had no takers for him and I only had £200 to spend saved from my milk round and paper round. I offered this the day before she was to leave to go to college and they accepted! They also agreed I could keep him at their farm which was five minutes up the road from my house and much nearer than Edgar Green's.

So this was my new horse. I did not have any transport for him though so I was really restricted in what I could do and where I could go. Just up the lane from the farm was a large communal park and spare green grass area. I used to go up there and ride him. I can't say it was schooling as such because at that time I no idea what I was doing. I had a lift to shows a couple of times from a lady down the road in her trailer, but Ebony did not really travel well in the trailer he would stress and sweat badly so it was a waste of time.

At this time my dad had bought a Welsh cob mare called Jenny. She was a driving mare and he had several different traps and carts which he used to drive her in. He also had one or two other horses, which were dealing horses, and we drove these together on a Sunday morning. I enjoyed the driving but really wanted to show jump and then my big goal was to do some eventing.

It was a waste of time keeping Ebony and a local girl was interested in buying him. I was very frustrated as I could not get anywhere and did not drive myself, of course. I sold him for £500 as he had actually been out competing and he was considerably better behaved than when I first bought him. This was my first profit on selling a horse. I enjoyed the feeling as it was, to be honest, quite a buzz.

I went with my dad to the Pannal sales and I bought another horse for £230. She was a young Welsh cob cross, seven years old and 15.2 hands high. She was a striking blue and white coloured. I got her home and she was very naughty and it was obvious she was scared of me. It took me a while to gain her trust and start riding her. I managed to get her to two shows to jump and she was a natural. Clear rounds and places in small jumping classes meant her value shot up. I sold her at a show to some people for their daughter. They took her there and then. I made £370 profit minus a few small expenses. This was great it was better than working and better than going to school!

Another few visits to the sales and successful selling netted me a tidy sum. By now though I had thoughts of motorbikes and girls. I was sixteen and a punk rocker. I still loved horses though and I knew they were in my blood.

I took a break from the horses. I was a proper punk rocker for a while. I joined the Police at seventeen and played rugby and golf. I also got married and had a son. It was not for long though and I found myself migrating back to the equine world.

My first pony: Romany Bay

My first dealing horse: Ebony

Appleby Horse Fair: washing ponies in the river prior to being sold.

Flash Lane: Appleby Horse Fair

My Dad and his Mare Jenny: Typical Sunday drive to a pub for a pint !

My Dads best ever job, Horses at Work Industrial Museum.

Chapter Three

I bought a horse from my dad called Ellena Shanghai Calgary Stampede or Ellie for short. She was a Welsh Section C pony and a lovely bay mare. She had been shown in hand a few times by a friend's daughter but it was for me totally boring. Showing has never turned me on.

She was bought for my son Jonathan but he was having nothing to do with horses, he used to beg me not to ride. I was gutted and I sold her again for a good profit. Incredibly, both my boys went on to become really very good footballers! Go figure. Later on when James, my youngest son, was fifteen, he discovered that there were a lot of girls around in tight white jodhpurs and suddenly discovered an immense interest in horses. It did not last long though.

It was at this time that I had applied to join the mounted Police. It was dead man's shoes though and I had to wait for someone to retire or die. After the miners' strike they put in plans to increase the mounted section and my application was in.

I was at home one morning as I was due to start on duty at 2pm. I had a telephone call from a sergeant from the mounted unit at Temple Newsham Stables in Leeds. Could I go that afternoon for an interview? I was over the moon. He called my boss at Toller Lane where I was based and squared it away.

I found my way there and went into the office. There to meet me was a sergeant, Bill Baker, and the Inspector Ronnie Prime who was in charge of the branch. They asked me about my history with horses and why I wanted to join the branch. The interview was very stilted and it seemed to me that they did not know what to ask me. I knew that the mounted branch preferred non-riders for some strange reason. I just answered truthfully. They were very concerned that I had horses at home and they were suspicious that it would interfere with my job.

I have not got a clue why these issues were in fact issues, to be honest. Surely someone with a lifelong background and ability to ride horses was a plus?

I was made a cup of tea and then shown around the stables. I loved the apparent formality of the set up there. In the tack room there was a great big mahogany display cabinet with all the ceremonial equipment on display. The horses that were actually in the stables all had matching rugs on and were beautifully clipped out. Their manes were all pulled and very smart. I was hooked.

I was told they had three more lads to see for the two vacancies that were available. So I had to wait. I went back to Toller and on duty in the vice squad for my second to last day as I was going back to beat duties. I stayed in the office as I had a load of paperwork to tidy up. I did not go back out that shift. I asked the boss for a day off the next day, Saturday, to run alongside the Sunday which was my day off. This was granted.

I was a bit down really as I loved what I had seen at Leeds and wanted to be part of it. On the Monday I was on afternoons and went in in uniform. I was given the Charlie Bravo Three car to drive and set off. I had only been out half an hour and I got the call to 10/3 (return) to the nick.

I went in and spoke to my boss, the Inspector, in his office.'Placey, what's this about you wanting to be a donkey walloper?' 'Yes Sir, it's a job I really fancy.' 'Well it seems they want you son, so you are to start next Monday at Temple Newsham in Leeds. Are you sure it's a good career move, going to the donkey wallopers?' 'Oh that's really great. Yes, I do fancy it, so if that's okay with you, I will go.' 'Yes that's okay with me, sorry to lose you but all the best. I will get the paperwork done but as I understand it you have to pass a course first so you're still on my strength here until you pass.' 'Right, yes, I will have to do well then and pass.' 'Ok then, back on the car and all the best. I will see you before you go'. 'Thanks boss.'

Back on the beat I was euphoric. The following week could not pass quickly enough. I had the weekend off, after getting rid of all my paperwork and outstanding jobs. I started my first day at 8 am at Temple Newsham in Leeds.

The house and gardens are mentioned in the Doomsday Book and the gardens were laid out by Capability Brown. The estate is currently owned by Leeds City Council, having been sold to them for a nominal sum. There are covenants on the property to ensure its continuing refurbishment and management.

To the left of the main house is the farm yard and the working farming museum. It is not somewhere you would have associated with the Police |Force. They had a small paddock to turn out the horses in. A main block of twelve stables and associated offices, changing rooms, hay barns, and the tack room. Outside, across a small yard, was a large indoor riding arena. The estate was enormous and riding around there was amazing.

There were two other stables which made up the mounted branch, one in Bradford at Bolling Road and one in Carleton, in Pontefract. When the three different forces, Bradford City police, Leeds City Police and West Riding police amalgamated in the seventies, the three stables came together under one branch. There was an Inspector, three sergeants, and twenty constables when I joined the branch. It had an establishment of twenty four horses. There was also a full time civilian groom at each of the three stables.

The reason I had got an emergency interview was that the lads at the Leeds stable were regularly going drinking in the local pub. They had been doing this for a long time. They were coming on duty, sorting out the stables and then going to the pub. The sergeant was aware of this and he went off early nearly every day to play golf. They never went out on patrol and the horses were turned out into the indoor arena or the paddock. It was widely known within the branch that this was going on and eventually the Inspector in charge had to do something about it.

They were caught one day by the Inspector in the local pub at 11.45 am. They each claimed they had been given time off, or other excuses, but it was a total load of rubbish. After an investigation, they were removed back to division and disciplined. This left a hole in the resources and hence the quick interview and course start date. On day one I met the other lad on the course with me. I did not like him because he confided in me that he was based in the fingerprint department, and that it was increasingly being civilianised, and rather than go on the beat again on shift, he was looking for a 'bolt hole' and this was it. He did not really like horses but he thought it was a 'piss easy number.'

I wanted to join the branch because of the job they did at the Orgreve coking plant during the Miners' strike and the performances I had seen at the football matches I had been to. This prat had been nine to five in an office for eight years. He was a lazy bastard looking for an easy ride. The exact total opposite of me and my ethos.

We were introduced to the horses and the yard and shown how it operated. In the afternoon we were taken to central stores in Wakefield and issued our mounted uniform. The leather riding boots we got were cheap and very stiff. They rubbed your ankles like mad. No one said anything, so they may not have noticed, but the next day I brought my own from home.

Later in the afternoon we saddled up a horse between us and we had a lesson on the lunge. This is where we ride and there is a long line from the horses bridle held by the sergeant on the ground. The horse goes around in a circle and is under the control of the sergeant.

This first lesson went without any problems. The other lad, though, could not ride very well and clung on. By the end of the first week we were riding on our own around the arena, I hadn't fallen off, but my mate had, a few times. We were riding in sitting trot all the time and much of it without stirrups. It was very military, the riding technique, and I got it straight away. Sitting in trot though, for an hour and half at a time, was very painful.

The daily management of the horses was intense, nothing was left to chance. They were all very fit and very healthy. One of them though was a killer! His official name was Whitley Boy, his stable name was 'Twitchy'. This was because everyone was very twitchy around him. He would bite or kick you at will, especially when it was feed time. I saw many an officer come flying over his door after putting his feed into his corner manger.

Later out on patrol I discovered that, if the traffic lights turned to red and you had to stand and wait, he would just go straight up on his back legs in a rear and walk forward. There was nothing anyone could do it was just his way. So as you approached lights you either slowed down or trotted on, depending on your reading of the distance to and the colour of the lights as you got near. You just had to hit green.

Another horse, Cavalier, was a Cleveland Bay breed and a stunningly beautiful horse. He was so good you could put anything in front of him and he would not be bothered. You could shoot a gun right under his tummy and he would just stand there, not flinch, and tut. He was the horse that went to the Horse of the Year Show for the Police best trained class. He was not scared of anything, he would walk up to the giant man on stilts so the rider could shake his hand. Go through the two giant dragons' heads that spat out smoke and up the rocking ramp.

On a Wednesday though, he could not be taken out on patrol because it was bin day. In those days people put their bin liners out at the end of their drives or gardens to be picked up. This was before wheelie bins. Cavalier was shit scared of black bin liners and would not move a step towards them!

Ambassador was a big thoroughbred cross horse and he was my favourite. Bay coloured he was very impressive. Skips were his thing though. If he saw one you had to turn around and go the other way or find another route. One thing was for sure, he would not go within 100 yards of one.

Saladin was the spare horse. He was bay and had a roman nose. He was an older horse and had been there and done it all. He was though, shit scared of his own shadow. At football matches he would stick to the other horse he was patrolling with like a limpet. You had trouble getting him to leave his partner.

Speed was named after John Speed who had been shot dead in Leeds. He was a very impressive big horse with no real quirks.

Senator was a small horse, probably the smallest horse in the yard. He had a great party piece though. If you touched him immediately behind the saddle he would launch both back legs in a big outward kick. It was very useful for scattering fighting yobs at the football. He was a small package that horse, but hard as nails.

Derwent was a lovely bright bay horse and he was Maureen, known as Mo, the Policewoman's allocated horse. He was lazy and had to be ridden quite hard. She was always washing his sheath and he hated it. He would shake his head up and down in a temper. All the horses, on a weekly basis, had their sheaths washed I hasten to add. It was not just the policewoman who did this.

The course continued and we started cantering and going out into the estate on mini patrols. I totally loved it. I felt completely at home with this job. I loved the horses and could not get enough of it. I was very proud to be part of this regime. I was more often than not early to work, just to be there. When there, I would be happy to do anything with the horses. I was good at pulling tails and showed some of the lads how to do it. I did not know though, that this was not going down well. I certainly wasn't trying to be clever or a suck up. They asked me to help them!

The lads I worked with were, as usual in the police service, quite big characters. One of them was very small. He had small man syndrome and was always whispering to others. What was funny though was that he thought he was a serious dressage rider. He reckoned he could speak German and used to give instructions to his horse in a sort of made up German.

He rode his horse around the arena at a very fast trot and you could hear him shouting at the top of his voice at his horse 'Nicer, nicer 'and 'Ya, ya ,ya' in a sort of mock pretend Germanic way. He also rode with his stirrups too long so his legs looked longer. In the sitting trot this made him look like he was bobbling about on the top of this big 17.2 hands high horse. I used to very quietly piss myself laughing, it was seriously pathetic but very funny. He used to quote from the books of Dr Reiner Klimke who was a famous German dressage Olympian. He read these books all the time.

Another of the lads already in post had been on the previous course to me and had got a place straight away. He was really strange, he went from hobby to hobby every week. When I started there he had just got a monkey which he kept at work. Apparently he had also got, in the previous few months, a hang glider and a top set of golf clubs which he only used once. The monkey did not last a month and he took it back to the pet shop. He later went on to sailing and bought a boat and also had flying lessons.

The most senior of the constables had been there for a long time. He was off duty when the other officers from Leeds had been caught drinking on duty so had escaped being removed. It was common knowledge though, that he too was a regular in the pub. He was a really strange cookie. He spoke very well for a Leeds police officer, it was almost a privately educated type of twang and inflection to his voice. He was also very polite. He stood out like a sore thumb.

He absolutely thought he was very good at the job, an excellent jockey and all round horseman. He treated everyone like they were his pupils and ordered us all about. Everything had to be done just so and correctly. Every time he farted, which he did with alarming frequency, he would exclaim 'Good arse.' His farting was embarrassing and also a bloody nuisance. Wherever we were he farted, and very loudly.

Much later on in my time at Leeds we went together, in uniform, to a local show whilst on duty. It was a charity show and the Police were invited to judge the tack and turnout class. We went together and the judging of the class went without incident. We then had a wonderful lunch in the marquee.

On the way out back to the van, a young girl was warming up for the jumping class and the horse she was riding kept refusing to jump the warm up fence. He just marched over and started to help her. She was, to be honest, useless, and so he insisted on getting on this horse in front of everyone to make it jump. I was so terrified and uncomfortable standing at the side of the arena. He cantered the horse toward the jump, it stopped. He went flying over its head. He ended on the floor with the horses bridle in his hand, the horse bolted off. I did too, back to the van. I was mortified.

Each of the stables, apart from Bradford, had a policewoman on the strength. The girl at Leeds was really lovely. She was just lazy. She looked after her own horse beautifully and was immaculately turned out. She would not though, do anything else for anyone else. She took her time over getting ready every day so if the horseboxes had to be got ready or washed out she would still be doing her own horse. Feeding round on an afternoon and skipping out the horses every hour or so she would be missing, cleaning her tack or getting a shower! So all the other lads did it. She got away with murder.

The Sergeant, Bill Baker, in charge of the stables was a very straight bloke. He was very quiet and kept his distance as the sergeant. You knew exactly where you stood with him but when he was in the mood he was a good piss taker and the banter was good.

The course went on and on and it was progressing very well. The other lad was doing very well to be honest, bearing in mind he could not ride at the start. He did love himself though and was always asking the policewoman out and chatting her up We were told, in the second to last week, that only one place was available at the end of the course and the other person would have to wait for a placement after the course ended. I was gutted. The thought of going back to the beat was horrifying

The end of course test consisted of riding the military number three dressage test and jumping three jumps with your arms folded. This was in front of the Inspector and one of the other sergeants whom we had not met yet.

We did attend a football match as 'strappers'. This term relates to people who attended any job but not in a riding capacity. Your duty was to look after the horses. We had to make sure that after the lads got mounted up, we rolled up all the tail bandages and collected the knee pads the horses had travelled in. We also had to fill buckets of water for them to have a drink when they returned and refill the hay nets on the back of the wagons.

My first football match was Leeds United at Elland Road. I was so hoping after that day that I passed and got a place because I could not wait to police a football match on horseback.

I did not know at this time though, that because I had showjumped previous to coming on the course, and I had horses at home, I was the talk of the branch. The rest of the officers at the other stables had been told I was a big head and although I could ride I was not that good and had ' bigged' myself up a bit.

I really had not. I did not know where this was all coming from. Someone was doing me a right disservice and mixing me a powder. I never found out who. I just kept my head down and got on with my job. I never mentioned my horses at home unless someone asked me. I never proffered an opinion about anything, again, unless asked. It got though, that I thought I had to constantly prove myself. This was a theme that followed me throughout my whole time on the branch. Something that greatly bothered me and still angers me to this day.

On the day of the test I was allocated Saladin, who was notorious at stopping whilst jumping. He did telegraph that he was going to refuse so I had a chance. My opponent was given Cavalier. Was this because it was only reasonable to give him a fair chance against me or was it so he could be given an unfair advantage over me? Probably just me being paranoid. I had mostly ridden Saladin through the course and he had mainly ridden Derwent.

I rode into the indoor arena and stopped in a square halt. I completed the military salute and rode the number three test. This involved trot, canter and walk. Rein back and full pass where the horse moves sideways using all four legs, crossing at the same time. I then went around the edge of the arena and jumped three jumps, folding my arms as I started the line of jumps. A final salute and out I went. The other officers that were watching clapped politely. My opponent went in. I couldn't see him but he went well and completed everything. I was told that the horse did not do a good rein back and he lost control of its quarters.

We were given feedback by the Inspector in the office. I had passed. Phew! I was very happy. I just needed to know now though, who had got the placement. The other lad passed too. After about an hour I was called in. I was on! I was so pleased. I shook all their hands vigorously and went back to the yard.

After he came out, my other course colleague shook my hand and was quite okay about it. He only had to wait a month anyway and he came onto the branch at Pontefract. I had the weekend off and celebrated. I started on the Monday at 8 am.

The quantity of kit I was issued with was enormous. I had a pair of leather black boots, six pairs of jodhpurs, three new jackets specially tailored for riding, and a long black Melton cloth cloak. This coat was like a skirt. They were long and went from the waist into a kind of blanket that covered the horse's quarters. My crash helmet was like a motorcycle helmet. It had a special piece of padding that hung down your neck to protect you. They had a visor and a microphone that came along your left cheek.

My allocated horse was Saladin, and although not the most exciting, I would have had a donkey and been happy. His kit was extensive too. He had stable rugs and a turnout rug. His saddle was a military type and they were good for the horses as they distributed the combined weight of the rider and the kit evenly across the horse's back. They were horrible for us though as they were like wooden boards to sit on. He had a military type bridle and a leather headcollar with a brass name plate on it. The truncheons we had were three foot long and had a leather scabbard that attached to the saddle. Battery operated lights were fastened underneath our offside stirrups and the leads led to a leather pouch with batteries in it, attached to the back of the saddle. All the leather saddlery was polished by hand.

Each horse had its own grooming kit kept in wooden boxes with their names on. These were washed very often. My own grooming kits at home would have been washed maybe twice a year but we washed the police kits every two weeks.

That first day, in the afternoon, I went on patrol with another lad along Halton Moor which is next to Temple Newsham. Nothing happened but it was very enjoyable. We had radios with us but did not respond to anything. We did not even report in to the local comms at Gipton nick which I was very surprised about. They had no idea we were about and, as such, a possible resource.

What became clear to me very quickly was that these police officers, who were doing a very good job, especially at football matches and serious public order incidents and searches, were in fact, in a bubble. They were so divorced from the real life policing, from where I had recently come from, it was unreal. They were rightly proud of their traditions. They also had a great deal of emotional investment in the job because of the magnificent animals they worked with on a daily basis.

The day to day partnership that was developed between you and your horse was paramount. It was just that I had to accept that mainstream policing was a thing of the past for me and I had great difficulty with this. We never, when on patrol, logged on with the local nick. They did not know we were there and patrolling. We did not respond to urgent calls even if we were in the vicinity.

The first Saturday football match I attended as a member of the branch was again at Elland Road for a Leeds United game. Sadly, and much to my annoyance, the police constable that worked full time in administration for the branch was down to ride my horse,

Saladin. He too was an old lag and I had to get the horse ready for him. I was the strapper for the day. I was even more annoyed when I later found out that he was on overtime.

I got the horse ready and all the gear he would need for him ready to box up into the horseboxes and went into the tack room for a cup of tea. This officer came in. 'Is he ready then, that Saladin?' 'Yep he is all done.' 'Good lad, good lad.' He was smoking a roll up cigarette and had a brown smock on over his uniform. 'Can you sort me these boots out an all? I haven't worn them for ages.' I was dumfounded. I know I was the 'new boy' but I had eight years of service in the job. I wasn't a bloody sprog (term for probationary officer) 'I hope you're joking.' I said. 'You're the strapper aren't you? Doing my boots is part of the job.' I just looked at him and said 'On yer bike mate. You'll want your arse wiping next.' I walked out.

My sergeant came and found me in the wagon where I was putting up haynets. 'Steve, what have you said to Gordon?' 'Nothing really I just said I wasn't cleaning and polishing his boots for him.' 'You're the strapper and new here so sort him out. He has been on this job longer than you have been in the job so you should have some respect.' 'Not a bother respecting him. I have got the horse ready and he is turned out properly. I am not though, polishing his boots, not a chance.' 'This is not a good start Steve, we have traditions here and you don't wanna make a name for yourself before you start.' 'Sergeant, I respect the traditions and my standing as the new lad here at the moment, but there is no way, no how I am going to polish another man's boots for him. I am not his valet and I am too long in the tooth for this rubbish.'

He walked away down the ramp of the wagon and into the stables. I was worried now, maybe I had gone too far but it was stupid, and in my book totally ridiculous. They brought the horses out and we boxed them up. Everyone got into the wagon and nothing was said to me.

This other lad, Gordon had gone in his own car so he could go straight home from the game. That meant he had just turned up, rode around the ground, and would get off hand the horse to me and go home without lifting a finger to sort out the horse before or after the match. This was very weird and not right to me. These officers who had been in the branch a long time were treated like gods, they were on pedestals yet they were just constables like me and the rest and had not, as I saw it, struck a bat of police work for years.

The match went off without incident. When we got back to the stables we divided our forces. Two did the horses, feeding them haying them up and settling them for the night. Two washed and cleaned out the horsebox and the rest cleaned tack and tidied up. One officer always stayed on until 8pm. The rest of us went to the pub. The conversation in the pub was always a bit slow and difficult with this lot. I found them difficult to make friends with.

Every Thursday was training day. Officers from Pontefract would come over to Leeds to train with us and the Bradford lads trained on their own. The Pontefract lads turned up. Their Sergeant was a right character and I got on very well with him. He later became the Inspector in charge of the branch.

They were so different from the people I was working with. The banter with them was good and they took the mickey out of each other mercilessly. I was so surprised. Their attitude to the training was light hearted and this made it fun. The serious element of the riot training we did was always paid due diligence, but beyond that they did some jumping and joked about. It was a breath of fresh air.

When they left though the bitching started from my brother officers. Oh my days, they were nasty and vicious about everyone that had been over for training. I was so shocked. This was a recurrent theme throughout my time on the branch but sometimes it became very personal.

I settled in well though and was thoroughly enjoying my time. I was sent onto a HGV driving course for a week. This was so I could drive the horseboxes. I had a good week except for the test on the Friday afternoon. I set of out for the driving school at Crofton. I turned right, as directed by the sergeant who was testing me, and came to a T junction.

I had a great cross view to the right and so, as it was clear, I slowed down selected a lower gear and carried on turning left onto the main road. I finished the test by reversing into a pretend garage made of cones. The sergeant said to me 'So how do you think your drive went?' 'I thought I gave you a decent drive Sarg, nothing major.' He said 'Yes, have you got your pocket book please?' I gave him my book and he opened it to the current page. He then formally cautioned me. I went cold and numb. 'What have I done?' 'When you came out of the driving school, you came to the first T junction, got a great cross view, and pulled out didn't you?' 'Yes I did that, why?' 'It's a stop sign there, not a give way only sign. You failed to stop so you have failed your test and I have to caution you for committing an offence.' I had no reply, I was just totally gutted.

I went back on the following Monday and re took the test which I passed.

Chapter Four

I really needed to get back on track to owning a horse of my own. I also wanted to try eventing. I did get involved in eventing, but in the first instance though it was as a spectator.

My friend Bernard who was a mounted officer at Bradford went with me all over, to the races and Badminton horse trials and also Chatsworth. I had known about eventing when showjumping as a youngster although it was seen as an elite sport enjoyed by royals and people with a lot of money. Badminton got me totally hooked on the sport. I thought the whole thing was just amazing. The attention to detail needed, the phases including the steeplechase and roads and tracks and especially the cross country just blew me away.

The first time I went to Badminton Bernard and I stayed in a lovely pub called the Cat and Custard Pot in the village of Sherston, nearby. I booked it and the guy who owned it was called Ken. He was from Sheffield and had been a steel worker. His wife Val was lovely and great company. We got to the pub at six pm on the Thursday. He showed us our room, it was a twin and comfortable. We just dumped our bags and went back down to the lounge.

Bernard asked if the towels were coming off the pumps and Ken obliged. So at six pm we had our first pint of the local brew Abbots Ale. At 3 am we were still on it. We had the locals locked in, telling stories and mimicking them and they loved us. On the way to bed I smacked my head on a low beam and knocked myself out. The next morning we had to be awakened by Ken as it was nine am and we were going to miss the dressage.

After a hasty breakfast we got to badminton. I had purchased tickets for the stand for the dressage and also the showjumping on the Sunday. We sat watching the dressage drinking wine all day in the sun, it was bliss Bruce Davidson from the USA was world champion at the time and his test was not good, in fact it was poor compared to others,

However, he was getting very high scores, people began murmuring and eventually this turned into boos. I was loving this, we had a right laugh, all these posh horse people behaving like football hooligans at Badminton Horse Trials! We walked the course later that day to sober up. I was totally taken aback at the size and complexity of the jumps, it was amazing.

Whitbred Brewery were the sponsors and had been for years. The big beer tent was run by Gilpins, caterers from Leeds. We knew Jeremy Gilpin really well through the police horses and got free beer vouchers which made it extra special. The cross country day was just fantastic and I took some time to appreciate the speed at which the horses were travelling. We walked the whole course including the steeplechase. We watched two horses over each jump and saw the world famous Tom Smiths walls, the Luckington Lane crossing, the Quarry, Huntsman's Close and the infamous lake of course.

The rest of that weekend went by without incident, although we consumed a life time of drink in the pub and also at the trials during the day.

The following year we went to the Chatsworth horse trials in Derbyshire. This was a 3 star International event and my heroine Lucinda Green won it. Whilst there though, we had an encounter. In the bed and breakfast where we were staying, a lady and her friend were also booked in.

When we got there they were in the lounge. Bernard, being the charmer he is, was chatting away and they quickly got out the photographs of their horse that they shared at home. It was called Pineapple or something like that. He was looking at every single photo, of which there were very many and chatting away I was thoroughly bored and wanted to get to the pub for a meal and something to drink.

The next morning at breakfast they were at it again making real small talk about nothing. I know you think I am just rude, but they were just banging on and on about horses and ponies in a very mundane and very opinionated way. One of the ladies, the larger of the two had two bowls of prunes for her breakfast which caught my eye. Later that day I saw them both at the horse trials and the larger of the two was chomping away on an enormous baguette. It was one of those foot long special things.

That evening I was having a bath in the shared bathroom. Next door was a toilet that again we all had to share. The door went and someone was in there. I thought it was Bernard and the noises coming out of that toilet were truly disturbing. It sounded like he was biting the towel rail in half! I got out quickly, dried and went to the door to await him coming out. My intention was to scare him and take the total piss out of his toilet noises.

As the door opened I jumped out screaming and laughing like a mad banshee. It was the baguette and prunes lady. She shit herself and then, when the realisation that I had heard her noises took hold, she died of embarrassment.

The following year in May we went again to Badminton Horse trials. I rang Ken but they had stopped doing bed and breakfast in the pub. He did arrange for us to stay in a cottage in the village. When we arrived Pauline, the landlady made it quite clear to us both that she never ever normally took in gentlemen but as Ken had vouched for us she had relented.

The rooms were fine and we went back downstairs for tea. The settees swallowed us whole, they were very comfortable and old. We were drinking tea and being very gentlemanly and polite when an old sheepdog came in and planted its snout right in Bernard's crotch.

What got me though was I had this thought flash in my head about Bernard still having it and being able to pull and attract an old dog. I got the giggles really bad, made worse by Bernard trying his best to quietly and politely remove this dog's smelly and very wet nose out of his groin. It was not for moving and Pauline was oblivious. I lost it and was laughing and spilling tea everywhere. I tried very unsuccessfully to make out I was having a coughing fit but it did not fool anyone. Both Pauline and Bernard just looked at me as if I was a total loony and, with hindsight I must have looked quite frightening.

We went out to the Cat and Custard Pot for a meal and another evening of drinking and debauchery. Pauline was not totally comfortable with this as she went to bed at 9 pm and did not want to be disturbed. We were not happy with this either, it was after all our holiday and break away from work. I was not going to bed at 9pm and I thought she was unreasonable to ask. She showed us the back garden and how to get in through the gate. She left a key for the back door on the lintel of the porch. We did promise we would not be too late!

At 2.30 am we were very drunk and could not find the porch. I was swaying and we were both trying to whisper but of course it was very loud.

'Bernard, Bernard this is it, it's the blue one' 'No it's not blue it's thish one here' 'Nah its blue honesht' 'shhhsh,t be quiet' 'I am being quiet, shtop going on bout it and find the owse'

Then the kitchen light came on and the door was opened very gingerly by an angry Pauline. 'Gentlemen it is very, very late and I am not happy' 'itsh okay Pauly we're here now, can we come in?'

The light reflected straight through her yellow pyjamas and she was naked. I pointed at her voluminous breasts and said at the top of my voice, although I swear I was whispering 'Bern, Bern, nipples size a bath plugs woo hoo big bath plugs'

The next morning and I packed my suitcase as did an angry Bernard. We went down for breakfast and she was not talking, she just did a lot of tutting and sighing. I apologised in a very sincere way and she did see the funny side of it thank goodness. We promised profusely to behave that night if she let us continue with our stay. The thing was, there was not a chance anywhere that we were going to get accommodation that weekend with it being Badminton. So after a suitable amount of grovelling and sucking up she let us stay.

We had a great weekend and enjoyed many more outings as mates together to the races and such. Later we went with the girls to Spain on a freebie holiday that Bernard and his partner Jenny had won in a timeshare scam. We had a ball that week too.

In Paris one October Bernard, Jenny and my then wife Sue and I were sat at a café on the pavement on the Champs Elyse. It was a warm day and we were having breakfast outside. It was very busy. There was suddenly a fair commotion and Liza Minelli came to sit down at a table with her entourage. Two of these were bodyguards. They had on dark glasses and dark suits. One had a long pony tail and one was bald. Pony tail came around our tables and when he got to us he excused himself and told us that Miss Minelli was not signing autographs and doing photographs.

I asked him what he was selling and he said he was not selling anything. He looked at me bemused. I told him he was bothering us and to go away. He repeated to us again about the autographs and photographs and I told him I did not know her and had no idea what or who he was on about. This went on for a few minutes, this guard explaining who she was and me feigning no knowledge of her. He went away straight back to her table. There was a lot of talking and whispering behind hands and she was staring over at us. I waved and she waved back. No autographs or photographs but Liza Minelli waved to me!

Chapter Five

I met Sue through the mounted Police. We had worked together before on a rape case in the police and she applied to come onto the branch eighteen months after I joined. We were just friends for a while at work until it became a relationship.

She had a young horse called Contessa or Tessa for short. This mare was 16.1 hands high and was by Augerman (Hanovarian) out of a thoroughbred mare. The dam had been given to the owner, Ronnie Wragg, as payment for a debt and he decided to breed from her. He bred four horses from this mare.

Ronnie and Kitty Wragg had a small holding called Blacup Moorend Farm just outside Cleckheaton, which was a small town between Bradford and Huddersfield. They fattened cows for market, had a few pigs and Kitty had a part time job. Sue got to know them through a mutual friend who had a horse there on livery. Sue helped Ronnie for a while and assisted him in breaking Contessa. She bought the horse from him some time later. Sue was just like me, horse mad, and had them in the blood and would do anything to be around them and that's why she was helping Ronnie.

The other horses bred from this mare were two mares and a gelding. The gelding, called Ocean, was sold to the Metropolitan Police and was a successful police horse. The other mare called Abby, had bad sweet itch so she was bred from. Baroness (Bonnie) had been sold on to a local dealer, Liz Pickering.

Tessa was athletic and had lovely conformation. She definitely had a mind of her own though and would happily go up on her back legs if she felt she was being 'told'.

Ronnie became a great friend and decided that he would breed or even buy horses and that Sue and I would break them and compete them for him. He wanted to start the 'Blacup Stud'. Sue and I were so excited about this and talked endlessly about eventing. We had such plans but sadly though, this was not to materialise as Ronnie was very soon diagnosed with cancer. The prognosis was not good and he died within months of the diagnosis. It was gutting for all concerned and a very emotional time.

Sue moved Tessa to a livery yard in the Shibden Valley in Halifax. This was because her very good friend Paula kept her horse there. The owner of the yard was a girl called Isobel Marshall. She was very talented on a horse and we became best friends over the next few years. She competed at dressage and eventing. Sadly she was taken very young and tragically, through brain cancer. It just strengthened my resolve to live life and love life.

The Shibden Valley was wonderful, it is a beautiful place and had some lovely rides. It had roads on very steep slopes and was fabulous for getting horses strong, fit and changing their musculature. We bought a house together in Northowram which is a village at the top of the valley and the local pub, the Yew Tree, was the focal point for everyone at the stables. Tuesday night was quiz night, we never won but had great fun and I have many fond memories.

Colin and Carol Lightowler were friends of Isobel and we too became firm friends. Their daughter Leanne rode and had a pony. We went to Badminton one year with them and it was boiling hot all weekend. The first night there we went to the Tunnel House pub and Colin got very drunk and hurt his ankle falling over some flower pots. He also fell out of his Range Rover at the cottage we had rented for the weekend. Percy's Cottage was wonderful, six bedrooms and a typical Cotswolds house with a thatched roof. We had a great weekend.

Princess Diana was there and Colin had a massive video camera permanently attached to his shoulder, he filmed her climbing down off a Land Rover. She had a wrap-around skirt on and it came apart. We saw, and Colin filmed, her pink French knickers. I said that the film would be worth a fortune to the press. Carol, who was a mad Diana fan, was having none of this and insisted, very angrily, that he delete it. He was furious and it was very funny.

I decided that I would go and buy a horse to bring on alongside Tessa. We scoured the Yorkshire Post newspaper as at that time it had a special horse selection and hundreds of adverts for horses for sale. I found an interesting one which was a 17 hand high five year old mare called Heidi. This mare was also by Augerman and seemed to fit the bill.

She was at a stables near Doncaster alongside the M18. We got there and it was a ramshackle, horrible yard with weeds and rubbish everywhere. A young lad met us and he was just full of it. He was going on and on about how good this horse was. She was in the field and it took him five minutes to catch her. She was not in the best condition and looked very fed up with herself. He jumped on from the ground and rode her around the weed filled field. She was upside down in her outline, a bit weak and not schooled very well.

She did though have very good paces and a look in her eye that said to me that there was more here. I sat on her for two minutes and thought, yes give this a go. He turned her back out into the field and sat down on a chair.

The asking price for this horse was £2500. Way too much. I said I would buy her and if he was interested I would give him £1500. He jumped up face to face with me and I actually thought he was going to hit me! He was not happy but I said he had my number and if he changed his mind he could call me. We set off back towards the car and he called me back.... Deal done, £1500 and he would deliver her the next day within the price.

She turned up at the yard and settled in well. She had quite a few problems though. She was very stiff and under developed through and over her top line. I tried working with her for about two months but I was not making any progress. She was a lovely mare. She put on weight and condition and her musculature developed. I decided that she was not going to event with me and so she was advertised for sale and sold quite quickly for £2500.

The next horse I bought was a massive mistake. A bloke called Barry, who Sue had known all her life, was a dealer. She, as a child, in order to get a ride on anything, used to go and ride all his horses and ponies and learnt quickly and the hard way. We got to his place near Barnsley and he had a lovely looking Trakehner liver chestnut gelding in for sale. It was unshod when we went to try him.

He was a big, good looking horse and to be really honest I bought him with rose tinted spectacles on because I did not sit on him. We just watched him trot up and down a stony lane. I broke every rule in the book but it was to be a big learning curve. The horse was sound for one day back at home, just enough time to let the dope wear off. The poor thing was crippled. I had him shod and he was no better so it was not a simple case of foot soreness. There was no point in paying for a veterinary inspection as the horse obviously had navicular disease in his front feet.

I was faced now with what to do. The dealer, Barry, would not have anything to do with us and certainly my £2500 was gone. I had to take him and 'do the journey' which meant taking him to the Rockwood Hunt Kennels for destruction. I was gutted. From that day on I had a different attitude and ethos to trying and buying horses.

My dad taught me many lessons in life, one which is sadly true but very hard to accept, and was learned over a period of time. When I had different ponies they were kept for a long time at my Uncle Phillip's smallholding in Thornton. I had a paper round from Monday to

Thursday and paid my mate Robert Newsome to do it for me Friday nights so I could go collecting milk money for Clifford and Nancy Brown. 6 am Saturday and Sunday mornings and I was out delivering milk until 10.am. At the end of this week I had the princely sum of £3 after paying Robert. I used to give my dad a pound each week to pay for the grazing for my pony. Eighteen months later, at a family Boxing Day clan gathering, it came out in a massive row that my Uncle had never charged my dad a penny for the grazing.

In the car going home with my Mum in tears, my dad turned to me and said "let that be a lesson to you son, never trust any fucker." It was certainly true with Barry the horse dealer.

I decided to track down the other sister of Sue's mare Tessa. She was called Baroness, though her stable name was Bonnie. We found her at Liz Pickering's yard in Wheatley near Dewsbury. I went on a Saturday evening to see her over the stable door with a plan to go back later and try her. Four years old and 16.3 hands high, she was the biggest of the siblings.

I was dressed up smart in trousers and shirt and tie with a jacket on because we were going to meet friends and going out for a meal. I looked at her over the door and she was a good looking mare. On the lighter side of build for me. Liz got her out and tacked her up. I explained I did not want to ride her as we were going out. She was having none of this and made me get on her in the dark.

She had a small woodchip covered area and one jump in the middle of it. I rode her around this so called arena and it was wet through. She put a jump up which was about 1.10m high and ordered me to jump it. I was laughing as I came into the jump thinking' I am going to end up in the shit here'. From a cold start, straight out of the stable, she soared over it, tucked her front legs right up and made a great shape. I was impressed and we bought her there and then. £3000 was the purchase price and I thought she was a bargain.

The £3000 had been hard saved and was supposed to be for a horsebox, but having lost £2500 on the chestnut gelding, it was all we had to buy a horse with. Some serious saving eventually bought Sue and I our first wagon. Bonnie and Tessa were going well at home and we were looking forward to competing. We had to blag lifts though from Isobel and it was very intermittent when we could get out so we had no consistency. A horsebox became paramount.

Near Batley was a cross country course and they used to have hunter trials there and you could hire the course for schooling. We went there for a hunter trial and I had the first experience of Bonnie going fast and out of control but clear. The course was not big but it was a mixture of fences from really small logs on the floor to large hedges and ditches. We set off and at that time we had no body protectors on.

Bonnie galloped off and jumped the first few fences under control but then having got the understanding of what she was being asked to do she just took off like a catapult. It was exhilarating in the extreme and left me a lot of homework to do. Tessa went clear too, until a ditch when she decided that she would stop and rear up a few times.

Back at home we were having weekly lessons with Isobel and the flatwork was improving very well for us both. We jumped them both, two or three times a week and hacked them for miles up the hills which got them really fit and muscled up.

Some friends of ours had a wagon for sale. It was blue and a Bedford TK. 4 cylinder, four speed. It was very difficult to drive as it was slow and you had to change gear so many more times than a 6 speed. It was a converted furniture wagon. We loved it. It was ours. We spent a whole day cleaning it out and purchased cushions and plastic cups, plates and cutlery to go in the drawers. It was very old really and, no matter how much we cleaned it, tatty.

We could now go anywhere whenever we wanted. We started jumping on a Thursday evening at Wood Nook Arena in Huddersfield and went to dressage competitions at Rudding Park near Harrogate. We had mixed results to begin with but going out competing and the horses totally took over our lives.

Our first proper One Day Event was near Harrogate at Beckwithshaw. It was run by the Harewood combined training group which was a riding club and quite famous in the area. The cross country course was a lovely introduction to eventing for the horses.

It ran along old turf and onto a disused railway track. Show jumping was in a field which was very undulating. Just to be there and have all the gear we needed and two nice horses was fantastic. We were very easily pleased in those early days and it was pure pleasure to be taking part. We did okay with clear rounds in the jumping and cross country but the dressage let us both down and we needed to improve this element. Back home we had more lessons and felt that things were getting better.

The social side of the involvement with horses was great too. We had made some special friends at the stables and every Tuesday night, when we were free, we went to the local pub for the quiz night and some supper. At Xmas we had fancy dress parties. Isobel was streets ahead of us in her level of competing and took her horse to Witton Castle in the north east to an affiliated one day event. I offered to drive her wagon for her and Sue came too to see what it was all about.

The day just blew us away. It was just brilliant how it was set up. The courses for the cross country were very professional and all the fences were dressed with flowers, solidly built and presented properly. There were trade stands and some of the top stars of the sport were there competing. We walked all the cross country courses and I was struck at how big and difficult they were. Quite imposing and very exciting. They ran all the levels at Witton from Pre-Novice, Novice, Intermediate and Advanced. The Advanced course was just unbelievable in its length and height. I was just mesmerised.

That was it, we were totally hooked and decided that the following year that we would join what was then the British Horse Trials Association and take part. The rest of that year we spent competing in every competition we could get to and every one we could afford. We had some success at local one day events and we felt that both horses were athletic enough and had the jump needed to be registered at affiliated level.

We completed a few One Day Events during the rest of that summer and had some success. Sue was placed second at Harrogate Equestrian Centre the week after they had the affiliated event there. I was placed at Rillington in the east of Yorkshire. We also went to Barton on Humber and both horses did really well and got placed.

Back at home, we spent an awful lot of money on equipment and saddlery for the horses. We also had to buy new skull cap riding hats, body protectors and stop watches for our arms. The stop watches were used to ensure that as we went around the cross country we made the optimum time.

The horses also had to have stud holes in their shoes which was an extra cost and we needed stud kits.

Getting ready for the events was as big a part of the process as the actual competition. Sue plaited the horses' manes and I cleaned out and plugged all the stud holes. We both did the horses tails and left them plaited and bandaged up. We did the wagon together and very often did not leave the yard the night before an event until quite late. The next day, competition day, we were always up very early and straight into it.

Show jumping and dressage days were much the same. As we were both serving in the mounted police we were very particular about our turnout. The horses were always immaculate. Blacup Contessa and Blacup Baroness were starting to do very well.

That winter we hunted them too with the Rockwood Hunt. We had several days out that winter season and they certainly learnt how to jump stone walls. The day after Boxing Day we started the fittening work we needed to do with them. Long trotting hacks and then eventually, canter interval training sessions two times a week became the norm. Schooling on the flat and grid work for jumping meant they only had one day a week off.

They thrived and we got to the terribly exciting part where we were going to register the horses and join ourselves with the BHTA. I had a very pleasant surprise at work too.

Chapter Six

In the summer, certain members of the branch attended Police Horse shows throughout the country. I had no idea about this showing which meant going away to different force areas and competing against them throughout the summer months. It was a very welcome, if not surprising turn of events. It was also a very closely guarded secret, but I couldn't wait to get the opportunity to go. Police days were enormous fun and we performed the musical ride and the activity ride. We also competed at tent pegging and pairs show jumping.

The police horse competitions were quite varied. The Best Trained competition consisted of riding a dressage test and then riding your horse down a nuisance lane. It was divided into three categories, novice rider, novice horse and the open. The dressage test was straight forward it was always the number three military dressage test and everyone knew it by heart. The nuisance lane consisted of ten nuisances such as a rocking ramp where the horse would walk up one side of a see saw ramp and wait for the ramp to fall down to the other side and then step off. A dummy was placed on the floor and the horse should not stand on it. You would have other stuff such as a motorbike starting up loudly as you walked passed it.

Each show, run by different forces, would have their favourite nuisance and we had to try and guess them and re-create them and train accordingly. Each nuisance was scored out of ten by the judge and your judge would score according to the horse's reaction to the nuisance. The scores from dressage and the nuisance lane were added together and the highest overall score won.

Pairs jumping was straight forward; two horses would jump together. You were marked by the judge on keeping your dressing that is staying as close as possible, throughout the round. We usually tried to keep knee to knee. Also, you lost marks for refusals and jumps knocked down.

My biggest win in this competition was some years later at the Royal Tournament in London. Me and my mate won! It was major. We were to be presented, with other prize winners, to the Queen Mother. Her Equerry took us all to one side and we were briefed very abruptly, and in my opinion rudely, with an enormous amount of condescension thrown in too, about what to do.

Standing at ease, as our names were called, we had to come smartly to attention. If the Queen Mother offered her hand we were told to lightly shake it and certainly not, under any circumstances, in any way, to grab her hand or squeeze it. If she spoke to us we were to answer quietly and we had to call her Mam, as in harm, not Mam as in jam. We had to practice this and the Equerry, who was right up himself, made us say over and over again, Mam as in harm not mam like jam.

She came along the line and as she got to me this Equerry said 'Pcs Place and Thompson your Majesty, West Yorkshire Police winners of the pairs jumping'. She came towards me and put her hand out. I shook it and said in my best Yorkshire Bradfordian 'aallriight'. The Equerry coughed very loudly in disgust and alarm. I just smiled and so did she. She gave us the shield we had won and stood for a photograph.

When she walked away I shook my head, I couldn't believe what I had said! I just panicked. My mate said 'Fucking hell Steve, only you'.

Tent pegging stems back to the cavalry days of Waterloo, the Raj and such. The cavalry would gallop amongst enemy camps with lances. They would spear, from horseback, the wooden pegs holding the enemy tents up thus collapsing them, and rendering the soldier's asleep inside impotent against an impending attack.

There was a white wooden peg stuck into the ground, 6" high, and you galloped towards it with a wooden lance carried across your front. As you approached the peg you would present the lance, drop it, and aim it at the peg, hopefully spearing it and raising it out of the ground. I loved this competition. The wooden pegs would be 4" across so at speed, on top of a horse, it was a skill to stab them and lift them. If the scores were ever tied they would turn the peg on its side so you were going for a 2" surface. Now that was skilful.

In the summer we trained to do the musical ride. This involved sixteen horses side by side in half sections. The riders carried lances with pennants on them. The lances would be stuck into a lance bucket which was attached to your right stirrup. They were made of bamboo and were eight foot long. The points were metal and very sharp.

We trotted in sitting trot and had about twenty movements including circles away returning back into formation. At the end of the arena we would split left and right and then cross over in a scissors move, being very close to each other. Half way through and we came into a formation in twos, head to tail.

We then performed a barn dance, moving away from each other on a beat, turning around on the horses' haunches and then coming back together. Then the music changed to a waltz and we would circle very tightly around each other and go forwards and backwards in pairs together and then backwards and forwards together on the beat. We then resumed the ride at the canter performing changes and circles around each other. We ended the ride coming together at the end of the arena in a long single line. We did a lance drill and charged forward a la charge of the Light Brigade.

The activity ride known as the 'Tivvy' was brilliant and I just loved it. We would go into the arena and gallop right around the arena waving to the crowd. We entered to the music 'Fanfare for the common man,' then the 'Robin Hood' theme struck in and other marching music. We then formed up into twos and jumped up a line of eight brushwood jumps. At the end we split left and right and jumped across the jumps very close to each other in a scissors movement. We then came down in twos, holding hands in what was known as the bridal arch. We split again and some of the riders stayed at the top end. We then came up the jumps in twos with horses coming over the jumps towards us and through the middle of us.

We carried on around the arena and pulled our stirrups off. You had to put loads of Vaseline on the top of the stirrup bar so you could get them off quickly. When everyone signalled they had them off, we jumped up the line of jumps with our stirrups held out at our sides. Then we dropped them in pairs on the ground and as we went around the arena we undid the buttons on our jackets. We again went up the jumps taking our jackets off and waving them above our heads. Back up the jumps and you put the jacket back on.

There was a little respite here as the ground crew put up on the centre jump, a big metal hoop covered in flammable material. This hoop was set on fire and we went up in twos and jumped through it. Jumps at the side of the arena were also set alight and we jumped over those too. The horses were just bloody fantastic and they did it very well.

The finale was special. As we were cantering around the arena, you leaned down and undid your girth, letting it drop down under the horse. The big trick here was never ever to do this on a corner or else you were on the floor, no doubt about it. You always did this manoeuvre on the straight long side of the arena. When the girth was gone you raised both legs over the front of your saddle and at the same time, with your strongest hand, reached behind and pulled your saddle out from underneath you. When we were all ready we would gallop up the jumps for the final time with our saddles held up in the air. It was knackering but totally exhilarating and the adrenalin rush was fantastic.

My first competition was at Staffordshire Police horse show. We were billeted at the Staffordshire show ground and I was riding Cavalier in the novice rider competition. Twenty eight were in the class. The dressage test went well and I was in fifth place at that point. The next day was the nuisance lane.

We wore ceremonial uniform for the competitions. The tunics were Victorian type with a high collar which had a lion head on either side of the collar. We wore cartouche belts too and were very smart.

The nuisance lane was fairly straight forward but you can never be complacent because the horse has a brain, and therefore a mind of their own. One of the nuisances was a candy striped BT tent raised up high and we had to ride straight through it. I bobbed my head down and in he went. Inside there were hanging streamers which you had to push aside. He was very good as he had not been in one of these before. He did though, stand on the dummy on the floor with his back leg as we went over.

I came fifth out of twenty eight and as the rosettes and prizes were to sixth I won a nice tankard and rosette. Apparently I was the first from our branch to get placed in a competition for some time. I was very pleased but back at home the knives were out again. Jealousy was horrible within the branch. Cliques were very prevalent.

We performed at a Police day in Roundhay Park in Leeds. The musical ride went badly wrong. The lad leading it alongside the Sergeant forgot it and took his side of the ride off on a tangent. They sort of got back in time for the barn dance and waltz but we had a right bollocking from the Inspector. The activity ride went well until the end, when two of the members of the ride fell off with their saddles in their hands. The horses were caught quite quickly and they were ok. We just carried on as it was virtually the end of the ride.

The fall out of this debacle was training and lots of it. Some of the lads did not want to do these rides, but thankfully lots did. We practised hard and I was chosen to lead the musical ride alongside the Sergeant. I had not asked for this, I could just always remember it. It was important to me to get it right all the time. We were on show and at some of the events serious proper horse people were there and looking at us very closely.

Blacup Baroness (Bonnie)

EGOR

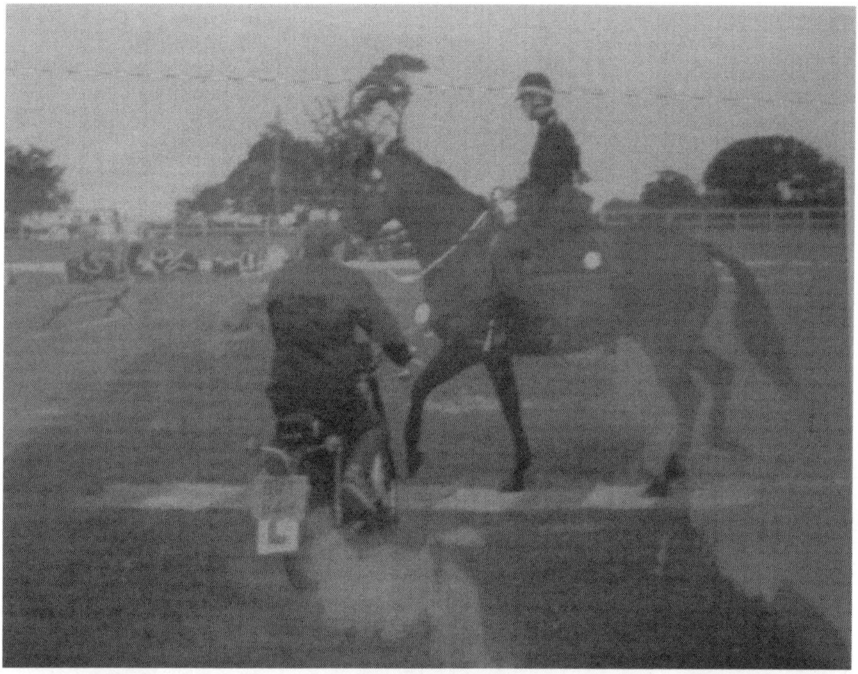

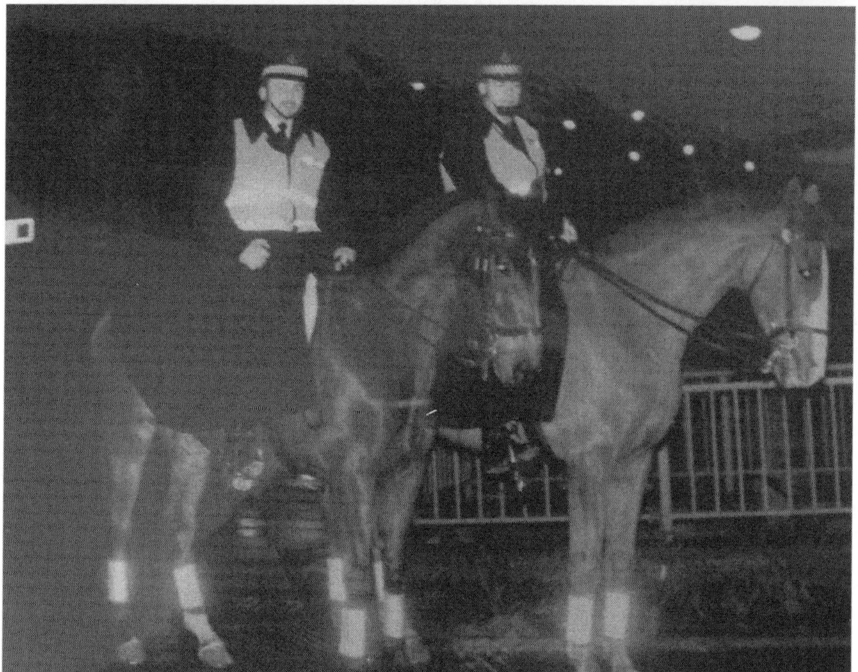

Remount patrol picking up my son James for the ride

The aim was obviously to win, but to get into the top ten was looked upon as a great success. Three day eventing was spread over three days and included the dressage test following a veterinary inspection trot up. The endurance day comprised of a roads and tracks section at a steady pace again within an optimum time. A gallop against the clock over steeplechase fences and then straight out onto a second shorter roads and tracks phase. On completion of this second roads and tracks you came into a ten minute halt box. It was then onto the cross country course. The final day was the showjumping run in reverse order.

Our first competition was at Winmarleigh in Lancashire. It was at Pre-novice level which is roughly a metre high show jumping and cross country. The feature fence on this course was a double of black and white lock gates, a mock-up of the lock gates you get at a canal. They were very upright and in the middle of a field after a long galloping section. We did okay and both horses went double clear.

We both had time faults on the cross country, earned by going too slow. Very pleased, we got home and were on a high. This high we experienced took three to four days to get over. It was an amazing feeling crossing the finishing line on the cross country having gone clear. It stayed with me for ever.

The rest of the season went without any problems. Sue was much better than me at getting the time right galloping across country. We did, though, struggle with the dressage. Tessa, Sue's horse did have a few alarming moments on her back legs when she objected to certain jumps. We travelled all over competing and visited Lancashire, Leicestershire, all of Yorkshire and into County Durham too. We met some lovely people and had a great time.

The first time we upgraded to Novice level was at the Harrogate Equestrian centre and we both did really well. I had a jump down in the ring and a small amount of cross country time faults. Sue was double clear but clocked up quite a few time penalties. The biggest buzz was the cross country of course, and going clear was a fabulous accomplishment.

Sue and I decided we wanted to go ahead and take the British Horse Society examinations to gain the Assistant Instructors qualification. We booked in for an assessment with Major Birtwhistle, the owner of Harrogate Equestrian centre. We duly turned up at 10 am on the day. Left in the waiting room for nearly half an hour he eventually came in and asked us if he could help.

I explained what we were there for and he had not got a clue. So without knowing us or ascertaining whether or not we had any idea about horses, he gave us a saddle and bridle each, showed us two horses and told us to tack them up which we did. We then rode them in the indoor arena whilst another lesson was taking place.

Fifteen minutes later he told us to dismount. He went onto say that we would be suitable candidates for the examinations although in his opinion we needed a great deal of help and instruction. £30 later we went home, totally bemused and feeling very hard done by and to be honest, ripped off.

A short while later we went back there on an evening with the guys from the mounted branch. We watched a display by the great John Lassetter and his gorgeous wife Charlotte. It was a very good demo and we then sat in the bar with them when everyone else had gone and got very drunk. The Major was a generous host and I think we drank his bar dry and so got our £30 back.

With a little support from the Mounted Police at work we signed onto a course at a stables near Sheffield. We attended once a week for lectures and a riding lesson. Stage One was taken quickly and we both passed. On the course we met a wonderful lady called Sharon Peshke, who had dressage horses at home, and her husband Kevin who was a top fashion photographer and into polo. She was so funny, Sharon, and one of those ladies that was always smiling, in fact beaming.

We went with her to take our Stage Two examination at RAF Finningley. We met her at the side of the motorway and went in her car, the dashboard was full of teddy bears and dolls, all good luck mascots. It must off worked because all three of us passed.

Sometime later we all went together to Bold Heath Equestrian centre in Cheshire and took the Preliminary Teaching exam and we all passed again. Stage Three, the final part of the AI examination, was taken at the Yorkshire Riding Centre. We went together and both the girls passed both sections. I was mortified to have passed the stable management but failed the riding. On the feedback Kate Kerr, one of the examiners, told me to ride as many horses as possible.

After I explained that on average I was riding three horses a day and was a mounted Policeman she went over to the other examiners to get the decision reversed!! I was gob smacked. Anyway, they did not and the fail stood. I was very pleased for Sue and Sharon but gutted for myself.

Two weeks later I went to Derbyshire to re-take the riding element. A lady there was a right pain. She was going on and on about the horses and the standard of them. She couldn't ride actually. She was given a great big horse called Mr Bones to jump. She was hopeless and was complaining about this horse like mad. It was pointed out to her that the horse she was riding, Mr Bones, was better known as Sanyo Technology and he had, in a previous life won the Hickstead Derby ridden by the great Harvey Smith. That shut her up!

On the flat I rode a large lazy horse and I was struggling. Janet Plant, the chief examiner, called me over and asked me honestly what would I do with this horse if I was at home, "Hit it" I said, "So hit it then" she said. I did, the horse woke up and went quite nicely.

In the jumping section they brought me out a small 15.2 cobby thing that they assured me could jump. I crossed the stirrups over the saddle to get me elevated off his back. I jumped him round and boy, he could jump. I passed, much to my relief.

The following year I decided to take the next level of examinations, the British Horse Society Intermediate Instructor. Sue couldn't be bothered with it so I went alone. I trained with a lady called Sonia Berry. She was very dry and really took the mickey at every opportunity, we got on very well.

I took the riding and stable management at the Yorkshire Riding Centre. In the conformation section I was teamed up with a Swedish girl who lived in Scotland. Gosh, the gob on this girl! She took over trying to answer every question. Marian Watts, one of the examiners, had to tell her to shut up.

They brought out an older looking horse and to me it was still looking very fit. We were asked to look at him and tell Marian what we thought. I was holding him and trotted him up for the Swede. She went on and on about this horse being old and weak, not having done much with its life and it being under developed. I couldn't believe this. She trotted him up for me and I went totally against her. I said the horse had a very well developed musculature, was still very fit and I also said in my opinion he had had a very useful life at probably a very good level.

Marian agreed and said the horse had competed at 3* level eventing with Christopher Bartle who had represented Great Britain in the Olympics at Dressage and went on later to win Badminton Horse trials.

We then went inside the stable block and were told to apply bandages to the knee and the hock of a horse. I took the front leg, the Swede took the rear. I put the opposite leg bandage on first for support, the underneath support bandage and then the gamgee and finally the figure of eight bandage. The Swede just put a simple bandage on the hock. Sonia was an examiner and checked mine saying it was ok. We had had fifteen minutes to complete this task. The Swede said "I would have put a support bandage on the other leg too and underneath the hock bandage" Sonia just looked at her and said "so why didn't you blooming well do it then?"

Outside each stable was a piece of square wood hanging down off a hook. Sonia asked me in front of the other candidates, what these were for? I looked at them, picked one up and was thinking quickly. I said "Oh I know, they are for jamming into the sliding stable doors to stop them sliding shut" "No don't think so" says she. Panicking now I said "Oh I know, got it, they use them to jam the revolving feed bins when feeding so they don't trap the horses noses" "No that's not right." Really panicking, I had not got a clue and had exhausted all my options.

A girl who worked there was in the stables. Sonia asked her what they were for, she picked one up revolved it around on the hook and it stuck out horizontally. "They are saddle racks for tacking up" said the groom. 'Blooming 'eck of course they are' said Sonia. "Didn't you know either, isn't that an examination question" I said. "No I hadn't got a clue, always wondered what they were for "said Sonia!!!

I passed the day. They did not tell you on the day at that level, you were sent a report and a certificate to your home so I do not know if the Swede passed or not.

I booked in not long after this for the teaching examination at Snainton Riding Centre near Scarborough. On the day I had a really bad cold, it was a stinker and I nearly called and cancelled myself for the day, but decided to go. I was sweating, cold and streaming. I got there and was given the individual lesson to do first. Gaye Bartle examined me on this and winked and nodded at me at the end. Good so far. Upstairs I went into a classroom for the oral examination. Greeted by Mr Tim Downs who had a fedora on and a clip board.

He squealed in delight at the presence of a man. It was, to be fair, rare that men took these examinations He started with the other three girls asking them about dressage, he was brusque. When he came to me he said, very condescendingly, that I looked like a show jumper.

He asked me, when teaching someone to jump an ascending fence, would I encourage them to get under the fence or take off further away. I asked for clarification in that is the horse a young horse ridden by an experienced jockey, or the other way around or is it, that the horse is experienced with an experienced jockey? He said I should just answer the question, I explained if it was a young horse I would encourage the use of ground poles to allow the horse a clear pathway to take off.

He picked up his clipboard and wrote a large x on it. He exaggerated this motion. I was appalled and lost my temper.

I said "Do that again."

He said "Do what exactly?"

I said "That big cross on your clipboard, do it again" I was shouting now.

He shouted back "What I write on here is for my record."

At this time Alec Lyle, who owned Snainton and was the chief examiner for the day came in. We had a row about it all and I went home. I got a report a few weeks later stating the obvious, that I had failed.

A couple of months later and I went back to take the exam again. I passed this time, although it was a red hot day and when I had to do the lunge lesson they sent me a volunteer pupil to teach. She was very tall, very gorgeous and had a very tight pair of white see through jodhpurs on which were very see through and a black thong underneath. Concentration was difficult of course, but I soldiered through.

Two years later and I had been on an advanced riding course through the Police. I attended Lancashire Mounted Branch and had daily lessons from Sue Pimbley BHSI. In conversation she found out I had my stage 4 exams and encouraged me to take the Instructors examination as there were very few men who did it. I started training with Sonia, Gaye Bartle and went out a lot with my vet for days at a time to see the latest techniques and drugs that were being used. I also spent a great deal of effort in the general preparation for the exam including attending Stoneleigh, the National Equestrian Centre in Warwickshire, for a two day training course.

On the day of the exam at saddlers' yard Stoneleigh, I stayed overnight in a motel nearby to be there on time and fresh. You usually take the exam in twos but a girl from Hong Kong had missed her flight and could not attend so I was on my own. Great, not the best start. The first section was assessing a horse for breeding purposes. This bit was examined by Sue Pimbley. I looked at the mare and seeing as I had done a lot of work with the vet on breeding and suitability, I discussed at length vulva conformation and the mare on offer. She was suitably impressed and winked at me.

The next stage was assessing a horse for purchase for use for Stage 4 pupils. The horse on offer was very young and weak looking. I just spoke honestly and said after a very brief look at it that I wouldn't buy it for the purpose of training Stage 4 students. I asked for him to be trotted up and he was lame so I stopped it straight away. That confirmed my thoughts.

The examiner was not happy about this for some reason and asked me to look at the horse's feet. He had heart bar shoes on and I told her this, though of course she knew and that was what she expected me to find. I had already made my mind up of course, before looking at the shoes as the horse was weak and would not have been able to cope with the rigours of Stage 4 training. I had not found the shoes though and so I did not think that had gone that well.

Next was my mini lecture. I had an overhead projector, a small audience and the examiner was Margot Tiffany, who I knew from training at Sheffield for my previous exams. I gave a lecture on slow releasing energy feeds for horses and especially their use in endurance horses. This was well received and she also nodded at me and winked.

Buoyed by this, the next session was the veterinary products test. Everyone had told me that in this there are numerous products on a table for use by a vet. I would be shown anything from the table and asked about it. I walked into the stable and there were at least three hundred bottles, sachets and bags of things on the table. The examiner, a tiny lady, asked me to find from the table something that would be used for treating ring worm.

I started at one end, taken aback somewhat. I thought it would take ages for me to find anything. I was searching and after a while she said I was not warm. I looked at her panicking. I started further up the table looking. I was looking for a paste or a topical wash but there was nothing. After another age I said "Please give me an idea where it is I will be ages searching". She replied "You are not even warm, keep looking." I sighed and carried on and she said "Not warm." This was ridiculous, I had been looking for seven minutes at all these packages, sachets and bottles. I said "Please just ask me about something on this table, anything at all, this is silly." "You want to fail? Keep looking," was her reply.

I jumped off the ground, both feet together, to the bottom of the table and said "Cold or luke warm?" then I jumped again to the middle of the table, "Warm now." Then I jumped again to the very end where I had not been. "Hot or not?" She was very alarmed now at this idiot panicking man jumping up and down in front of the table bellowing at her. Carol Broad, the senior examiner came in and asked what on earth was going on? I let her explain and she told lies, saying I had lost my temper and had frightened her.

I explained that I had not lost my temper and then told her my side of the story. Carol told me to go get a coffee and calm down. By now though, I had had enough of this nonsense, bade them all good day and went home. That was the end of my involvement with the British Horse Society.

The second season of eventing started really well and we were very soon upgraded permanently to Novice level. This involved bigger jumps and the cross country courses were bigger, technical, and the optimum time was tighter.

We started the horses off on walking work the day after Boxing Day again and progressed to trotting and canter interval training. Competitions for jumping at Wood Nook Arenas and dressage there too, as well as Wikefield Farm on the outskirts of Leeds went really well. Wikefield had a good cross country schooling course as well so we went there frequently. The Harrogate Equestrian Centre also ran affiliated competitions and we schooled there as often as we could.

I also attended my first Rockwood Pony Club Camp as an instructor at Beverly racecourse. A full week of teaching a group of kids working towards their Pony Club C and C+ tests. I had a ball. The days were spent getting the ponies ready after mucking out, an inspection of turn out and then out onto the racecourse or across the road to a large piece of common land known as the Westwood for lessons on the flat and jumping.

Evenings were brilliant fun with the other instructors, made better when I got one of the kids to open the jockey changing rooms by crawling through a louvre window after I had removed the glass from. Once in I put on the sauna and we all had saunas for the rest of the week.

I had taught Oliver Townend some years earlier at a rally. On that first camp I had him again in my group and he was a funny cheeky little bugger but he had an ear for learning and a feel for his pony. No one could have known then of course what was to come. His amazing success on the world stage was founded firmly in that pony club.

On the Thursday we took them all to Bridlington for the day. Gaynor Greenhalgh the DC wanted all of them to go onto the beach to play games but the kids who were over thirteen were not happy about this at all. I acted as a go between and she agreed I and two other instructors could take them up to the fun fair.

This went really well until three of them came off the Wurlitzer looking very green and threw up over the beach wall. The problem was that on the other side some twenty feet down on the beach were people sunbathing.

Chapter Seven

We were stabling the horses at Shibden on livery and were happy. The wagon though was parked some way away at our friends' place and it was a pain travelling to and fro. A friend of ours, in the pub one night, was talking about a yard for rent in Coley Road which was in the next village. My ears pricked up and I asked some more questions. The next day I drove up and had a look at the yard. It was very decrepit with a few old railway carriageways scattered about. There were though, twelve stables and a big barn, an arena and some fields.

That evening after work Sue and I met there and we had a walk round. A lady came across the small road outside and asked us what we were doing. It turned out she was Angela Awan., she was married to Dr Awan and they owned the yard. Two hours later and we had rented the whole place. She originally wanted to rent individual stables on a DIY basis but we convinced her one person renting would be better for control and financial reasons. There was fifteen acres of land and the arena was 55 meters by 20 meters. Utopia!

Sue had reservations but I was totally up for it. We moved in a few weeks later after we had spent hours cleaning it up, emptying dirty stables and weeding the place. We brought the wagon there too and I made us a private tack room at the back and we later put in a hot water system.

Over the next few years we changed the yard by getting rid of the old railway boxes and putting up new boxes in their place. We extended the arena and built a small schooling cross country course. The land was clay and in the winter it was very wet so we had to carefully manage the grazing.

The hacking was still great as we were only two miles from the Shibden Valley. We also had a field down the road, which we could use for cantering and interval work at any time as it belonged to the council and it was left fallow. Coley Road was a quiet backwater between Bradford and Halifax. It was all green belt in the area. Coley Road church, which was next door, was built in the 15th century and it had a very interesting history, especially in the Cromwellian period. Coley Hall was just down a private track alongside the church and had an underground tunnel to the church to allow for secret and then illegal worship by the family during the Civil War.

We hadn't thought about taking liveries but when we were approached by a couple of people to bring their horses on a DIY basis we eventually agreed. A girl called Angela was the first livery we agreed to and she moved in with her big black Hannovarian horse and a young girl came with a pony. Word got around and over the next few months we became full and had a waiting list. The income from these horses paid all the bills at the yard and also paid for the keep of our two horses, so it was a winner.

That season was interrupted by the yard and all the work we had to do. Although we were going well, on the whole, it was not a planned out season that lead us to upgrading or to achieving our goals. Sue and I also began to teach and earn money. Sue did the Pony Club every weekend and I had some private clients at various times. It was all working out very well.

We changed the wagon too. Our beloved old Bedford made way for a green three horse Leyland Daf 45. It was quite smart, and best of all, it had six gears. Our final event of that year was at Bishop Burton College of Agriculture. This was notable for the fact that Sue had a crashing fall in the water fence but was ok. We were parked next to the great Mary King, she had King William there, and we had few chats with her throughout the day. She was lovely, encouraging and very friendly.

Sue was okay after the fall, no damage or injuries, Tessa had just tripped on landing. Bonnie though was becoming a real problem. She was so strong across country and a bit kamikaze to say the least. She would go headlong at full gallop, and as the fences at Novice level were more technical I needed a good deal more control than I had. I decided to hunt her and had a day with the Badsworth hunt near Wakefield. Big mistake, she was even worse, it just blew her head and she gave me the ride from hell. She was plunging and careering about and just wanted to gallop headlong out. I went home and bid goodnight at one o'clock that day.

Sue had a great day, Tessa was a superb hunter and took to it like a duck to water. Sue hunted quite a few days that season and when it was the Frickley meet with lots of jumping, she was working so I took Tessa, what a day I had! We were up the front jumping everything and she was just fabulous. I ended up going for tea with Charlie Ward-Aldham the Master. We went up to his loft above the stables at Frickley Hall and had a stew and lots of beer and wine. I drove home in the wagon with Sue's precious horse on board. If she knew how much I had imbibed she would have been furious.

Over the years we had many liveries come and go, some went and then came back. We had a mass exodus one Christmas of eight liveries who all left to go down the road to a farm. The farmer had converted a shed into stables and that was all he offered, stables and grazing, no tack rooms, storage for rugs, no arena and no supervision. They also had to park their cars out on the road. We had a car park.

He was though, £5 per week cheaper than us and so they left. Sue was really upset but my attitude was, sod them, if they want to go you can't stop them. We very quickly filled the empty boxes and one by one over the next few months each one of them asked us if they could come back as they had made a big mistake. I churlishly would not let them return or use our arena, even for a hire fee.

Paul was by far the worst livery we ever endured. He came with a fabulous big grey horse called Oscar. He was a body builder bloke who DJ'd and also, we found out later, managed strippers. He was on the dole and claimed as many benefits possible for his four children that he had at home. I cannot say he looked after them because he didn't. He hardly ever rode and it's a fact that when Sue and I were at the yard he rarely was. When we were not there though he certainly was.

By this time we had girls working for us as grooms and Kirsty was our head girl. She was lovely and very gentle and soft in nature. It eventually came out that this Paul was insisting on his horse's food being weighed and during the day he was having him brought in with a large haylege net and put into an different stable as he did not like the stable he was allocated. He was also a plain nuisance to the girls throughout the day.

When I found all this out I confronted him about it and we had serious words which resulted in me giving him notice to leave. He certainly did not like being stood up to and most certainly was not use to and did not like the word 'no'. He eventually apologised and asked to stay. I foolishly relented.

He had a thing for Sue and made it very obvious and over the time he was with us he did make overt approaches. He was always late with his livery payments and it was a constant problem to get the money from him. He was going hunting one day with another livery we had, a lad called Richard. They were going in Richard's wagon. Hunting was cancelled due to extreme fog and so they decided to cook a breakfast in the horsebox which they promptly set fire to. The fire brigade attended and the wagon was a right off.

Paul came to a sorry end when, owing three weeks livery and despite him pleading poverty, he attended the Christmas Do we had for the whole yard at Sandal farm in Thornton. He spent the evening glaring at me and giving me evils all through the meal. He was obviously spoiling for a fight. During the dancing, which all the girls were up for, he went and started suggestively dancing with Sue. He was giving it large and was embarrassing. Sue sorted him though, she said very loudly "Paul, we have two rules at Coley stables, one is pay your livery on time and the second is you don't try and shag the wife". He left, three days later his horse was gone and we never saw him again.

One evening Sue and I were on our way home from riding police horses at an evening football match. We saw, as we approached the yard, that the lights were on in the hay barn. I stopped the car outside the gate, vaulted it and ran into the barn. Sue had started to call the Police. I ran in and found one our liveries and her boyfriend naked in the hay. Embarrassed does not cover it.

Joyce was a nurse, a lovely lady in the main, and her husband Wilf was also a very nice man and we became friends. Joyce had a lovely big bay gelding called Stevie, he did have a cloudy eye but it did not bother him. She was happy hacking him although he was a handful. Sue had a sit on him one day and liked him. She started riding him and then took him competing for Joyce who loved the "owner" status.

She bought Sue a set of cross country colours to wear and nothing was too much trouble for the horse. She also made wonderful food for us when we went eventing. There was a big problem though, she could not stop bitching and talking about us behind our backs. All sorts of stuff was coming back to us via the other liveries. She was quite nasty sometimes but most of it was puerile and ridiculous. We did have a quiet private word with her but she moaned about this too and it got back to us.

Things came to a head one Saturday. She worked at the GUM clinic on a Saturday morning in Brighouse. She would always call and ask who wanted fish and chips from a fabulous chippy nearby. One day the order was called through and we were all in the portakabin which we had in the yard for liveries to get a drink and meetings and such. Joyce arrived with all the fish and chips and we were all busy dishing them out, passing red and brown sauce and making tea and coffee.

It became apparent that there was one portion short and as Joyce had had a falling out with another livery Kim the week before she admitted that she had left her out. Kim was good about it saying it did not matter and she walked out. I went into the kitchen and got a bin liner, scooped all the fish and chips into this liner and gave it to Joyce and I said "we don't do this here Joyce, everyone gets included or no one". I left then. Her husband came up later shouting about the amount of money she had spent on food and we ended up having words.

A couple of weeks later and Stevie was on the clipping list for the day but he was last on the list. I had one particularly difficult one to do and we had to sedate him which meant the last two did not get done as I had to get to work. Behind my back Joyce went off on one and was calling me lazy and a rip off merchant as her horse was costing a fortune for little reward and that he was always last to be considered for anything. She did not want to but she left a week later.

Louise was a young lady in her twenties who came to us with two horses she had bought for herself to event. They came on full competition livery and one was already Intermediate level and the other was a Novice. She had obviously paid a lot of money for these horses from a professional rider. The horses were soon followed by an Oakley Supreme horsebox. We were very impressed and for two weeks she came every day schooled them and fell into our training regime where every Tuesday and Thursday the horses were jumped, either at home or we took them jumping. The rest of the week was either hacking days, canter days or schooling days.

We sat down with her and planned her season, she was hoping to upgrade both horses and then go onto some three day events. All was good until she stopped coming. She literally one day did not turn up and we never saw her again. Some men came to take the wagon away and after a phone call to verify this I allowed it to go. Then the horses were picked up by someone from Cheshire to go to be sold on.

We were offered a job by two local girls who were sisters, they had a mare and yearling at foot at a stud farm in Newbury. They wanted the mare back and as a payment for picking her up we could keep the yearling. It was a big bay colt called Bayleaf. We agreed to this and went down one Saturday to fetch them. We only had two stables free at the time and so they were bedded down and made ready. One of them was on our own yard the other in the DIY block.

A couple of weeks prior to this, a lady called Jane brought her daughter's pony to us on livery. The pony was called Bothy and it came covered in lice and in a very poor state. We cleaned him up and treated his lice, his feed was managed for them as they did not know what they were doing and he began showing great improvement.

We got to Newbury and picked up these two horses. The colt was a big, well made youth and we liked him. We got stuck in traffic on the way home and did not get back until nine pm. The stable on our block was not a problem for the colt and he settled ok. The other stable for the mare though was full, it had a grey pony in it. I was fuming. I rang our head girl and she did not know anything about it. I had to go to the field, bring in a gate and make a temporary stall for this pony so we could put the mare in her intended box.

The next day all became clear, Jane had arranged for the pony to stay overnight as Poppy had a friend having a sleepover. Charming. I told Jane how out of line she was and she apologised. She had not mentioned this to anyone. She did try make amends with a bottle of Bollinger, which was nice.

When the six weeks school holidays came about the Nanny started bringing Poppy, who was only ten years old, up to the yard and leaving her there all day. This was no good as we could not supervise her and it was dangerous, especially when she started walking home on her own. I tried to explain that we were not a nursery and couldn't have her there all day, on her own unsupervised and that she was walking home through a long quiet country footpath. They moved the pony away fairly quickly and left us with the feeling that we had let them down.

The colt, Bayleaf, was being prep'd by the vet for castration when he told us that he had a disastrously bad heart murmur. We were devastated. It was checked again over a period of days at frequent intervals. It did not get better with exercise or at rest. We had to make the decision to have him put to sleep. I have often wondered if the girls knew about this problem and that is why they gave him to us so readily in payment for transporting the mare back to Yorkshire.

All was not doom and gloom with liveries, we had some lovely people who stayed with us for years and we made a lot of money from them in livery costs and extras such as clipping and teaching. A nucleus of constant, settled liveries makes for a happy yard. We did learn quite quickly that you cannot become best friends with people for whom you look after horses. It is fraught with danger and fall outs can be very costly. But, there are exceptions to every rule. Darrel came to us on livery within year two of having the yard and stayed with us for years. He is a life- long friend and we went through every emotion with him. Tragedy and so many laughs.

He had a chestnut mare that he was bringing but just the weekend before she was to arrive she did a tendon at a hunter trial. He got her out on loan to breed and we set about buying him a horse. The first horse we saw, he bought. Solomon was a bay gelding four years old and very under developed. He was weak and I did not want him to buy him. He did though and he came to us and settled very well. He cannot have had him more than five weeks when he got kicked in the field and shattered his forearm. Oh my days, it was devastating. I held him in the field whilst Sally the vet shot him. The kennels picked him up and I was inconsolabe. Darrel was very philosophical about it but I am sure he was as devastated as Sue and I. We set about finding him another horse and went to Sue Clark's. She had a giant chestnut gelding called Tommy Riley, he was Irish and very well made, he was tried and vetted and came home.

This horse was a nightmare. He became called "Tommy bastard Riley". He had a mind of his own and would not do anything he did not fancy. We went schooling with him to Harrogate Equestrian Centre and in the field he just stuck his head in a hedge and refused to come out. Darrel was trying so hard to pull him out of the hedge but he just would not. Sue and I could not move for laughing. Darrel laughed too but he was almost hysterical. It was the very beginning of the end, he went hunting and did well and that was his career.

Back to liveries. One thing for sure is, that you could offer, within the price, gold plated stables, with en-suite shower rooms and a Thai massage after they have ridden and it is still not enough. They would still find fault and complain. The most ludicrous incident with liveries came with the Meadows girls:

Lynne and Gail Meadows were mum and daughter. They approached us for summer grazing for their driving pony. We agreed and they brought it down. They then asked if they could store their harness in one of the tack rooms and we agreed. They then asked if they could bring the cart they used down and store it in the garage we had to save them transporting it every day, and we agreed. This was a lot of services for a grass only livery of £10 per week per horse. Anyway, they seemed nice people and we were happy to help.

Sue and I were going on holiday in July. It was one of a very few we took during the eventing season which runs from March to October. We would normally have a week at either end. We flew on the Friday and I had asked my dad to keep an eye out on the yard if he was passing. The next day, the Saturday he did just happen to pass and stopped and called in when he saw a large white transit van in the yard.

A young lad was unloading speakers, wires lighting stations and decks. My dad asked him what he was doing and who he was. "I am here for the party mate, I am the DJ" "What bloody party?" says my dad. A car turned up and a man started making a temporary bar and unloading drink right in the entrance way to our barn with our event horses in it.

It was, as it turned out, Gail's sixteenth birthday and as they knew we were away on holiday, her parents had decided that our yard would be an excellent venue for a large party. My dad, bless him in no uncertain terms got rid of the DJ and the barman and awaited the Meadows family. Mum Lynne was first, she arrived with large pans of chilli and rice, bread and dips. She was told unceremoniously that the party was cancelled. A massive row erupted and my dad called me. He eventually got me and I told him no way had we agreed to a party. My poor father was at the yard until 9.30 pm that day turning up to sixty people away with various amounts of alcohol. Thankfully, on our return home they had gone.

Chapter Eight

My first full winter on the mounted branch went very well. Football Season was the biggest part of our job. We policed Leeds United, Bradford City and Huddersfield Town. We also regularly policed Featherstone Rovers, Castleford Tigers and Wakefield Rugby League. On certain matches we acted as mutual aid to Derby County Football. These were good days out as we always got lots of overtime. We always worked with South Yorkshire Police on these games and they were great fun to be with.

Fighting at matches was a big problem and a few incidents stand out. When we got to Elland Road, the home of Leeds United, we would get straight out onto patrol. We had two officers in Elland Road itself, and two in the west stand car park in Lowfields Road. Six officers would be alongside the east stand, as that was where the main big concourse was, and the place where all the busses despatched the Leeds fans from the city centre.

Away from the ground there is a pub called the Wheatsheaf, and this is where the hard core United fans gathered, so we always had two horses there too. The visiting fans, on official coaches, would be taken by motorcycle escort to a big parking area that was on the other side of the M621 motorway. To get them to the ground we would form an escort with officers on horses and on foot either side of them. We always had two horses in front of them and usually one behind. The worst part of the journey up to the ground was to take them underneath the motorway. We had, literally, just enough room to bend down under this flyover, on the horses. The fans would always chant and jeer under here because of the echo effect.

It was a bloody good horse to walk under there with all that noise. We had quite a few incidents under that flyover. God knows what Health & Safety would say about it nowadays. When we took the visitors up Lowfields Road alongside the east stand we always had idiots from the Leeds lot having a go. This was usually where it all kicked off and serious fighting was not uncommon. The visitors were taken onto the top of Lowfields Road, where it met Elland Road, and into the south stand which was where the visitors were housed.

When the game kicked off at 3 o'clock we went back to the horseboxes and lined up. On the order, every other horse would take steps forward one horse's length. We were then ordered to 'make ready'. This meant that all together we swung our legs over the horse, remaining standing on one stirrup. At the next order we all lowered ourselves to the floor. It was called a formal dismount. It was quite impressive. Horses were then boxed up with hay and they were always rugged up so they were warm and happy.

We had delivered to the horseboxes, by one of the dog handler vans, a doggy bag in which we had sandwiches, a pork pie, crisps etc. The fleet of wagons we had then did not have toilets in them and we had to go in the back of the wagons for a pee. We used to shout 'watering the horses'. If you needed to do anything else it was a long walk around the ground to the toilets in the police cells inside the ground.

At certain big games we would walk around the ground into the west stand and watch the match. We got back onto the horses twenty minutes before the end of the game. This again involved a formal mounting procedure, which was the reverse of the dismount. Everyone on the branch had to be able to mount their horse from the ground.

At the end of the game we always had eight horses across the gateway into the south stand to hold back the visitors. This involved the horses standing, heads facing in, across the big gateway and then we had officers behind us on foot. The visitors were used to being held back at all grounds and they were, in the main, well behaved. They just really wanted to go home. If we had trouble outside though it would mean holding them for a long time and then they would get arsy about the wait.

When we got the order we would reverse the horses out of the gateway and form an escort for the supporters back to the coaches. This was where we could have big trouble with the home fans waiting for them. We had to be on our toes at this point and getting isolated could be fraught with danger.

The visitors who had come on the special trains from the city centre were provided with buses back to the train station, and every now and again they would refuse to get onto them, preferring to walk. Well we could not have a load of supporters walking on their own back into the city centre, it was just a recipe for bother. We had to escort them.

The police always tried their very best to get them onto the buses but sometimes it was futile. We never escorted them straight into the town centre. Oh no, fuck them, we walked them at least three miles further than they needed to go. We were on horses so it was okay for us. They were knackered by the time they got to the station. Home fans would be at the station waiting for them and we regularly ended up on the station platform sorting out fighting fans. We had to be very careful though as the concrete on the concourse could be like a skating rink for the horses.

At that time, arresting people at football matches was not common amongst the mounted branch, this changed a great deal in the seasons to come. The ethos was that really we were there to escort and be a preventative show of strength. When it really kicked off though, we really came into our own. Sunderland at Leeds was my first taste of major trouble.

It was Boxing Day and we were all on duty as trouble was inevitable. The Sunderland lot turned up in all manner of vehicles. One big white transit van came along Elland Road and mounted the big concourse outside the east stand. We went straight to it as did other foot units. The driver was absolutely pissed. He could not stand up. He was arrested and most of the other young lads inside the van were also lifted. The back of the van was littered with bottles of beer and vodka. One of the foot units drove it away. The buses bringing supporters off the trains turned up and we were waiting for them. We had horses stood alongside the doors of the buses to stop them getting off randomly, and to try our best to keep control of them. On one of the buses the upstairs emergency window was opened and the supporters were jumping out. They were grabbed. Officers travelling on the busses were outnumbered and could not do anything. We formed a cordon alongside the vehicles and let them off. They were chanting and jeering at the top of their voices.

The Leeds fans were gathering and counter jeering. It was very noisy and other horses were called around from other parts of the ground. We moved them across the concourse towards the stand turnstiles and then the Leeds lot charged. It was pandemonium. We formed a line quickly, facing the home Leeds fans, and walked towards them.

Most supporters were twenty yard heroes, they would stand and motion you on towards them. As soon as we moved toward them they would run off. It was pathetic. As we moved in a line all together the fans moved backwards. They still chanted and jeered and the noise was amazing. We just pushed them backwards towards their own stand and they went inside the ground and the crisis was averted. Gold Commander, the man in charge on the day, radioed through his thanks to us for our efforts.

We went to the visiting coaches to escort them up. We had to wait whilst units were put in place across the big gateway at the bottom of the east stand as this was where all the Leeds fans congregated. We set off with them and I was alongside, on the right, which was going to be nearest to the east stand. The supporters on the coaches were just pissed. A lot of them were struggling to walk, let alone get into the ground. If you were in drink and considered drunk you were not allowed in the ground, but there was no way we could bar all this lot.

Under the motorway they chanted and shouted as usual and we kept them in order. As we got to the ground, I realised that there were an awful of Leeds supporters waiting. The radio was going mad and we were told to draw truncheons, which we did, of course. We were also told to put our visors down. As we drew level it went nuts. The Leeds lot just jumped at them, running into them kicking and punching anything that moved. There were females and kids amongst the visitors but no one got away. We just started cracking skulls and charging into these idiots. I knocked a few over and Ambassador was great, standing on people and knocking them down. I think he enjoyed it!

It was over as quick as it started really. They were no match for the horses and our truncheons. Order was restored and we got them into the ground. A few minor scuffles were dealt with and the game kicked off. Some of us were left on horses to patrol the ground. The others boxed up for a break.

We knew that the end of the game was going to be very busy. I was on the south stand gate to keep them in. They were not happy at all and were jeering and pushing from the back, towards the horses. We stood our ground and the horses were just magnificent. The noise was unbelievable. The Leeds lot were not for dispersing. We got the other mounted units outside the ground near to us in support.

After half an hour though we had to let them out. The ones for the buses into town were allowed out first. Officers on foot funnelled them into the buses but they went nuts. Kicking the windows in and climbing out to fight the obliging Leeds fans. The others waiting for the coaches were going mad now too, as they could see this going on. One or two got out and the rest surged towards the corner where they had made their escape. Saladin, bless him, did not stand. He went backwards and they were out. We reversed out and into a major fight.

The Sergeant was patting the top of his head which was the signal to go to him. We did, and formed a line again. We just walked towards them at first. It was like a scene from an old black and white Western in a bar. There were men fighting as far as we could see. Officers on foot were in a line too, behind us, and as we walked, we just either walked over people fighting on the ground or we knocked them over. A gradual realisation that we were there took place and people started moving off. Bricks were being thrown now from further up the road. We kept our line very well and moved them away from the ground. It did not matter at that stage where they went, we just wanted to separate them and disperse them.

We couldn't get the visitors marshalled to get them to the coaches. They had to get there under their own steam. There was still a lot of fighting going on around the corner towards the M621, and we were sent there. We actually, in a line, charged a great number of Leeds fans, who were throwing bricks. It was adrenalin busting, charging up the road on horses in a line together.

I had my truncheon out and the blood was pumping through my head. Do not get isolated was the number one rule, and no one did. We got rid of them over the footbridge across the motorway. We stood funnelling them into the walkway until they were all over. Two lads on foot were left to make sure they did not get back across.

We were stood down at 6.30 pm and finished work at 8.30 pm that day. We got a letter from the Gold Commander on the day stating his immense thanks to us for a job well done.

At Bradford City we always escorted visitors to and from the transport interchange in the centre of the town. This was a long way but we did not have too much trouble with the escort. They were noisy, depending on the numbers. Bradford were in the lower leagues so an average gate of 3,000 was very manageable compared to Leeds where the average there was 27,000. Huddersfield was an old ground, similar to Bradford. It was outside the town centre and one main road ran from the train station to the ground. Not many visitors came on trains at all here. It was mainly private cars and coaches. The coaches were brought to the ground and the supporters disembarked from the coaches straight into the ground. It was easy there to police. At the end of the game we went into the ground itself to hold the visitors back until the home lot had gone. It was a sloping ramp we stood on in the ground and the horses were never really comfortable here. They would jog on the spot and move from one side to another. They never really stood still in comfort.

I never knew why we attended the rugby matches. The crowds here were completely different from the football crowd. They were families in the main and the young lads attending would have a drink but they were not tribal at all. I never had an arrest at rugby and cannot remember any trouble at any of the matches I worked. I had always enjoyed playing rugby and played rugby league a lot. I did not though, enjoy watching it. We used to take the horses into the ground and watch the games on horseback or we would take off our cloaks and put them over their backs to keep them warm and watch from the ground. Most of the games were on a Sunday and I found the duty quite boring. There was only ever two of us on duty at these games.

Chapter Nine

Two things happened with our first season hunting with the Badsworth. We met Rupert Cox and Sue Clark and discovered team chasing. Our first team chase after Christmas was at Marton cum Grafton and it was a baby course. We managed to get into a team of four and walked the course. Virtually everyone we knew was there.

I went second and Sue agreed, reluctantly, to go fourth in the team. We finished all together and though we went fast we did not get placed. I was hooked on this team chasing and the competitor in me came out. It was very simple too, you turned up, warmed up went like stink across country and then had a few sloe gins.

Back at home, we managed to get a team together from the liveries and we went to Frickley Hall. Now this was a different ball game, the courses were enormous compared to the week before. We were undaunted but the liveries were shitting themselves! We made it round though, with me in front leading and Sue going second. She did try to get in front of course, but I was not having that.

Team chasing over the years was great fun, we were called the Coley Roadrunners. Although some of the team names left a lot to be desired, the Cunning Stunts and the Badsworth Bitch Pack being examples. There was a team, for about three seasons of four girls riding side saddle, they were fabulous and great to watch. We won some and also had our share of falls.

One year, we were sitting on the ramp of the wagon, having already been round and we were drinking Sloe gin and various concoctions when Karen Dixon, an Olympic three day eventer asked us if we wanted a ride round again on some horses she had brought? She had entered a team, brought the horses but did not have any jockeys. Yep, we were up for this so Sue, Darrel and I just got on these strange horses.

They were very green. Sue fell at the third fence. As I sailed over her, she was on the ground, and I shouted to ask her if she was ok. She shouted that she was and to get on with it! After we finished Karen came to our wagon to check on Sue and we talked about the horses, then she dropped the bombshell that they were only recently broken and newly onto to her yard. I was not best pleased, but I thought Sue was going to kill her!

A few seasons later and I was on a young horse making a team up with Trish Heaps who was leading. Trish had bought a horse from me in the past and had ridden around Bramham International Horse Trials. She is some jockey and in the nicest way possible, totally nuts, very bold and brave, she just went like stink across country. She would scream back over her shoulder for us to keep up. We were at the Burton and part of this track ran along an old railway line. Half way along we had to turn sharp left and jump over an enormous jump made of telegraph poles in an ascending line that led to a serious drop into the next field.

Everyone was up in arms about this jump and representations were made to the organisers. They announced that they would modify it. We set off and when we got to the jump it was just the same, though they said they had 'modified' it. They had put a sign in the ground, handwritten it said "kick on from here!"

I had met Sue Clarke through my work in the Mounted Police, having been to her yard to try some Irish horses as potential police horses and Darrel had bought 'Tommy Bastard Riley from her. I bumped into her again out hunting with the Badsworth. She did hirelings and supplied a lot of horses for the hunt. Sue was a dealer of the old fashioned school, in other words she would sell anything for a profit. Everything had a price and she would not suffer fools in any way.

Because Baroness was mental out hunting Sue offered me rides at any time. She even paid my cap as long as I did not mind what I was riding. They would often be fresh off the boat from Ireland or very green. Hunting days at her yard were great fun as the people hiring horses, and there were some serious characters, always came early and she would, within the price charged, cook everyone a full English breakfast. Sue was also a great baker and her cakes are legendary.

So winter Saturday mornings were, when I had a day off from football duties, spent at Sue's having a fabulous breakfast and then getting on whatever horse I was allocated for the day. I had some rides that would make your hair curl.

The Sinnington breakfast gallop was a case in point. I got there and we had breakfast, whiskey porridge, champagne and Guinness. Out we went into the field where the wagons were parked and I asked Rupert, who was the head lad which horse I was riding? He just started laughing. I asked again and he said it was called Hardy.

He dropped the ramps and opened the two side gates. I jokingly said to him in a very posh voice "come on my man, get me my horse off this wagon what, what." He just laughed and said "no way mate, you, have to get on him on the wagon." I said in an ordinary voice "fuck off I am not doing that". I was told then that the only way to get on it was on the wagon, there was no chance of getting on it on the ground.

So, after a few choice words I climbed to the top of the ramp and Rupert gave me a leg up on this horse who began shaking. I got my feet in the stirrups and bent over along his neck. Rupert undid the head collar and took it off. Boom! This horse just jumped out right across and down the ramp and then on landing it just buggered off across the field. God knows how, but I stayed on. I tried my best to stop him but he had gone. I circled him around the field and slowly got the circle smaller and he stopped.

I walked him about until the rest of the field were mounted. He was 17 hh this horse, and lovely dapple grey. The gallop was very well organised, different members of the hunt took us off in groups of four over a long flowing course with a good mixture of fences.

This bloody horse crashed straight through the first two fences, I thought I was going to crash and burn. He did, however, pick himself up and start jumping. By the time we had finished he was jumping really well. I could feel that he was actually making a good shape and using his shoulders really well. I ended up taking this horse home and, after a few months and some unaffiliated events, he was sold into hunting for a good price.

Timbertops was the name of Sue's yard. It was a big place, lots of stables and a big bungalow where they lived. Sue also did film work for TV and film productions. Over the years I bought a few horses from her and I rode many a horse for free out to hounds. Rupert is a great bloke and we have remained life-long friends. He knows horses and has produced some lovely horseflesh in his time. He is a big character and tells a great story.

A consummate professional, Rupert adapted and made sure the clients got what they needed. I took some clients on one occasion. Leanne was the thirteen year old daughter of my very good friends Colin and Carol. We went to look at a lovely 15.2 hh bay horse. Rupert, assuming that the horse was for eventing, rode him in a lovely outline and was going on about how well he moved and what a great test he would do.

I pointed out that the pony was for polocross and he went straight to a tree, broke a branch off and began whizzing it about like a polocross stick shouting about how it was trained to the stick and would be eminently suitable for polocross!

I went down the yard one day and all I could hear was Rupert screaming like a loony. I went around the corner to see both Rupert and Sue with scarves wrapped around their faces, boiler suits on, wellington boots and gardening gloves. They were clearing out a mobile home caravan that a groom used to live in. She had left to go to America for a job with Camp America.

The caravan was just disgusting, duck and cat shit was all over the floor. It stank. I looked in the Belling electrical cooker and it was full of dirty knickers. Rupert was gagging and bagging up the bedding and he screamed again, from under the pillow he produced a great big black rubber dildo! The funny thing was though, it had a massive fist on the end. That was it, Sue hitched the caravan up to the tractor, towed it into the field and set fire to it. We went in for tea and cake.

Over the years I have had a few deals with Sue. She is still going strong although she does more filming work than dealing. She has a variety of animals from a deer to a fox that she hires out to films and TV production companies. She has sold a great deal of horses to clients all over the country including the Police Force mounted units.

I went to look at a very nicely marked skewbald horse one day. He was 16.3 hh and five years old. I was quite taken with him although he did not move very well. After a few conversations she did eventually admit that he was in fact a pacer. Donald was a horse I was looking at for the police, he was a lovely big stamp and she told me he had just come over from Ireland where he had been hunting. She had forgotten though, that I had hunted him some months earlier and that he had high ringbone!

Rupert is freelance teaching now and still a friend. He has ambitions to get to the Horse of the Year Show in the Working Hunter class and I went along in 2012 to give him a hand at Bramham Horse Trials. He was competing a lovely big grey horse he owned and had

Field Mastered on. I introduced him to some quite posh friends and one of them asked him if he was nervous? Back came the reply "I am as nervous as a paedophile in Toys r us" always a conversation stopper our Rupert!

Chapter Ten

In March, a year after I had joined the branch, we had our internal competition. This was a full day of competing against one another to choose the showing team for coming season. It took place on a Thursday, which was our normal training day. A judge from another force was always invited in so that it would be fair. The training was intense and we did patrol as normal, but in the afternoon we rode again practicing the dressage test and our own home made nuisances.

There were not only individual honours to be earned, but also the three stables were competing against each other so your stable honour was to be fought for and a year's bragging rights. Not everyone competed, it was an individual choice. Most of the officers did take part though.

My first Internal was judged by the Chief Inspector from Lancashire Mounted Branch. He was a Scottish man with a very red complexion. He was well respected though. I was on Ambassador and I thought I had done a reasonable test on him. I was very disappointed with my score. The nuisance lane did not go well either and I came 3rd in the novice class. In the tent pegging I did much better coming second.

Leeds won the day overall and it was very enjoyable. A meeting was to be held the next week to discuss and choose the team for showing. I was dying to get on the team. It meant a lot of training and going away at weekends, more or less the whole summer, to compete against other forces. The social side to these competitions was also legendary.

The following week, after a great deal of speculation and sadly an even greater amount of bitching and gossiping, the meeting took place. I was chosen to go to Newcastle, Liverpool and Stafford but not on Ambassador. It was decided that Speed, a big, gorgeous

Cleveland Bay who had the musculature and features of a stallion, was a better prospect. His rider did not want to go away to shows so I had the ride.

Well, the talk about me reached new heights over this. It was not nice. I naively thought we were a team and that we supported each other in every respect. I was very wrong though and I had had enough of the carping. I went to see my Sergeant and chatted it through with him. He couldn't have been less interested. He told me to suck it up and get on with it. I was gutted. It was a problem throughout the whole branch. A policewoman at Pontefract was in the frame as being the main protagonist against me. She would never speak to me and always gave me daggers on training days. I had been told that at one particular football match she had been quite vocal about me and not in a nice way.

I debated whether or not to try and pull her about it and iron out what the problem was. I was told not to waste my time. She had been a civilian groom before actually joining the police and getting onto the mounted branch. She had the sergeant at the Pontefract stables wrapped around her little finger and got away with murder according to the lads who worked there. I never ever got to know what she had against me. I did not know then of course, but my position on the mounted branch was to become in serious jeopardy later in the years of my service because of her!

Newcastle Show was a great affair, they put a great deal of effort into it. There was a dog show at the same time, and a flower show, so there were a lot of public in attendance. They had a tradition that as you rode around the dressage arena waiting for the bell or the horn from the judge's car to go in, a sergeant came to the entrance at A. On getting the signal to enter you stopped at the A marker and the sergeant offered you on a silver tray a nip of whiskey. It was called a 'nippy sweetie'. I took my nippy sweetie and went in to do the test.

Speed was a lovely horse but he was a plain mover. He did his best though as he always tried. The nuisance lane was straight forward and he did really well. There was a man on stilts and you had to go up to him and shake his hand. He did not like this though and we did not get a very high mark. When I saw the sheet afterwards we only got a 2 out of the 10 available, which I was disappointed about as I did actually shake the man's hand.

I was not placed so it was a bit of a shame really. The placed riders got lovely silver plates, bottles of whiskey and really big fancy rosettes. None of the other lads got placed at this show either. Back home there was an inquisition and of course, according to people who were not actually there, it was my bad riding that was the reason I did not get placed!

The next show was in a month's time at Liverpool. We did a lot of training in the afternoons and we were in good spirits as we set off. Liverpool mounted branch was based near to Stanley Park. This park was between Liverpool and Everton football clubs. Their stables were very old fashioned and almost Victorian. It was a nice place. The field where the show was held was enormous. The show was in conjunction with their annual Police day and the place was buzzing.

Speed did a great test and I was lying in joint first place with a Lancashire Police lad. Lancashire were always the ones to beat out showing. They had a dedicated team and were very hard to beat. The nuisance lane went well and I came second by two points lost at a motorbike that was revved up loudly as you approached it.

I was over the moon and one of our open riders, Dave on Cavalier, came second too. The tent pegging did not go well. Because of his bulk and his build Speed did not gallop well enough to get a good mark. I didn't peg him anymore after that. A lad from Bradford came fifth in the pegging so it was a good show for us.

Back down to earth at work and we had to go to Highroyds Hospital near Menston. This was a very large hospital for people suffering from mental health disorders. Elderly people were always going missing and we were regular visitors to carry out searches at the hospital and the surrounding areas, which were agricultural and large wooded areas. There was also a lot of moorland so we were ideal for this job. We searched for a couple of hours for an old lady in the morning when we got there. We had been invited as usual into the hospital for lunch. We were stood in the queue waiting for the buffet-type lunch and I thought I would be very funny. I turned to one of the lads in the queue and said 'Don't stand still too long son, they might be stock taking'. My colleagues all laughed but a Doctor in the line did not see the funny side of it. He had a proper go at me. He was very indignant and to be honest a bit over the top.

I tried to calm him down but he fancied himself and started raising his voice. I was trying to be calm and apologise but he was not being talked down. Eventually I gave up and turned my back on him. He carried on berating me and it was our Policewoman, Maureen who shut him up.

Back out on the search, we were crossing some farmland and there were dead sheep all over the place. I counted ten in one field and there were another three in a stream. This was not right and I radioed for a lad from the local nick to come meet me. The farmer was well known and a trouble maker. He was anti police and not a nice person.

Undeterred, I waited again for a while until the photographer got there. We took photos of the dead sheep. I later got in touch with what is now DEFRA and we went to see the farmer. He was obnoxious, but I did him for failing to dispose of carcasses. This was a new one on me but he did get fined £1800.

The search was negative on the first day and so we went back the next day. We were looking for an old lady and all she was wearing was a nightgown and some slippers. She was found by two officers near a stream. She had a plastic bag over her head. It was a suicide. We went back there quite a few times over the years. I kept my mouth shut in the lunch queue though and I did find a man who had hanged himself in a tree.

As the year went on there were very strong rumours that the branch was going to be significantly increased in size and that we were getting a new boss at Chief Inspector level. In the running for this post was the Inspector from South Yorkshire mounted and an Inspector from the burglary squad in Bradford. The lady Inspector from the burglary squad had horses at home but no mounted experience. The Inspector from South Yorkshire had been a sergeant in our force and had moved on promotion to South Yorkshire.

He was appointed and started at the back end of the year. He was a great big bear of a man. Very larger than life and good at his job. We did not see much of him to begin with but things started moving very quickly. We were to increase manpower from twenty two constables to thirty two. Three sergeants and an Inspector, and him in overall charge. Horses were to go up from twenty two to thirty six. I was really excited as this was a major change for the better.

Chapter Eleven

Our third season eventing with Bonnie (Blacup Baroness) and Tessa (Blacup Contessa) started in the deep snow at Brough horse trials in Penrith. It was snowing when we set off but undaunted we went. I remember going cross country with the ground covered in deep snow and the snow falling sideways as we went. It was drifting too against some of the fences.

Osbaldeston in Lancashire was a superb facility. The dressage arenas were situated in a flat field with loads of space. The jumping was in a large purpose built indoor arena with a big viewing gallery and a café and toilets. The cross country course was easily accessed and it was always fair, straightforward and bold. It encouraged you to run at the next level and was a great introduction for Novice level.

Norman Barge and his family ran the events and nothing was too much trouble. The only downside was the parking. We always used to park in the car park but it did get very crowded. Both horses had been there at Pre-Novice and therefore their Novice runs would be familiar and a not too stressful upgrade. I went first on the cross country and we were sailing, going very well until the water fence. Bonnie being bold, and at times stupid, just launched herself over the log into the water, she then crumpled on landing. Her front legs just disappeared.

I was wet through, got up and saw she had cut her knee open really badly. On walking back to the wagons some people came up to me and said three or four horses had fallen at the water. The vet came and saw to her. He confirmed that he had treat a few horses following falls at the water. I sought out Colin Furness the TD (Technical Delegate). Colin was a lovely man of the old school and gave a great deal to the sport of eventing. I had changed and put my wellies on. I waited between horses and went into the water fence. I was walking amongst boulders and picking them up and showing them to him. The surface of the fence under the water had broken and that was why horses were falling. He was apoplectic and was shouting at me that nothing was wrong. We had a right old row and Colin, incensed at my cheek, jumped into the water wearing his brogue shoes and moleskin trousers. He grabbed the boulder I had in my hand and threw it away. I was laughing to be truthful, at the nonsense of this.

The next horse, ridden by an American girl, fell, right in front of us. She seriously hit the deck and cut her face, the horse also tore its leg open. Thankfully the fence was taken out. I loved going there and over the next few years the place played a major part in my life!

Ivesley equestrian centre at Waterhouses in County Durham was quite a happy hunting ground for me. I won there and had several placing's over the years. You entered the centre via a beautiful tree lined drive, the trees were hundreds of years old and made for quite a welcome. They ran Pre-Novice to Intermediate classes and the course could be trappy in places. My only problem though was the prizes. I won a Pre-Novice and got a tin of hoof oil. It didn't improve really the further you went up the scale.

My first Intermediate on Bonnie was here a year later. I lost an over reach boot somewhere and went back to all the fence judges to ask if they had found one. I got half way around and at the drop fence into the next field, followed by a sharp right turn to a timber wagon, the judge there had my boot. "Were you the chap on the chestnut?" "Yes I was. How did you remember me with all these riders jumping over the fence?" she said, a bit startled "You were the only one gripping your saddle shouting Shit as you went over." I laughed but did think, you`re right, she is uncontrollable at times.

We entered Withcote 2 day Novice event in Leicestershire. This was our first venture into the full three day programme. I was so excited I could hardly sleep. We put extra training into play and ensured everything was done perfectly. On arrival, the event was held at a big dairy farm. We had, in those days, to be weighed prior to cross country. Some of the little girls went to the scales with saddles and very heavy saddle cloths with lead weights in them. I just walked down in my jodhpurs and boots.

At the briefing I was again excited as was Sue. They put us on big flat straw wagons and we sat on straw bales as they took us around the roads and tracks. We had booked stabling and were placed just down the road from the event. A local pub was within walking distance and so we were well catered for.

The horses settled very well and we had a good night. The next day we both did the dressage tests and then the showjumping. We did ok and were both mid table but inside the top twenty. Sunday was the endurance day. We had written on paper taped to our arms, the times for the kilometre markers so we could make sure we were on time, and of course our stop watches.

I set off on the first roads and tracks with no problem and then at the finish we were counted down for the steeplechase which was around a field with the fences placed within the fence line. We hit the second fence really hard and I thought we had had it but she recovered and went off at 100 miles per hour. When we then set off on the second road and tracks Bonnie could not understand and wanted to gallop the whole way round. Try as I might I could not settle her.

When we got to the 10 minute halt box, the vet couldn't get a pulse. He said it was a woosh and that unless she came down dramatically I would not be allowed to go. We washed her down and drowned her in water. She did come down to within the accepted heart rate and so we set off on the cross country. A flowing, up to height, bold course. It was made for us. She flew round, we did hit a big hedge that had a hidden telegraph pole in it quite hard. At the Ha Ha at the back of the garden to the main house she slipped into it rather than dropped. I just could not hold her.

I did not get placed but was not bothered, I had just loved the whole thing and was desperate for more. I had though, to sort out Bonnie's jumping. Sue did really well too on Tessa but she had a moment on the second roads and tracks where she stood up a few times and cost herself lots of time penalties.

Back at home and we had a phone call from Tracey Dillon asking if we would like to have lessons with Yogi Briesner. Yogi rode for Sweden at the LA Olympics and was placed in the top ten at Badminton numerous times. He went onto become the performance manager for the eventing teams for Britain and of course the successful London Olympics.

At this time he was visiting Tracey's yard for a week on a monthly basis. Tracey had won the under 25 years championship at Bramham Horse Trials and she was well known in the area. We were quite excited to be invited and our first lesson was a great success. He had us working on control, which was something I really needed. When he saw the two mares jump he was very impressed with them. His communication skills were fabulous, nothing too complicated, he just generated and instilled a confidence in you.

We started going twice a week in the week that he did come up and although it was a fortune to us it was, we thought, very well worth it. Bonnie responded quite well although we discussed at length bits for cross country. He rode her a couple of times and jumped her too. Yogi thought she was a definite 4* horse if we could sort out her exuberance across country.

I never did and at the final event that year at Bishop Burton we were Novice and across the country, I have to admit, she was out of control. It was a bit frightening.

Chapter Twelve

We started the next year at Witton Castle in County Durham. This was a fabulous venue catering for Pre-Novice to Advanced. It had a panoramic view of the cross country course and as it was the first real Advanced track of the season and as a pre-Badminton run it attracted the who`s who of eventing.

Sue and I entered the Novice and we were up against the greats on young horses. In my class were Ginny Leng, Ian Stark and Mary King. Sue was up against Lucinda Fredericks and Blythe Tate. It was a fabulous day out for us and although we did not get placed we did go double clear.

I was sat on the edge of the ramp, catching the early spring sun, when Heather Holgate, mother of Ginny Leng nee Holgate came around with four dogs on a lead. One of the dogs took a dislike to me and bit my ankle. I remonstrated and she apologised very profusely. The upshot of this altercation was that I managed to blag myself a week`s training at their yard at Acton Turville near Badminton. A few weeks later, and stopping in bed and breakfast nearby, I presented myself at the yard. They had a rotweiller dog who lived in the tack room and she hated me. I have never done well with dogs, or geese for that matter.

On the first morning Alison, the head girl was showing me around the yard and describing all the horses, most of whom had some sort of injury or other and were used for the working pupils. I looked over a stable door and there was this 16 hh thoroughbred looking horse, over at the knee and looking poor. I said "is this another injured old one?" Alison snorted and said "certainly not, this is Master Craftsman". That did not go down well I can tell you. Master Craftsman or "Crafty" as he was known, had won Badminton and been to the Europeans and the World Equestrian Games.

Later that morning I stood in the arena with Dot Willis, Ginny's trainer, and watched her training the working pupils. I had a ride on a very young Welton Houdini. He was a five year old grey horse who went on to win Badminton. The rest of the week followed much the same format. I learned loads of stuff that week, nothing was too much trouble for the horses and the attention to detail was phenomenal. I took home loads of ideas about our yard management and changed the daily routine for the better.

At this time we also got a massive stroke of good luck. Tom Seymour ran a saddlery in Ripley just outside Harrogate. He had been there for years and was well respected and well known. I had been tasked with finding a saddler for the mounted Police at work and approached Tom about supplying saddles for the job. He was keen and eventually sold over fifty saddles to the branch. He specialised in Kieffer saddles from Germany and Sue and I loved them.

To be honest, I went to see him off duty hoping for some discount on a couple of jumping saddles as I had got him the contract for the police. He said he would like to sponsor us. I was over the moon. He took sizes and told me to go back in two weeks' time. At that time I had an old battered Volvo estate car and when I went up to see him I was in this car. He gave us that much stuff I had to drop the back seats to make space. I was totally overwhelmed. Both horses had five different types of rugs each, boots, saddle cloths, travel boots, headcollars and numerous other pieces of equipment.

I was almost in tears when I got back to the yard and Sue was in tears when she saw what we had been given. Tom was a very quietly spoken lovely man, he did drink a lot though and when we knew he was coming to an event we made sure the drinks cabinet was fully stocked. I think he was quite lonely and sadly he passed a few years later. He looked after us though and he was a proper gentleman. We had discounted dressage and jumping saddles. I loved the Kieffer saddles, they were very well made and stylish.

The next event we entered was at Brigstock in Derbyshire. The problem with that was that it was the final selection trial for the Barcelona Olympics, which we did not know when entering. It was again the who's who of eventing and for Sue and I, a disaster.

Bonnie went into the dressage with her tongue hanging out of the side of her mouth and had a dreadful test. She jumped well though and was clear showjumping. In the cross country Bonnie was much the same as before and it was getting ridiculous, there was just no stopping her at all and she would not listen. Sue did a good test and was clear show jumping, however she fell off at the fourth fence when Tessa threw in a rear of serious proportions and then galloped headlong into the fence. Both were okay.

It was now getting to the point that with Tessa, Sue was having too many problems and we decided to sell her. She was sent to David Bartram near Thirsk. David was a dealer of some note and competed regularly at HOYS and Badminton.

Just before she went though, we were contacted by Spillers horse feeds. We had been selected to have a lesson with Robert Limeuex who rode for England but transferred to Canada for the Olympics. This was all sponsored and we got goody bags and it was going to be filmed. We readily agreed and went to Birchinley Manor near Manchester. Birchinley was an enormous indoor and outdoor showjumping venue. Purpose built, it had a fabulous café, seating gallery and parking facilities. The shame here though was the clientele, but more of that later.

We turned up at the arranged time and although we had been asked the level and ability of our horses we were put together with two baby horses that were green. Undaunted in he came, he did not ask us any questions about the horses and went straight into putting poles on the ground at intervals right down the centre line of the indoor school.

They began to film and he started us off straight into serpentine canter movements changing leg over each pole as we got to them. Bonnie and Tessa coped ok although I was gobsmacked at what we were doing. The other two did not fare as well at all and one of the ladies had had enough fairly quickly. She stopped, got off her baby horse and left. It was a disaster to be honest but we got polo shirts, baseball caps and bags of feed so it was worth the effort.

Tessa had been at David's for a month but had not been sold, so we went up to see her and it was red hot. Sue was wearing denim shorts and trainers and a strappy top. David was saying basically that the mare was not as good as we had said. He said her jump was not too great and that on the flat she did not move very well and should be a lot cheaper.

He was riding her a bit sloppy, Sue was furious and demanded to get on her. She rode her in shorts and trainers. She quickly had her going beautifully on the flat with extended and medium trot and half pass and then rode her up to a very big hedge and jumped her over it into the next field. She then re-appeared over this fairly big hedge back into the field where we were, got off, handed her back to David and said "stop pissing about David and get her sold, she is a bit special". I was so proud of her and David's attitude to us changed instantly. A week later she was sold to go hunting with Liz Verity, Field Master of the Bramham Moor.

This little session at Thirsk rekindled my love and buzz of dealing. We discussed it and decided to have a go. One Tuesday evening, not long after at Osbaldeston in Lancashire, there was a Viewing evening. This is where people brought their horses and had five or so minutes to show them off in the indoor arena and afterwards you could go and ask about them and try them or arrange a viewing later.

We were sat there, not really thinking there would be anything to buy, when into the arena came a 17 hh black mare. She was stunning to look at. Riding her was a tiny girl. She rode around on the flat for a while and then a man, who it turned out was her father, put up a jump. .He just stuck it up at about 1.05m. She trotted up to it and I said to Sue "if this horse jumps that from trot we are buying it". She did jump it and made a great shape. An hour later and Mystique was ours. She was seven years old, so a little old for us really but she was very low mileage having competed in showing classes.

On the flat she was seriously fixed on the right rein and Sue took ages to make her soft and loose. Jumping, she was very talented, brave and bold. She was a proper mare in the stable and you had to be very wary of her as she would frequently bite and now and again she would peg out at you.

I was still competing Bonnie and we had some very near misses. At Scunthorpe Horse Trials we ran in the Intermediate and at the drop to a skinny on one stride, she crumpled on landing and scrambling up, jumped it from a standstill. My heart stopped. We went clear and the last fence was an enormous Kleenex tissues box with the middle cut out. It was causing all sorts of problems with horses stopping or getting the width wrong and banking it. Bonnie flew it even though, at the fence before, which was a coffin, we hit the rail in very hard as she would again not listen to me. She was so bold and brave she was one of only a few to go through it.

The next event was our nemesis and for me the final straw. Jervaulx Abbey in North Yorkshire was a lovely event. The terrain was hilly and the going, being old turf, was always brilliant. We set off on the cross country after a clear show jumping and a good test. All was going really well until we came around a copse of trees where there was a double rail, bounce, single rail complex. I was trying again to slow her down to make sure the speed for the bounce was okay. She was not listening to me at all and jumped the whole thing in one. I screamed like a big girl, stopped her, got off and swore that I would never cross country her again. I have never been faint hearted across country and to me eventing was about the total buzz of setting off and finishing any course. This though, was suicidal.

Sue and I discussed at length what to do. She wanted to have a go on Bonnie, being lighter as a rider, she thought she might respond to her. I was entered at Henbury Hall in Cheshire in the Intermediate and so we changed riders. She was very brave, my wife, to sit on this horse at Intermediate level for the first time, well brave or stupid.

Henbury Hall was an amazing venue. You did dressage on a beautiful polo field and the show jumping was under trees on very uneven ground. Sue had a rail down but the cross country was really good for her, she flew round clear. Prior to going though, she was retching into a bucket at the bottom of the ramp, she was so nervous.

I begged her not to go, pointing out that this was, after all, supposed to be fun, but as we were so competitive there was no way she would withdraw. We got an amazing picture of her bouncing into the water jump. Sue sensibly decided that she couldn't cope with her and so she was handed back to me.

Fortunately for me, it was not long after this that Mrs Verity telephoned and asked about Bonnie. Being the full sister to Tessa, whom she loved, she wanted to buy her. I explained that she was not an easy ride across country and this did not make her ideal for hunting. She was undaunted and explained that John Gill who was a Whip and Field Master would ride her. I asked her an awful lot of money for the horse and she came to view. I was riding her around the arena and Liz, not a lady to trifle with, asked to see her jump. The girls put up a single pole at 1.10m and I walked her towards it, clicked my tongue and Bonnie just sailed over it. "That will do you won't it?" I said. She was sold.

Mrs Verity did say that she wanted her for hunting only and that if she did not make a hunter she would breed from her, having a policy of never selling her horses. Not long after she was sold I was at Osmaston in Derbyshire as Sue was competing in Pre-Novice on Mystique. Bonnie was there entered in the novice class. I spoke to the girl riding her and said she should not be sat on her as she was dangerous.

She was having none of it and was quite rude. I listened to the commentary and at the fifth fence they hit the shit. She was ambulanced off the track but thankfully was okay. The following hunting season no one could ride one side of Bonnie and very sadly, I thought, she was sold to Portugal for show jumping. I was very sad at the outcome for this lovely horse, she had been a pleasure to own and had taught me so much.

Shortly after she was sold I went to Doncaster Bloodstock sales and I was looking for a nice young horse to buy to replace Bonnie. The third lot of the day was an enormous 17.2 hh five year old. He had run in a bumper at Market Rasen and had obviously not made times or any running. He was a big ugly brute of a horse and sadly his racing name was 'Come on Jonnie'. He had though, in his favour, an enormous languid walk and he strutted his stuff around the parade ring.

I followed him in and in those days the minimum bid was 500 guineas. He was introduced and no one bid. He started at 1.000 and was quickly reduced to 500 to get him going. I bid 500 and even though the auctioneer tried his best to get him away, he was not making anything and was knocked down to me at 500 guineas. I was very pleased and followed him to his stable. I had a good look at him and saw he had both central upper teeth missing. Curious, the girl with him knew nothing about him, or she was not saying. I went to the canteen for a coffee and an Irish man came over and asked me if I would take profit on him. I was tempted but he told me he was full brother to Party Politics who had won the Grand National. He was by Scorpio and would be very promising. I politely declined.

Two days later at home and I had a phone call from another Irish man and he offered me good profit but I decided I would keep him. He couldn't believe I had got him for the price I did. I re-named him Big Ben and so he became Blacup Big Ben. He settled well into the yard and the routine. Grid jumping him, it was soon clear he did not jump anything, he leapt, and you had to stay with him or hit the deck.

The first time I took him jumping was in a British Novice class at 1.0m. He was double clear and I was very pleased with him. Nick Stoker, a show jumper came over in the cafe and told me to stop pissing about and get him in the Foxhunter. I told him he was only five and green but he said he was a natural and I should take him in. It meant staying very late on the Thursday night but I did put him in the class. He had the first down as it was a bit of a shock to him but then went clear.

His first event at Pre-Novice was at Bretton, Denby Dale near Wakefield. This was a joint venture with the local college and was a very popular event. I later served as the health and safety officer for this event for a couple of years. I went up the centre line in the dressage and some horses were walking past, having completed their tests. Ben went vertical, I couldn't believe it!

I took my Patey hat off and hit him with it up in the air, looked at the dressage judge and she motioned to me to carry on. I finished the test and was properly sulking back at the wagon. I was ready for the jumping and moseyed on down. Walking around the warm up collecting ring with the reins tucked into my folded arms I was feeling pretty down. Laura, our head girl, came down and told me I was, at that stage, second in the dressage on a score of 31. This made me get a grip, shake my head and warm up properly. He went clear and also on the cross country he just flew around. I was third, won a headcollar and some sweets and went home a very happy man. At Osmaston we won the Pre-Novice. Darrel had come second in his section and won a grooming box, lovely big rosette and a saddle cloth.

They called my name out and I took off my hat, walked forward as everyone was clapping, and was handed a Bakewell pudding, yes a bloody Bakewell pudding! For first prize. I was gutted. I broke it up and we ate it whilst the rest of the prize giving was on. The next day at the yard Darrel parked his Discovery in the yard with all his prizes displayed over the tail gate! Funny bugger our Darrel.

Darrel had bought a fantastic horse to replace Tommy Bastard Riley called Mr Brigham from Hilary Jannion,, who owned Masta Rugs and then went on, with her husband Raymond, to start the Equi-trek trailer and horsebox company. This horse was gorgeous to look at and a superb event model but he was very quirky out of the stable.

Darrel is a life- long friend, he is very funny and great company. He is though, tighter than a coat of paint on a wall. He was fed up with buying rugs for his horse so he went around the charity shops and bought a load of old blankets. He bought a very old singer sewing machine and made some rugs for his horse, we just pissed ourselves.

He spent hours making his first rug, came to the yard and proudly put it on his horse. Mr Brigham being very, very indignant, just ripped it in half within less than a minute of having it on. Darrel was caught pinching rubber bands to plait his horse with, they were at that time only 50 pence for a bag of 200.

On a more serious note, we went with the Badsworth Hunt for a day out to Wentworth House which is a stately home. The hunt had not been allowed to go there for years and cross their land and so we were told to be on our best behaviour. We were galloping off across the main parkland in front of the house, it was beautiful and very picturesque when Darrell and

Richard, another of our liveries, just set off towards a big herd of deer and scattered them. They got such a rollicking from the Master and it was very embarrassing. God knows what they were thinking.

He went cross country schooling on his own one day to Stamford Bridge near York. Here was a fabulous UK Chasers course and we used it a lot. Much to our chagrin, he went alone. Quite a few hours later and with no reply from his phone, we telephoned the owners and they went looking for him. They found Darrel lying unconscious on the bank and Brigham was grazing nearby. He had come off quite hard, knocked himself out, injured his kidney and his spleen and generally bashed himself up good style.

Darrel being Darrel, drove himself home and went to work in the restaurant he runs with his lovely partner Petra. Years later, at Allerton Park, riding another horse, he came out of a sunken road and hit a tree. He went to work later that day and three days later conceded to go to hospital where he found out he had broken his shoulder. Tough lads us Yorkshiremen.

With Ben at his next event at Skipton a few weeks later, we had a slip up on the very steep bank down to the water fence and he stopped. I could not really blame him and he finished the course still in the time, even with a stop. I was very pleased with this horse and at home he was quite a character. I upgraded him to Novice for the next event at Witton Castle. The grass arena for the jumping was really slippery and he was not very confident. It did cause a lot of problems and clear rounds were at a premium. He had one down and then cross country it's fair to say, he skipped around. I was so pleased and thought I had a 3* horse on my hands. Nothing fazed him, he took everything in his stride.

Not long after Witton and I was interval training him in the field down the road from the stables, which we always used, and he stopped suddenly with a big grunt. He was very lame.

The vet came and after a few examinations it was decided that he had torn his hamstring. He had pain killers, box rest for a while and then I turned him away. He eventually came right but would not event again. He did two seasons of half days with the Rockwood Huntsman, Clive, and then retired to a hacking home near Harewood in Leeds.

How quickly dreams are shattered and how quickly things change. I was so upset about this lovely big stupid thug and I have often wondered what would have been. One of my best memories with Ben was at the Badsworth breakfast gallop. I was at the front with Charlie Ward-Aldham who was riding Burrough Hill Lad. This horse had won the Grand National trained by Jenny Pitman and on retirement she had sent him to Charlie to hunt. We jumped everything on these two and it was special as we were riding a winner and the brother of a winner of the greatest steeplechase race in the world.

Red Rum, was the greatest Grand National winner ever. He won three times and came second twice in this greatest race in the world. He came to Bradford Police stables for an overnight stay. He was retired now and was in town to open some betting shops the next day. The lad with him left for his hotel at 8pm knowing he was happy and secure.

Not a chance! Some of us went back to the stables and got him out into the yard. We only had a headcollar on him but we just had to sit on him. We took it in turns sitting on him in the yard. He was fine and happy but it was the chance of a lifetime. Two of the lads also took some of his tail as a keepsake.

Aldaniti, who also won the National with Bob Champion, came to stay over too. He had bandages on and was very frail so we left him alone. We just had a cuddle.

Chapter Thirteen

Whilst I was competing Ben, Sue had been having a mixed time with Mystique, she was really a show horse and she did not like to gallop flat out. She was talented with jumping but she was never happy galloping across country. We decided to sell her and advertised her as a show horse.

A lady called and arranged a viewing. On the day a Volvo estate car pulled up with four ladies in it. They had a gaggle of children and assorted pushchairs, none of them were dressed for riding. It was obvious to me they were on a girly day out.

I asked them who the horse was for and why they were not dressed for riding. The lady in question said she was wanting to see the horse ridden and perform and if she liked it she would come back and try her. Mystique was all plaited up, bathed and looked fabulous. I told her to go away and come back when they were prepared to try the horse properly.

These girls were not happy, but nonetheless I sent them away. It was a very typical scenario of my time in horses, dealing and selling and sadly the whole of the next twenty odd years were peppered with idiots and tyre kicking timewasters. Thankfully though I have met some fabulous people and sold horses all over the country and the Continent. Mystique was sold a few weeks later to hunt and show.

We both needed new horses. I had a mare called Sophie who belonged to a very good friend of ours Danute Lawson. Sophie was homebred and, to be honest, a bit small for me. I had good fun with her competing unaffiliated and also in show jumping and dressage. Sue loved this horse and we decided to buy her from Danute and that Sue would have her.

A few weeks later, one Saturday night, Sue declared she had seen a horse advertised in the Yorkshire Post near Bolton. She had called about it and we were off to see him. I was not up for this as she would possibly have two to ride and I would not have anything. We went though and when we got there the women that greeted us was absolutely plastered. She also had a foul mouth. Her very slurred opening sentence to us was "I hope you're not timewasting cunts or else you can turn round and fuck off". Charming!

Vincent was a lovely looking grey, 16.1 hands high and five years old. He was obviously not a happy horse, he was tied up in a stable made out of wooden pallets and looked miserable. I looked at Sue's face and knew then that he was coming home with us. Drunken lady got him out and tacked him up. Well actually she gave us a saddle and bridle and told us to "fucking do it yourselves".

Sue rode him in a sort of arena and I made a jump from beer barrels and some fencing rail. He had a very ordinary jump, to be honest, but we could not leave him there. £1500 later and he was part of the team. He was difficult to ride and really not our type of horse. He was a daisy cutter and did not move freely. He came to us very stiff and didn't ever show a great deal of improvement.

It was decided that we would sell him to a lovely home but he needed a CV first so Sue asked John Thornton to ride him. John and his partner Richard Howard had a very successful yard at Carlton Husthwaite near Thirsk. John is a fabulous jockey with a great feel for a horse. I have known Richard since my pony days and we used to compete against each other at Aire valley. He has competed at HOYS himself and was with David Bartram for years before he met John. One thing about Richard is that his horses are always, without fail, immaculate. They are produced to the highest standard and he is a real horseman. He is also outrageous and very embarrassing at times!

Sue and I were at the Great Yorkshire showground once, at the Hunter Improvement Society annual sale. We were sat in the stand and Richard and John came in below us. I wolf whistled them trying to be funny and they then set about having a very loud argument between themselves as to who exactly I had whistled at. I was very red and wanted the earth to swallow me up. Sue was very amused. Many years later at Northallerton Equestrian centre, I was warming up alongside his now partner John Guy when Richard shouted over at the top of his voice, "Hi Steve have you had a shag lately?" Going very red I shook my head to indicate no. Richard shouted again at the top of his voice in front of everyone, "John get off that horse, I will hold it and you can give Steve a blow job, he is well bagged up". They are great company at a dinner party or hunt ball.

The arrangement was that we would take Vinny to the event and John would just sit on him. His first event was near Carlisle and he went clear cross country but had a fence in the show jumping. Then, at Bishop Burton he was 10th which allowed us to advertise him. A lovely girl from Hull bought him for the university team events and he did well with her.

John went onto compete a fabulous horse called Thrintoft Win and they completed Bramham 3* International together. The poor horse had an untimely demise, breaking his neck in a freak accident in a trailer. Later Richard and John split up and went their separate ways. Richard is now with John Guy and they produce horses out of a lovely stable yard near Bedale. They are proper horsemen and their horses are beautifully produced and turned out.

One year I went on the Friday to Burghley with them. I normally was up and off by seven am to get there so as to not miss anything. I went to their house at eight thirty and Richard was ironing his shirt. At something after nine we left. Richard was driving and he never went faster than 50 miles per hour. He also refused to go into the outside lane of the

A1. I was quietly very frustrated. I was proper pissed off when twenty minutes from Burghley Richard pulled into the little chef for an Olympic breakfast!!

When we eventually got there, sometime after lunch we did have a great day and as is traditional now, we called on the way home at the Wetherby Whaler for a fish and chip supper. Good times.

Chapter Fourteen

I had seen Egor at Witton Castle, ridden by Joanne Kay and was impressed with him. He was a 16.3 hh liver chestnut and had two white socks on his back legs and a stripe down his face. He was a Warmblood and moved beautifully. He had three very expressive paces and a very tidy jump.

I made enquiries with Joanne and she told me he would be for sale. I went to Rawdon Hall Farm in Rawdon, just outside Leeds where Joanne lived with her husband Roger and son Tom. They kept a few cows and did agricultural work on a contract basis but their living was derived mainly from horses.

Joanne had completed Burghley and Roger was very well known and respected in the equestrian world. He had been instrumental in forming the Hunter Improvement Society and was a judge at county level and had ridden point to point and to hounds for years.

Sadly, Roger died a couple of years ago and at his funeral it came out that his first wife was an international model and that Joanne had been a back-up dancer for Pans People on Top of the Pops! Joanne became our coach for a number of years. She would turn up at our yard with an amplifier and a car battery and a microphone. She would use the amplifier to shout at us, a hard taskmaster but honest and fair. She once shouted at me whilst I was riding in the arena, calling me a "wanker" in a very loud voice, just as an elderly couple walked past on the roadside!

When I first met Roger he was getting on in years and had retired from riding. He had a distinctive flat cap and walked with a tall shepherds crook and could be seen at many a venue, team chase and event. Very well spoken and a real charmer, he was also very dry and funny. I became good friends with him and Joanne and I had a great deal of respect for them. Roger was also outrageous and regularly came out with treasures.

He was commentating at the unaffiliated Beckwithshaw one day event and was saying outrageous things about people setting off cross country. They tried to get him out of the commentary box but he had locked it and wouldn't stop. They had to cut the wires to the speakers to shut him up. One of the nicest things he said about a large lady going around on a cob was "Don't bother timing this pair because that pony will take hours carrying her around the course". He also forgot to turn off the microphone in between his diatribes and he was so naughty and un- pc with his observations.

At the Scunthorpe horse trials some time later I was warming up for the dressage and he was there watching. I was called through and was riding around the arena awaiting to be belled in. He was stood against the rope that divided the arenas from the warm up and there were lots of people there watching. He called me over. I went to him and said "Hi Roger, I am just going in" he said "Stephen, would you take some advice form an old horseman?" I replied "Yes of course Roger" and he said at the top of his voice with a big smirk, "Stop riding like a wanking policeman". I could do nothing but laugh all the way through the test.

I tried this Egor horse at their place, had a lesson on him with Joanne and I was very taken with him. He was quite backward feeling in his movement, one of those horses that does not feel as if they are going anywhere but in reality they are moving very nicely. We agreed a price and he was mine subject to vetting.

The vet we used for all our horse was Peter Schofield from Hird and Partners. They had a full veterinary equine unit about three miles away from our yard which included operating facilities. We had a great deal to do with them over the years and we took horses in, post operation, to look after them for the owners, on their recommendation.

Peter came with me to Rawdon to vet Egor. He did the preliminary examination and he asked him to be walked away from us and then trotted up in hand. He looked un-level and not sound. I was gutted. Peter examined him again and asked for him to be trotted. He did not look right. We couldn't work this as there was no heat, swelling or anything to point towards him not being right. Tom was leading him up and so there was Roger, Peter the vet and myself stood scratching our heads.

Joanne had gone into the house to make tea and bring biscuits. She came out carrying mugs and various packets and asked what was wrong. We told her, and Roger told Tom to trot him away again, which, much to his annoyance, he did. We all stood watching the horse intently and then Joanne said at the top of her voice, "You bunch of wankers!" we all took a sharp intake of breath. "Look at the bloody clip, call yourself a vet and you two call yourself horsemen".

The penny dropped. Roger had given this horse a blanket clip and one side was much lower than the other, seriously lower, and this created the optical illusion that the horse was un- level. Peter was so embarrassed, I jokingly said "Bloody hell veterinary, do you need glasses"? The rest of the vetting went well. I paid for him and very excited with my new horse, brought him home.

He was a complete twat. He just stood and kicked the stable door twenty four seven. Nothing could stop him. I put carpet on the inside of his stable to soften the noise but he still did it. He was also stubborn, and if he decided it was not a day for working, he would not work.

A week after I had him I took him to Pony Club camp at Beverly racecourse but after two days Sue had to come and pick him up, such was the noise he made through the night he kept everyone awake.

The rest of the camp went well. I had a ball, although on the first night I was drinking someone's home brew and got very drunk. I was allegedly walking around the dormitories declaring my undying love for Gaynor the DC. Later in the week I was bored with teaching the group I had which was the B test group and so it was quite intense. I invented out on the Westwood a game. We split into two teams and had a blue club jacket in a tree. One group were the cowboys defending the jacket and the other group the Indians who had the task of capturing it. This went down a ball. If, you were an Indian and tagged with a whip by a cowboy you were 'dead' and we just had to get that jacket. We were all whooping like Indians too and we caused quite a stir.

Later in the week I was going through the process of shoeing horses with a small group and they were individually telling me the separate tasks. One girl explained how the farrier started by taking off the shoe and then I asked Oliver what came next he said 'My farrier says ooh my bloody back let's have a cup of tea'.

Egor had first event was at Witton castle where he had already been. I was in the lead after dressage and show jumping by a mile. All I had to do was skip round the cross country for a win. We set off over the first fence and then you galloped sharp right over the second, a log. The course then took you down a steep hill in between trees either side of the pathway that everyone took.

Not Egor, he jumped the second and I steered him to the pathway, he plunged me to the right and took me off through the trees. I managed to stop him although my face was cut on the branches, and then whacked him as we went down the hill. A sharp turn right over a wall and you went out onto the course at large. He never stopped at anything but he just would not gallop. I had to ride him very hard and I was exhausted when we finished. I had a boat load of time penalties and was very fed up. Sue, however, had done really well on Sophie for fifth place.

His next competition was Osbaldeston. Again in the lead after dressage and show jumping. I had fed him competition mix to improve his energy levels. I set off across country and we got to the fourth fence, a garden seat with stuffed toys on it as the sponsor was a company called Tebro Toys.

Just as we got to it he went to jump it and in a split second he stopped dropped his right shoulder and catapulted me into the fence. I sat on the fence and kept hold of him. I jumped on him off the seat and set off again. Half way across the field, no fence in sight and in mid gallop he stopped dead, dropped his right shoulder and put me on the deck. I lay there in the sun looking up at blue sky thinking, 'Bastard, what have I done to deserve this?' Egor stopped trotting away, turned around trotted over to where I was laying and straight over the top of me!

That was it, no way was I going to forgive him and despite protestations from Sue and the girls at the yard, the following week he was advertised in the Yorkshire Post. After a couple of weeks a lady called and arranged a viewing for her daughter. She told me that this poor girl had had to have her face re-constructed after being kicked in the face by a young horse.

They arrived and the girl had a metal cage around her face. She was also quite big, having put on a lot of weight whilst in hospital. I rode Egor on the flat as they wanted him for dressage. She asked to ride him and I thought this would be interesting. She made him talk, boy she was a jockey. He went so well for her and after a lot of chatting they bought him. I really enjoyed waving him off with one hand and the money for him in a carrier bag in my other hand.

Another trip to Donacaster Bloodstock Sales and we bought two horses. A small 16hh bay gelding called Joe and a larger 17hh chestnut called Simon. Joe was not up to much so we sold him on within two weeks   Simon though was a big upstanding youth, liver chestnut and he actually moved really well.

We had by now, had quite a few Thoroughbred horses from the sales through the yard and we had developed a great system of producing them. We had a definite system and rules for buying them too. If they had raced more than twelve times or they were younger than three or older than seven we did not buy them. If they were the flat whippet types of horses too we did not bother with them. The chunkier the better for us.

The first week they were allowed to settle in and were turned out and lunged each day just lightly, but over the week we built them up so they would go into side reins and this worked well. The next two weeks they all hacked out up the roads and steep hills which improved them really well, especially in their head and neck carriage. They all went out in knee boots in case they slipped on the very steep inclines and they all had Market Harboroughs on. These allowed them to fall out with themselves and not come against the riders hands. They also encouraged them into self- carriage within the neck as most of them were very upside down when we got them.

You could always go back a step too with this system if needed and they were all treated very much as individuals. The next two weeks they began their schooling and jumping work and this is when we chose which, if any, to keep for eventing and the rest were sold. Selling horses this way paid for the sport we loved so much, and our training as the costs were astronomical.

It was not always plain sailing of course and we had many times when the horses ate and we did not. One Christmas we sold our furniture to pay for Christmas and help keep the horses going over the winter. Our friends came to visit and brought their garden furniture so we could at least sit down.

Colin, our friend, owned a carpet import business and he offered us a job one day to deliver some carpets for him to Penzance in Cornwall. It was cash in hand and enough to enable us to tax our cars for six months so we agreed. We left at 6 am to drive his wagon down, got stuck in fog near Birmingham and got to the place nine hours later. What I did not know was that the bloke at the other end did not have a forklift and I had to help him handball off the wagon, thirty big rolls of carpet into his warehouse. I was exhausted.

We set off home and our sandwiches and flask coffee had well run out. Sue had driven some of the way down and went up into the sleeper cab to get a rest. She could sleep on top of a wall or on a washing line, that girl, and I never saw her again. We got stuck again in Birmingham and got back to the yard at 2 am. Colin was laughing like mad and shaking his head, he took the tachograph out and tore it up. We got the cars taxed though.

I liked Simon, he was a nice character and moved well. In fact he moved very well. He was totally chicken shit with jumping though, he was just not having it and even though I persevered it was a non-starter for eventing. I advertised him and had a right job moving him on. The first lady that called and arranged to view name dropped everyone and their aunty. She knew Captain Mark Phillips and goodness knows who else. She also talked with a gob full of very large marbles. She came with a red Discovery and matching red trailer. She had on all the gear, topped boots, jodhpurs and hat. She barked at her aged mother to get the video going and was asking question after question. I rode him for her and he went very well. She eventually stopped talking and got on him which was an operation in itself. She had only gone a few strides and Simon went upright. She screamed and tugged him tighter in the mouth, she was scared to death.

She was very rude and would not accept the horse was too much for her and that she was quite the novice. It took her seconds to wrap up and bolt for the gate.

The next person to try him was my very unfortunate brother Craig. Craig, by his own admission, is a novice. He came to try him in the arena and rode him very well. He did think, though, that he was too much for him and I said he may as well ride him back into the yard.

There were some boulders painted white on either side of the pathway to the arena, and as he was leaving, Simon stumbled very badly and threw Craig, who was just caught unawares, onto the floor. He landed flat on his back with his right arm under him and if that was not bad enough he landed plum on a white boulder right between his legs. Poor lad was black and blue and needed a wheelbarrow for his bollocks.

The third viewer was a lady called Angela. She came from Buttershaw Estate in Bradford which is where they made the film Rita, Sue and Bob too. It was a very rough area and she was a very typical Bradford girl. I was really not sure about her but she turned up with a huge black guy and explained he was her boyfriend. She insisted on riding Simon straight away and I was having a good natter with Errol the boyfriend. He was the chief security man for the Arndale shopping centre in Manchester city centre. They lived in the penthouse flat.

Angela rode very well and was looking for an unspoilt dressage horse to bring on. That was it, boom, sold! I had to deliver him to a yard alongside the M62. We agreed the price and also £40 to cover the diesel for the delivery. All was well until I got to the destination and found she was not there. She had left the money to buy Simon but not the delivery money. I started putting him back in the box to come home and the girl at the yard spoke to Angela and agreed to pay me the money. Shame really but that's people in horses. She did do very well with Simon, getting to Medium dressage so I was very pleased.

Chapter Fifteen

The new Sergeant at Bradford had only been in post for about six months and he was sent a new horse to have on a two week trial. I did not like this horse. It was six years old but very weak. His musculature and frame were that of a four year old and he was a late developer. He actually coped very well with the routine within the stables and in traffic and he was doing okay.

We did a school visit together. At school visits we always spent some time explaining our roles and also did a bit of training. We would get the kids lined up along the playground about thirty feet apart. Then we would ride the horses between the lines of kids and get them to clap and stamp their feet. The second time we went between the lines of kids we got them to clap, stamp their feet and cheer. Finally the kids, who loved this, would take their coats off and wave them, stamping and shouting and making a right old racket.

The horses were great and just walked through. The new horse on trial did very well this day and went through four or five times at full crescendo.

At one school visit a really gorgeous teacher told me she had horses at home. I asked the kids at the end of the visit 'Who would like to see Miss ride my horse?' The kids went mad and were chanting for her to get on. She hitched her skirt up revealing suspenders and stockings and I legged her up. It was a good visit that one.

At the end of the first two weeks of the trial for this new horse, we had a fairly low key Bradford City evening match on a Wednesday night. The sergeant, being very pleased with him, decided to take him to the game.

The horses had a piece of leather padding that went over the top of their bridles and it extended down their noses as padded protection. This also had a clear perspex visor attached to it which went around their eyes. They always wore knee pads just in case they came down on the road by slipping or being pushed.

At the game it all went very quietly and the horse was really good. Normally with new horses we only rode them until the kick off and then boxed them up or took them back to the stables. At the end of this game this new horse was still out. It had been very good though. We were on escort back to the town centre with about fifty visiting supporters.

The new horse was in the front as a lead alongside a more senior horse. At the top of Mannigham Lane, where it became Manor Row, there is a major set of traffic lights. The lights turned red and we were waiting at the junction and all was quiet when this new horse reared up fully onto its back legs. It went so high it lost its balance and came over backwards on top of the Sergeant. When it got up again it had rolled about on the top of him too. It just stood there looking bemused.

The sergeant was in a poor way, he couldn't move and we had to get him ambulanced away. The horse was led back to the stables off another horse. We got back to the yard in a state of shock really. It had all happened so fast. This horse had been very good and coped really well. The sergeant was very poorly. He had split his pelvis by seven inches and damaged his lower back. It was touch and go whether he would walk again. The horse was sent back to its owners.

Eventually he did walk, but in a shuffle. He came back to work after six months of re-couperation, but was never happy. He eventually was retired, medically unfit. It was a salutary lesson for us all. Horses have a mind of their own and therefore can be very unpredictable.

In the inquest that followed we all decided that it must have been the reflection in the eye guard from the traffic lights that spooked the horse and made him rear. On analysing the incident it was the only thing we could all agree on that was the likely cause.

During the time he was away, the senior constable at the yard was made acting sergeant, even though he did not have his examination qualifications to be a sergeant. This was an in-house move and totally against police regulations. He was a total bloody idiot this man. He did the most ridiculous things and made everyone's life a misery. Power corrupts! Watchman, my horse in training was taken away from me to go to Wakefield and I was given a new horse. She was a big black mare about 17 hands high. She was a five year old when she turned up and very plain looking. It was decided by our new boss that she would be called Portia, as everyone wanted their pound of flesh from the Mounted Branch, as they had of Portia in the Merchant of Venice.

Portia was very good, she accepted Police work with ease and was a pleasure to ride and train. The quiet nature she had made her an exceptional prospect for showing too so I was giddy about her.

At the internal competition the following March she won the novice horse competition. I tried the pegging but she just couldn't gallop. She did the activity ride training and although I fell off her a couple of times when taking the saddle off she eventually got good at this and we did all the displays that year. When I fell off her in training a couple of times it was when I dropped the girth off and went to take off the saddle. She simply stopped mid canter. This threw me right up her neck and onto the ground.

Every year we had a practice display prior to the big displays. This was in front of hundreds of school kids. This particular year we were at Scott Hall Fields in Leeds. Hundreds of kids were walked or bussed into the fields and sat around the arena we had marked out with cones. We had a portakabin with a PA system in it and one of the Bradford lads, Robin, was great at the commentary. He would whip the audiences up into a right frenzy.

We were all warming up in the arena area for the musical ride as all the kids were getting seated. I noticed that a lot of the lads were all warming up at one corner of the arena. Some of them were stood still and looked like they had run out of petrol. I went over and asked 'Is everything okay?' One of the lads said 'Don't stare Stevie, but look at the teacher on the corner sat down crossed legged'. I went over to the corner and there sat on the grass, cross legged in a white skirt, was a very attractive teacher. Her skirt had ridden up and we could all quite clearly see she had no knickers on! The Sergeant rode over and gave us all a quiet telling off and told us to get out of there. He particularly meant me! I had only just got there, the others had been stood looking for ages! Typical.

Chapter Sixteen

John Norton was a racehorse trainer based in Hoylandswaine near Barnsley. We made contact with him at the sales and he had some nice horses in. Mainly jumping horses, they were bigger built and made good event horses. We had numerous horses from him but by far the best was a bay gelding who was four when we bought him. He was called WUG, pronounced 'double u gee'. WUG had been bought from America as a yearling by Robert Sangster for £120,000 guineas and we paid £600 for him. Some drop that, but he had only run one bumper at Newcastle and had not done well. He was though, by the famous Salmon Leap.

Sue fell in love with him and wanted to keep him. She began her campaign and he did really well, very trainable and a lovely person. He was a very definite yard favourite. He was always in the ribbons and won or was placed numerous times. We did not want to upgrade him though as he had to be for sale. Sue Bartle approached me at Thornton le Dale event and asked about him.

What a saga this turned out to be. She came six times to try him and after the third time Sue had lost all interest in trying to sell him to her. She brought Lady Sarah Tetley-Hall to look at him, videoed him numerous times and from head to foot. When she brought Chris, her hubby, I was riding him around the arena and I could hear them arguing about who was going to ride him. Chris was saying it was for her so she should ride it, she just wanted him to ride it for her. I stopped riding him and said "For fuck's sake one of you get on this horse or go home". Chris got on for a couple of minutes and said he approved. So that was it, sold subject to vetting, £4800

The vet was supposed to be coming on his own and Sue following in the wagon with the money. She turned up with the vet in his car. The preliminary examination of him took place with what seemed to be no problems. The vet left his clipboard on the top of the dog kennel whilst he went to the loo. I read it and it said 'lovely horse no problems'. He took bloods and I thought that was it. They both went to the car and were there for a good twenty minutes.

Sue came back down the yard and said "We like him Steve but feel that he needs a bit more working up on his frame." I said, "So has he passed then or no?" She replied "Well we like him but he needs more work, he will pass him if the money is better." I was furious but kept a lid on it. "Well he is sold subject to vetting Sue, so if he has passed you owe me £4800 and you have bought a horse." "Well, I have all the facilities at home to improve him and so we need to talk on the money." "Sue, he has been placed in every Pre-Novice he has been in and you don't have any better facilities than me here apart from a horsewalker, so what are you wanting to pay?" "Well we were thinking more in the line of £3500".

That was it, I stomped up to the vet waiting in the car and he wound the window down. "Simon has this horse passed the vetting five stages or not?" "Well we just feel that he is weak in parts and" I interrupted him, "Simon you are the Vet, it's nothing to do with you the money or whether or not he is passed if the money is less. Has he passed your vetting or not?" "Well erh," he was stammering. "If he has not passed, what have you found clinically wrong with him?" He did not reply, just looked at Sue who was stood on the passenger side of the car listening.

I said "Do you two know what I do for a living?" "No" they said, " I am a policeman, and if you two don't fuck off right quick I am going to arrest you both for attempting to obtain a pecuniary advantage by deception." He went grey, she jumped in the car and they pissed off very quickly.

A lovely young girl called Helen, who was profoundly deaf, was coming for lessons with the Pony Club to our yard. She had lessons using a special microphone system. The horse she had was not very good though as it was spooky and bad tempered. She impressed us though as everything was immaculate, she kept her horse and herself beautifully. She tried WUG and loved him. Over a couple of weeks Sue sorted out the sale and he was sold to this lovely girl. Over the next three to four years she won over 200 red rosettes for everything from dressage to working hunter classes.

It was a perfect match. It all ended very suddenly though and tragically. At a one day unaffiliated event out on the cross country course, just half way over a fence, he collapsed and died. He had had a heart attack. Helen was in hospital for two weeks in a coma, we were devastated. She has made a full recovery though and is still riding and competing.

We had another tragedy on the yard which had a profound effect on me. Mr Brigham, Darrel's horse was a lovely person, but as I said, he was very quirky. He would not be turned out, with or without another horse and if we did get him out he was totally stressed and then just would not be caught. Darrel and I built him a special paddock and put extra high fencing on, similar to a stallion paddock, but that did not work. He just kept charging the fence and trying to jump it or he just stood still and never moved. I could not work him out at all and try as we did, we sort of knew something was brewing.

Darrel suggested tethering him, not happy about this at all I managed to get a chain and collar from my dad and we led him out to the field. I had bashed in the stake a good four to five feet and normally that would suffice as a tether for any horse. Not Mr Brigham though. As soon as he was let go he ran to the full end of the chain and just yanked out the stake. Still attached, he bolted through the field and through the stone wall. He disappeared over the horizon and I was dumfounded. An hour later we found him a fair way away, his off fore leg was shredded.

The vet came and it did not look good, the prognosis was guarded but we got on with repairing him. We used a length of guttering as a splint and waited to see. Three months later and he had made a full recovery. I dare not turn him out again but Darrel, being philosophical about it told me to do it. I turned him out with baited breath and he walked to the fence and just stood there. After watching him for ages we left him be, he seemed calm but just stood still, it was really unusual behaviour. When we went to get him in he jumped into the next field and then came to us at the gate. Stressed, I was just happy to get him in.

The next day I put him out again and he just stood still. I left him alone. He was okay for about an hour and then as I was walking about the yard I saw him. He just took off to the end of the field, jumped the big wall out onto the road, ran straight passed a field full of livery horses and careered off down the road. I followed on foot but heard the bang very soon.

When I got down the road there was Mr Brigham laid in the road. A VW Passat car was at an angle across the road and it had a massive horse shaped dent in it. The police came and Chris, the vet from Hirds. Brigham was twitching, we moved the rug a bit and it was obvious his front and back end had gone. Chris put him out and I just burst into tears. The man in the car was lucky, very lucky but he was okay. The policeman that turned up I knew, and he kindly agreed to go speak to Darrel and tell him what had happened.

I went home, nothing could make me feel good. It took me months to get over this horse. I am normally very pragmatic about horses and the end of them, but boy, this totally floored me.

After the sale of Blacup Egor and the untimely retirement of Blacup Big Ben my eventing career stuttered somewhat and even though I had lots of dealing horses to ride, I did not have a special one. Sue had a few to choose from, but again they were for sale and were sold as soon as we had buyers.

We were all looking now for horses, Darrell, Sue and I. Darrell went to try a horse at Richard Howard's yard and he agreed to buy it subject to vet. We went with him and Peter, the vet on the day. The horse he had agreed to buy had had a leg and it subsequently failed the vetting.

As we were waiting for the vetting to conclude Sue and I had a look around the yard. Half way down the line of indoor boxes was a 16.1 hh bay roan mare. 4 years old, she was home bred and called Shuzannah. John showed her to us and jumped her. She had huge scope and moved beautifully. Sue tried her and that was it, given the stable name Tootsie, this lovely mare came home. £4500 was the most we had ever paid for a horse.

A few short weeks later and Darrel had a new horse too. Mr Milligan was very similar if not almost the double to look at of Mr Brigham. A tall 16.2 hh bay gelding he was lovely and was also four years old. Easy to deal with, you could turn him out without any problems.

We did go look together, Darrel and I, at two other horses prior to finding Mr Milligan. The first was a HIS approved horse that had shown in ridden hunter classes, or so we were told. The lady selling him was pregnant, which was the reason for the sale. At Bedlington, the other side of Newcastle, it was 120 miles. We got there and I knew Darrel had interrogated her on the phone. In the yard was a very smart looking bay gelding looking out over the door. The lady was there and very pregnant. I opened the door and got him out, all looked well until I saw his off fore foot.

I said somewhat angrily "This horse has a club foot love." "It`s never bothered him." "He has a clubbed foot, how on earth can he be ridden, he is a cripple." Darrel never said a word, I think he was stunned. I laughed and said to him "All the questions you asked, didn't you ask if it had a club foot?" I got a bit annoyed and the lady ended up giving us £20 for petrol to go away.

Word gets around very quickly in the horse world and Gaye Bartle called Darrel with a very promising horse. Back in the car again we picked up Gaye and went up to Piercebridge to try this 'Lovely young horse' she had really sold to us in her description. He had evented previously very well and had a great track record but now the girl was going to University so he was sadly for sale.

We got there and the horse came out of the trailer tacked up and ready. It was a bag of bones, had an obvious breathing problem and looked like it had totally broken down. Darell`s turn this time. It was a good forty five minutes back home in the car to drop Gaye off and he berated her all the way back.

Sue and I went to Doncaster sales in the hope of a cheap horse for me. We had a new wagon which was a Dodge 5 horse with a Perkins Cummins engine. It was painted red, white and blue and had all the toys. We loved it. We could both drive HGV wagons as we had passed the test in the police. I drove to the sales and on one of the very few times we never bought anything we set off back to the wagon to come home empty. Sue asked for the keys and I said I would drive, but she insisted.

I was proper fed up at not getting a horse and fell asleep by the time we hit the A1 to come home. I woke up a while later and asked how long we had been going. Sue looked flustered and when I saw the signs for Lincoln and Newark it dawned on me and more importantly her that she had gone south for quite a distance. The language was blue in that wagon and she just stopped in the middle of the A1, climbed across me and told me to drive. It was a long way home and cost her £60 in diesel but I had great ammunition. I have often dined out on this story and have embellished it to say that when I actually woke up we were only sixty miles from London which is not true, but fear not, she had her revenge later.

I had heard of Les Moorhouse through various people, but mostly because he manufactured really great horseboxes and the Police had bought several off him. He did always have some very nice horses in and he sourced them from Ireland. We went to see him one Tuesday the week after the great Yorkshire show. The first horse I tried was 18hh and a gorgeous chestnut. It was beautifully schooled and had been placed at the Great Yorkshire show in the middleweight ridden hunter class.

I was instantly in love with him and was riding him around the arena when Sue came in on a bay gelding who was smaller and looked fat. I jumped the chestnut and although he did not give me a great feeling I was still smitten. Sue was riding this bay horse and I was not paying any attention to her. She jumped the horse over a pile of railway sleepers that were in the middle of the arena.

She shouted at me "Placey, stop messing about on that thing and get on this!" I ignored her as I was on my dream machine. She shouted at me again and so I swapped horses and got on the bay. The chestnut was quickly taken away at the behest of Sue.

Connundrum was 16.3 hh and four years old. He was well made and actually a very good looking horse. He moved well and his jump was very big and gave the feeling of boldness. I jumped him a few times and each time he felt better and better. I had found my horse. The only sticking point was the price, at £5500, he had not done anything and was very green. The chestnut was £7500 and I had not actually asked the price prior to getting on them. Not a chance of paying that sort of money. I made an offer of £4500 which I thought was fair.

Much to my surprise he agreed, the horse had a five stage vetting from Ireland and as we never insured any of our horses I did not have him vetted. I met Les at the car park of a pub called the Bridge Inn half way up the A1, paid for him and brought him home. The next day I had a hack out on him with Laura our head girl on a dealing horse. We were going down the road with me on the outside when a big skip wagon came past very close, he was only four and the wagon made a right noise with the chains clanking and the skips on the back banging about.

He never moved, was not in the slightest bothered, and just took it in his stride. I patted his neck and said aloud what I was thinking "He is a right little wazzy boo boo this one". That was it, his stable name and he was for ever more called Wazzy in the yard. His official name of course was Blacup Connundrum.

The next week, due to work commitments, I turned him out with another horse we had in to sell. I looked at him every day and on the Friday of the following week he was stood still with his head up in the air at an odd angle. Something was wrong. His near hind hock was the size of a football. It took me ages to walk him into the stable and then Peter, the vet came. He had had a kick and the synovial sack was torn surrounding the hock. We got him to the operating theatre and they were just amazing. They went into total professional mode had him sedated and a cannula in his neck in no time and in he went. Peter is very honest and direct and told me it was touch and go.

The next few hours were not good, we were all on tenterhooks about this lovely new horse. He came out ok and Peter said the hock had been flushed and repaired it was a wait and see as to whether or not there was any infection. He came home the next day and we looked after him in great detail. He did recover well and was okay. Wazzy was doing well although it took some time to get him fit again and back into full work.

We had another horse in for sale which I had bought from a farm in York. He was a thoroughbred cross Irish sport horse and when we got him home he started with locking patellas. This is very alarming when you first see it as the horse comes out of the stable with their back leg totally straight and they cannot bend them. If you back them up the leg unlocks and they are okay. Many young horses get this, it is when the medial ligament over the patella slips due to not being formed properly. We had Peter down and he operated in the stable. We had to strictly follow the recovery regime as the horse affected can be permanently damaged if you rush the recovery.

We were very lucky really over the years, bearing in mind the amount of horses we had through our hands. We had little need for the vets to attend, most of the small niggly things can be dealt with in house. I like to think that our lack of injuries is the way we looked after them and the strict regime they were on.

I was once sat in the café at Birchinley Manor one Thursday evening, having already jumped and was having a plate of their famous chips and gravy. Sue came into the arena and was announced over the speakers. A lady sat at another table with a group of people said "Oh it's one of them Blacup horses, they are always immaculately turned out them and they always look really well." I was very, very proud at that moment.

Chapter Seventeen

Later on that year I was moved to Wakefield to train horses and new recruits. On one of the horses, I was in Wakefield city centre, and we were going very well. This was another grey but he was a lovely horse, six years old and enormous. As we were walking up Westgate, we were in the right hand lane of two and a double decker bus came past on the left hand side of us. This was unusual, as most of the time the horses were only used to traffic along their offside to the right.

This young horse panicked and ran sideways to the right, away from the bus. The bus was, to be honest, quite near. As he went sideways he hit the crash barrier in the middle of the road. He fell over this and took me with him onto the other side. It was a bad fall and I was trapped underneath him. He got up and trotted off.

My right leg was killing me. Someone caught him, unharmed, which was a great relief. I managed to get back on him and went straight back to the stables. My right leg was black and blue and he had grazes along his shoulder and right foreleg. He did become a good police horse but it just went to show what a difficult job it could be.

At a Bradford game one Saturday, we were escorting the visitors through the city and we were trying out a new route. The daft thing was that this route went right through the main shopping area. We were doing okay and as we went along the top of Westgate one of the new lads, riding Cavalier, had a problem.

The fans had managed to surround him and were pulling at his reins. This really upset the horse who jumped into the air off all four legs and then went crashing through a big shop window. The shop was Fads decorators and the window was a big picture one with a display of beds and bedding in it. The glass shattered as the horse went through it sideways. The supporters erupted into cheers and jeers. Cavalier was floundering in the bedding and tins of paint. How he had not been cut in half by the window glass I will never know, but he did not have a scratch. I remember looking over at my sergeant who was just sat on his horse shaking his head in disbelief. Either that, or he was thinking about the paperwork he would have to complete for this little shindig.

People used to say when greeting the horses 'Oh he is lovely, did you train him?' We used to say 'No love we buy them fully trained and then we bugger them up.'

Things had now settled down at home as we all had horses at four years of age and we then had to prepare them for the following year to start their careers off. We still had a few horses in for sale and the dealing part of our business was going well.

Two major incidents happened though, in quick succession that kept us on our toes and often made us think about what we were doing. On the whole we were surrounded by lovely people and had great friends. Some customers left a lot to be desired but our philosophy about complaints and any unhappy people was to give them their money back and take back the horse, depending on what was the problem of course. People who had, in our opinion, a legitimate reason for the horse being returned were treated properly. Others though, were not. Thankfully these were very very rare.

We had a livery called Mandy and she had a sweet pony called Misty. Mandy ran a café and was doing well. She lived in a flat above the café and had a boyfriend. All was well and she was pleasant to have around the yard until one evening we were at home having supper when Mandy came and knocked on our door. She had come to explain that her boyfriend had ended the relationship and that as he owned the building that housed her flat and café she was very vulnerable and may have difficulty keeping Misty.

Sue counselled her really well and over the next three months we lived through the breakup with her, as she regularly visited and poured her heart out to us. We cooked for her and on a couple of occasions she stayed over. The problem worrying me though was that she had not paid her livery bill. I asked her about this eventually and this small, sweet, emotionally distraught girl changed immediately. She rather nastily told me I would be paid and that she was going through a shitty time. I felt a bit rough having asked her but the bill was over a thousand pounds.

She had become friends with Rachel, one of our grooms, and the following week they went out on the town in Halifax. The weekend after they went out again on a blow out in Leeds. It was the weekend that livery bills were due so I called her and asked for a meeting. She came and Sue and I spoke to her and in strong terms outlined the fact that she owed £1200 for livery and had been going out and not spoken to us about paying. She was very sulky and did not commit to any payment agreement. I knew then that this was going to go wrong.

Rachel, rather sheepishly, told me a couple of days later that Mandy had made arrangements to remove Misty on the Wednesday morning at 7 am. I was furious, beyond furious and padlocked the stable top and bottom bolts. I was there at 7 am to meet her and we had a right old row. She stomped off and returned an hour later with an enormous black fella. He was like the side of a house and they came down the yard.

I walked to the tool store and picked up a metal shovel expecting the worse. He spoke to me very calmly and gently he told me I wouldn't need the shovel and that he had come to try help sort out the situation.

I explained to him my side of the story and that I was disgusted that she was going to spirit the pony away and not pay me when we had given her so much help. He told me she needed to sell the pony to clear her debt. I am not stupid and there was no way she was going to make good her debt if the pony was allowed to leave. Just then he spoilt it as he told me that Mandy was going to report me to the tax man, the council and the VAT. That was it for me. I told them both to leave the yard.

Vicky Walker, who I knew very well, turned up with a trailer. She had agreed to buy the pony not knowing the true extent of our problem. It was eventually agreed, after a lot of shouting, that Vicky would still buy the pony but pay the balance of the bill to me and the residue to Mandy. A couple of weeks later and I turned up at the yard to find Mandy sat in the portakabin having a coffee with the girls. I told her to leave in no uncertain terms.

I went on my own to Doncaster sales as Sue was working. There was nothing of any note but right at the end of the sale was a big Irish grey gelding called Murphy. He was five years old and by Embla George, a very good sire of jumpers. He was common and a big hunter type. I bought him for £1500, got him home and then realised there was something not right. Peter, the vet, confirmed he was a shiverer and I had dropped a bollock. Sue was not happy I can tell you, but you win some, you lose some.

Shivering is one of those misnomers that no one can explain. It is a problem associated with the nervous system and makes the horse have great difficulty picking up their back feet, especially to be shod. In extreme circumstances they have trouble walking.

Murphy had the problem, but very slightly. Laura had him to ride and show jump and he did very well. He was a very good safe hack and I cub hunted him a few days with the Rockwood and he was very well settled, to both, hunting or hacking. I advertised him in the Yorkshire Post stating quite clearly that he was a shiverer and therefore at £2500 he was half his real worth.

The phone was red hot and the first to see him was a lady called Nadine Jimmison. She wanted a safe hack. Her husband, who had never ridden, sat on him in the arena to demonstrate how safe he was. She would not hack him and refused which surprised me. I explained shivering the best I could and she agreed to buy him there and then. She came back an hour later with the money.

She signed my receipt which stated she had not had him vetted, that he was a shiverer and was buying him as seen and tried. I delivered him for her to somewhere near Doncaster three days later. Had I known then what was to come to pass, I would have run a mile. Three weeks later and Nadine called me to say she had big problems as the vet had told her he was a shiverer.

I explained that she knew that as it was on the advert and the receipt. She was hysterical and her husband came on the phone threatening me. I hung up. I have never taken to threats and for me the conversation is over if you start threatening bodily violence. It also strengthens my resolve. Sue said, and quite rightly, this was not going to be smooth and that trouble was ahead.

A few weeks later and I was issued a summons to County Court, not for the £2500 for the cost of the horse but for £44,000 for damages and injuries caused to Mrs Jimmison. Sue quite rightly shit herself. I was so angry, it was ridiculous. What followed then was seven years of total tomfoolery.

She was claiming that the horse had thrown her in a ditch and had damaged her neck. She further claimed that she had had to have the horse put down due to his very bad state of health. I was a dealer, and under the Sale of Goods Act, the horse was not fit for purpose. It took fifteen months to get to a court hearing and I had a fabulous barrister called Gerry Heap who had horses and understood the job.

Before we all went in for the hearing, her solicitors went in first and asked the judge to be disallowed from representing her. She was a nightmare client and refused to pay any bills. This was allowed and the case was stood down. Twelve months later and we attended court again. The same thing happened and her new legal representatives asked to be stood down. This again was agreed and we did not get through the court door. I was now though, getting twitchy as my costs were in excess of four thousand pounds.

A year later and it was listed again for court and the day before it was cancelled as she was ill. In the meantime, the case bundles were now numbering four. Four full files of evidence and claims and medical reports. We did get into court in March, five years after I had sold the horse.

Her husband was first and he just kept pointing at me claiming that I had ripped them off. He came across as aggressive and nasty and the judge stood him down. She went into the box and gave evidence that she did not know the horse was a shiverer. She also claimed that he was not a safe hack and that he had thrown her in a ditch and damaged her neck, rendering her suffering badly and that she had been left with very limited movement.

When asked if she had been on a skiing holiday the previous month, she said she had. When asked about the day she fell in the ditch she gave a very eloquent description of what happened. When Gerry asked her about the domestic disturbance that day at her house, when her husband had throttled her and had been subsequently arrested, she was speechless.

The judge stopped the hearing, told both barristers to stand up and referred them to trial bundle one, page seven, the receipt which she had signed. Her lawyer could not say anything. He threw out the case and awarded costs to me. He also went onto say that the case should never have been allowed and that it was a travesty that it had taken so long to come before him. My barrister estimated, conservatively, that her true costs of all this, over the years were in the area of £52000 which she now had to find.

Chapter Eighteen

In November prior to the court case with Jimmison I was detailed to go to Bradford for the Remembrance Sunday march to the Cenotaph. It was great this, as we had ceremonial kit on and it was a proud moment to lead the veterans in their march throughout the city centre. We lead the parade and pulled off to one side as they did the prayers and speeches awaiting eleven o clock. The last post was sounded and all went quiet to stand for the two minutes silence.

I saw a man walking towards us. Hundreds of others were stood very still in respect and you could hear a pin land. This man though, walked up to the mini bank in the wall next to me and started beeping the buttons. I quietly said to him 'Stop that pal, it's the two minutes silence.' he said to me 'Why should I? I want some money.' 'Have some respect my friend, it's the two minute silence.' 'Nah, not for me mate, I don't care.' The big clock on the town hall had chimed so the silence was over.

I walked my horse over to him. I lifted him off his feet and told him he was locked up. The look on his face was a picture. Two foot lads, who had also seen him, took him away for me. It was only over the road so we went to the Bridewell on the horses and my mate held my horse whilst I went inside and sorted him out. He was eventually fined £250 and bound over to be of good behaviour for twelve months. The little shit.

Wazzy and Tootsie were very quick learners, they were also very trainable. We could not event them the year we bought them though as they were only four. We took them to dressage competitions and show jumping at Birchinley Manor and at Wood Nook arenas. Both were in the ribbons and were doing well.

We could not wait to event them and as members of the Harewood Combined Training Group Riding Club we attended team training to get onto the eventing team for the club at the regional competition. These competitions were held annually and the winners from the area final went to the National Championships at Offchurch Bury. The competitions were fierce and much revered.

We attended four training sessions at Rosemary Search's yard near Harrogate. Rosemary is simply a lovely lady. She was also later the owner of the Olympic silver medallist Opposition Buzz ridden by Nicola Wilson. The yard was a fair distance for us and the training sessions were on an evening so it was always a late finish.

Even though we attended the training sessions we were not picked, other members of the club who had not attended training were. We were really pissed off with this and joined the West Yorkshire Horseplay club. This club was new and had been formed by friends of ours who lived in the Huddersfield/ Wakefield area.

We were selected for their team and we attended the Queen Ethelburga's College for the competition. Sue and I and two others, Jo Wiper and Wendy Ellis were in the Novice team. We won. Sue and I had a double clear, great dressage and I was second individually, the other two team members were the same, double clear and good dressage.

There was a nasty and childish objection by the Harewood club stating one of our riders had carried a whip in the dressage and therefore the team should be disqualified. Thankfully someone had video recorded all our tests and this was thrown out.

So off we went unexpectedly to Offchurch Bury where the National Championships were held. We had a great weekend and both our young horses did really well. They were green though and I had a run out at a skinny after a stile thing, and Sue had a stop at the drop fence to a skinny.

It had been a great learning experience for them both though as they stayed over in strange stables and the track was up to height and asked good questions.

Back at home and Sue had her revenge for the wagon going south on the A1 incident. We went every Thursday night, or as often as we could to Birchinley Manor show jumping. It was a fantastic purpose built place, although it had a chequered history. We got there and entered the horses. I entered Wazzy into the British Novice class and went to get changed. Sue was also in this with Tootsie. As I put my leather boots on and pulled the zip, the thing came off in my hand. Bugger, I could not put my boots on and had no spares.

We had an argument as Sue had invited herself to ride Wazzy for me. Not a chance was my stance, but as I had paid the fee and would lose it. I agreed between gritted teeth that she could school him round and at least he had had a work out. Don't get me wrong Sue was an excellent jockey and I have always admired her. We were though very, very competitive and so her riding my horse was a no no. There was no way she would let me ride Tootsie.

There were forty eight in the class and yes, you have guessed it, she won on my horse. My days, I could not live this one down. I was not allowed to forget it for ages. I went to the yard and Wazzy was in the stable tacked up. Laura told me that Sue was coming to school him properly for me! It also got around everyone else and so at competitions I was often asked if I was warming him up for Sue.

At Imber Court for the Metropolitan Police Horse show that summer I had a serious bit of silliness. On the Friday night we were in the bar and drinking. We drank an awful lot and I was with a big group of people from all different forces. Sat next to me was a Met lad called 'Ragarse'. He got this name because he was very scruffy and so was his horse.

We were drinking and it was my round. I asked him if he wanted another and he declined, saying he had to go as he was doing the guard next day. 'The Guard, what's that?'

'Changing the Guard at Buck house'. 'Bloody 'ell I would love to do that.' 'Come on with me then, you can do it I will stay I bed.'

That was it. I got into the van with him and went to Knightsbridge Barracks. We spent the night in his small room. Him on the mattress and me on the bed base. The next day I got up and put on his uniform and borrowed his boots which fitted thankfully. Downstairs in the mews there was a pair of grey police horses tacked up and ready. I got on one with Ragarse laughing his head off.

The police woman that was with me was a scouser. She looked at me and said 'Who the fuck are you like?' 'Hi, my name is Steve from West Yorkshire.' 'Ragarse, what the fuck's going on here?' Raggy just smiled, winked and said 'My mate wants to do it, look after him.' 'Fuck off, we will get the fucking sack, you idiots.' She said. I said 'I am mounted at home and can ride, don't worry it will be fine.' She was mortified but the whistle went and we had to move off. The horse I was on was older and very much used to doing this duty. He could have done it with his eyes shut.

We set off down the Mall and onto the large concourse outside Buckingham Palace. Then it dawned on me, or was it that I instantly sobered up? I don't know but I was suddenly quite worried about what I was doing. Jackie was her name and she was barking at me to wheel right or left, keep with her and go along the frontage. Tourists were everywhere and taking photos of us.

We picked up the band and led them along the mall and into Buckingham Palace, dropping them off behind the gates where they played their music as the soldiers were marched in to change over.

It went really well and back at the stables I handed to horse over to the grooms with a big pat. Jackie did not say anything. She stomped off leaving me with Ragarse trying to work out how to get back to Esher to the show. I was taken back to Epsom and got changed and sorted. My lot had left for the show with my horses thankfully and I got a lift there with the RAF. One of our lads was with them too having pulled one of the RAF girls that night.

Back at the show we did okay, but not great that day. I really enjoyed my little adventure. I can always have changing the guard at Buckingham Palace on my CV.

The rest of that year we kept the babies ticking over. Darrel was doing really well with Mr Milligan too, he was in the ribbons at different events. In the winter we cubbed them all and had a few half days out with the Rockwood.

After Christmas we started proper fittening work with them and we also went team chasing. The first one we went to was at Factory Farm near Huddersfield. We went clear and fast and it felt great. They all three jumped really well. Wazzy gave me a great feeling. The next one was at Marton cum Grafton, just off the A1 near Knaresborough. The open course here is very comparable to a mixture of Pre-Novice and Novice fences. It does have one massive hedge which, on the take-off side is about 2`6" but on the landing side is a good 8` drop. It is quite famous and as you sail over there are always a lot of people watching you land. I have seen some fairly spectacular falls here. We flew around the course and the hedge was no problem for Wazzy, barely five years old he took it brilliantly and we galloped off to finish the rest of the course to much applause.

The rest of the preparation went really well, we did the Novice course at Frickley and Sue, Darrel, Richard and I won which was a fabulous feeling. Much sloe gin and red wine was consumed. Wazzy and Tootsie got the two double show jumping clears required for a regional qualification at British Novice level and they were jumping regular clears at Discovery and Newcomers too. They had also been placed in dressage competitions. Weekly training with Joanne was going well too.

Sue suggested that we only do a couple of Pre-Novice events and then go straight into Novice level. I was not so sure but Tootsie was more than ready. We started at Osbaldeston for the first event and we both went double clear but time faults across country cost us a placing. Still, we were over the moon with them. At the next event we were both placed and Darrel won so all was really good.

I got a call from Lynne Tolan asking us to help her out at Osbaldeston with a little demonstration to the North West British Horse Society members. She was a little vague about it but we were happy to help and agreed to take both our young horses. We were to be given diesel expenses and she also asked if we could take the girls who worked for us as helpers in the arena.

Lynne is an ex-policewoman, she was actually a Detective Chief Inspector and was very well regarded within the force. She rode at events and has had some beautiful horses over the years. She is now a dressage judge and still competes at a very good level. When she retired from the force she became the North West development officer for the BHS.

When we got there she dropped the bombshell that there were between 300 and 500 people coming and it was actually a lecture demonstration by the one and only Lucinda Green. Lucinda was a hero of mine, a superb horsewoman and prolific winner at the top level of the sport, she won Badminton six times, a feat never repeated. She is also very attractive.

Sue and I were miked up with Madonna type microphones. Lucinda gave us a briefing and asked a lot of questions about the horses. When we went into the arena there were an awful of people watching, the seating gallery was packed out and I knew a lot of them. We were the first guinea pig riders and following were two Intermediate horses and riders and Tracey Dillon was last, on her own, with an avanced horse.

We started off slowly, nice and easy on the flat. It is amazing but when you're in this situation you very much raise your game. I felt I was riding an awful lot better than normal. Lucinda started some basic grid work jumping and was asking us questions all the time. We answered through the Madonna mikes and soon got used to them, in fact I forgot it was there.

As we progressed with the jumping she asked me why I had a martingale on Wazzy? I could not really answer, I suppose I had just been conditioned into always wearing one for jumping. She took this off as she said it was inhibiting him. The grid was now at a metre in height and both horses were jumping really well. I went down the grid, which by now comprised of a bounce to a two non-jumping stride distance to a parallel and I got it all wrong. The stride before take-off, I had not got right at all. As I went around the corner at the bottom of the arena I said to myself

"Stephen, stop riding like a big wet fanny and get a grip"

The sound of laughter coming from 300 plus people surprised me. Lucinda asked me if that was Yorkshire equestrian terminology. It then dawned on me that the Madonna mike had let everyone hear what I had said! God I was so embarrassed. I remember looking over at Sue who was just sat on Tootsie shaking her head.

The rest of the demonstration went fantastically well. We ended up jumping both horses over a single bucket in the middle of the arena, standard fare for demonstrations in those days. I had loved it and was so proud of my young horse. Lucinda joined us in the bar afterwards and we had a really good evening with her.

Not long after this and we were asked to guinea pig ride again at Stockeld Park near Wetherby. This time it was for Ian Stark. Ian again was a prolific winner at Badminton and the Olympics. I suppose his claim to fame is a one, two at Badminton with two wonderful grey horses. He also took on a horse from Ginny Leng called Murphy Himself. Murphy was one of those horses that was a freak of nature. His jump, athleticism and speed were just unbelievable. How Ian stayed on him at times I just do not know. I was at badminton when they bounced the Luckington Lane Crossing, which, if you saw the distance over two enormous hedges, is an unbelievable feat.

This was a much different demonstration as there were thankfully no microphones and only about seventy people there. It was a karma moment for Sue and I as it was the Harewood Combined Training group who were hosting the event and they could not find anyone else to do it. So bearing in mind we had been overlooked for their eventing team and we had beaten them at the Regionals, it was sweet.

Ian was great to work with and he ended the demo by having Sue and I bouncing through a grid of seven cross poles at a metre high. I really enjoyed the evening though the horses were very tired at the end.

Sue decided that her first Novice was to be at The Great Yorkshire Showground event. I was very against this as it was a very hot summer and the going was rock hard. She went clear though and within the time. Tootsie, her mare, had an incredible engine as she was not the most athletic of horses. I chose Skipton to go to for our first Novice and we had a great ride around. The horses need to be fit for this event as there are some very big hills to negotiate.

Near the end of this course is a trakehner fence. Everyone who events has a bogey fence, these fences are mine, well and truly. I had to walk straight them past them when walking the course. If I looked into the bottom of them I would hook and hook and stop or lose so much momentum we would be climbing and that was not fair on the poor horse.

We both went to Holker Hall in Lancashire for the next Novice. This was an amazing event as it had loads of trade stands around the main arena and when you rode in to the jumping it felt like you were at a major championships. It was a major loss to the circuit when they stopped. We did well again here although Wazzy had three down in the jumping phase and I was very disappointed.

At Henbury Hall in Cheshire I had a great dressage and was in the top three after this. We went clear show jumping and I was pumped. We set off out of the start box and we were flying. The adrenalin was flowing very freely and it was a great feeling.

At the top end of the course I had a serious directional failure. I flew one jump, went to the left across a field and came to the wire field boundary fence. This was not right so I turned around and went back the way I had come. Back at the fence and I went right through some trees and ended up back near the horseboxes. This was not right either so I went back to the fence and went straight on and came very quickly to the next fence. I finished the course but by now had about sixty time penalties.

It was a bloody long way home in the wagon, especially as Sue had been torn a strip off by the steward over something and nothing.

She was ordered to go to the Secretary's tent and meet the steward. This lady was old school very posh, very, very loud and rude. She spoke to Sue about her use of the whip but was so condescending and over the top, I was surprised Sue stood for it. She just adopted a 'let's get it over with' stance and accepted this woman shouting at her in a very threatening manner. Thankfully it became clear quickly that it was not Sue but another rider, although of course there was no apology forthcoming.

We were good really over the years. Apart from my run in at the water fence at Osbaldeston, we never got into trouble at all throughout our time eventing.

I began to have a problem with Wazzy. It developed over a very short period of time but it was disturbing. He was of course just a five year old, and although I felt at no time was he under undue pressure or else I would have eased off, he started dropping his right shoulder and dipping out in front of a show jumping fence. He never did it cross country, always while show jumping.

I was at a loss as to what to do. At Winkburn Horse Trials he did it in the arena and I fell off. I was furious. I got straight back on and brought him round to the fence again and he jumped it. The commentator and judge sounded the horn and said "335 we think you should retire before you bleed to death." I stopped, looked down and I was covered in blood, my jacket and my number bib were red. I did not know where this was coming from though. I got back to the wagon and it was underneath my chin, I had a big tear. I had to go see the doctor and he told me to go to hospital. Sue was still to compete Tootsie and a young horse in the Pre-Novice so I couldn't go to hospital as we were in Nottinghamshire.

The doctor could not do anything and I was bleeding quite a lot. I used an ice block from the cooler box in a towel. When we got back home I left the girls to do the horses and went to hospital where I had three stitches inside the wound and five outside.

At Wood Nook arenas in Huddersfield I booked a jumping lesson with Peter Mellor, He was a show jumper and evented too. He and his wife Gillian ran the arenas and still do. The place was a focal point locally for competitions. I have spent many an hour there competing. I told Peter what the problem was and when he finished laughing at my black and blue chin he put up some fences.

We began and Wazzy was jumping really well, he did not stop and do his new trick at all. I was fed up, bloody horse! We had a break and he gave me a length of alkathene blue water piping explaining that if he did do it I had to hit him with it very hard. This piping will hurt a horse more than any whip available.

We did a few more jumps and he did it. I managed to stay on and he shouted "Hit him". I did, just a couple of times and I knew he felt it. I jumped him again and he jumped really well. I never used a whip on him again. He never did the drop and spin trick again either.

Chapter Nineteen

We were on duty at a concert in Roundhay Park in Leeds by Genesis. It was a great concert except for the eight hours of fighting the Leeds United yobbos put us through. I was reunited with Ambassador. We got to Roundhay Park at twelve after a meal at the Carrgate stables.

We got mounted up and started to patrol. Everything was good and running smoothly. We stood down for a break at 3 pm. Mounted again at four pm, people were everywhere, milling around and queuing to get in.

It was getting dark at seven p.m. and the concert support act were on. We had South Yorkshire mounted branch in support and therefore we had thirty horses. The radio was buzzing but it was menial stuff about meal relief and parking issues. The concert was in full swing. All of a sudden, and from nowhere, came the radio message 'Control, there are about three hundred lads walking up from the lake towards the long side fence'.

And so it started. We were deployed straight away to that part of the park. As we rode down alongside the fence we heard them before we saw them. Chanting 'We are Leeds, Leeds, Leeds. Marching on together were gonna see you win la la la la la la la we are Leeds'.

They came up towards us and they were fired up. I estimated about two hundred but there were more. We tried to stop them in their tracks with four horses but they ran past us towards one of the big gates in the fence line. On top of the fence were stewards and they quickly shut the gates. They charged the gate and were kicking out at it. Some of them were trying to climb the fence but there was no way they could get up. It was about ten foot high, made of tank tracking and too slippery.

We radioed for more urgent help and some more mounted units got there. They would not be cordoned though and the main body of them ran off towards the Mansion House and gardens where loads of nice people were having picnics. As we got there in sections of four horses, they started throwing bottles and stones from the gardens. It was raining bottles. 'Heads, heads' was the shout from the foot units as this lot started to land.

We were told to withdraw whilst the lads on foot started to clear the picnickers away. They were though, most put out, and did not want to move. The main group of yobs ran off again past us back to where we had come from. We were told to give chase and follow them. They were thinking now that this was a great game and it became a cat and mouse situation. Attempts to breach the gates or fence were being made all the time. They were determined to get in free, either that or to disrupt the concert.

By now Genesis were on and going well. The sound was great and the band were very good. People in the gardens were really angry at the trouble and started remonstrating with us. We were stood at twenty feet gaps along the fence with our backs to it. One woman came over and had a right go at me. She was shouting that we were the cause of the bother and that we should go home.

As she was having her rant at me she was hit by a bottle. I said to her 'I didn't throw that love. I suggest you get out of here'. She soon got out of it, dragging her family with her. The situation did get out of hand for about two hours. We were struggling to get this group together and control them. Gold Commander was apoplectic trying to get control. We needed more horses but they were reluctant to deploy them in case it was looked upon as overkill. Members of the public were getting hurt and several were ambulanced to hospital.

One man, trying to protect his kids, had a go at some of them and was mass set upon. Two or three were arrested but the main lot got away. We were moved away from the gardens near the Mansion because the ground was really difficult to move in. It was all rose gardens and lawns. We were destroying them charging into this group.

We moved to the long side of the arena where we had first encountered them. They came around towards us again and there were definitely more than two hundred. They were stood chanting. They knew they could not get in and so decided to make a stand and just chant and be stupid. The South Yorkshire Mounted were at last deployed and they came around to meet us. We now had twenty four horses so we charged them in a line, truncheons drawn.

As per usual, they were cowards and turned and ran. We followed them at a distance instead of getting into them. The line we held worked, as we pushed them away from the fencing and arena out into the park and into the dark. We lost the lights from the arena and it was difficult to see them all. We just kept pushing them away towards the end of the grass. Absolutely nothing was said between any of the mounted lads but we all knew exactly where this lot were going.

We kept pushing them and herding them in this big group. Eventually, those at the very back began to shout and we could hear the splashing. We increased as one now, the speed with which we were moving them. I was loving this and was laughing out loud. We trotted at them now and it was so easy. The ones at the back were really screaming now but the momentum was there. They were all going into the lake. It was shallow up at that end but it was muddy and filthy. A panic started now amongst them but we kept them going. The ones nearest us at the front stopped and stood still, we got angry with them and tried to keep them moving but they were certainly not for going into the mucky lake.

It took about an hour and a half after that to round them all up and escort them out of the park into the top end of Oakwood. The fire had gone out of them by now and some of the sights were heart-warming. Wet through, and covered in shit, mud and grass. For me it was a great piece of police work and we all congratulated each other. We were stood down after the concert at eleven p.m. and I had been on Ambassadors back without a break for seven hours straight.

Not long after the concert by Genesis we were on duty at Bramham Park on the outskirts of Leeds. Bramham hosts an annual International Horse Trials three day event. We performed the musical ride on Friday and it went very well. On the Thursday though, which is the first day of the competition, there were just four of us riding around the park. This was really a PR day to meet and greet and the public who were all horse people and just loved the horses.,

I was having a lovely old day, the weather was great. I was on Commodore, a big Cleveland Bay and was partnered with Maureen. The horses were looking great and we had a lot of admirers.

So we were very surprised to get a general radio call from the mobile police station based there to attend the trade stands urgently. We trotted off and found about twenty people shaking and rocking a burger van. I went into this lot straight away and shouted at them to move away. The group was nearly all ladies and they were incensed.

The burger van was advertising venison burgers. Venison and game were on sale. The problem was though, that it was situated next to an Animal Sanctuary stand and part of their display was an enclosure which had a small pig and a very small young deer in it for the kids to meet and pet. These women, or some of them, had thought that the deer was for the burgers and it had all kicked off. The burger van was soon moved.

Chapter Twenty

All three of us entered the Novice 2 day Championships at Chepstow in Wales. We were very excited and the preparation for this was very serious. If we went clear across country and completed we only needed two Intermediate runs and we were then qualified the next season for a One Star International three day event. We took the wagon with all three horses in, but Darrel took his trailer to sleep in and carry the bedding and feed we needed for three horses for four days away.

The first thing of note was the £12 it cost to get across the bridge into Wales, £12! They should pay us to visit. I was disgusted. The second thing was that we were one of the first ones to arrive at the racecourse and therefore parked far too near the hospitality tent which meant no sleep until the early hours of each morning.

The next thing was Darrel struggling to blow up, by mouth, his lillo. He had forgotten the foot pump and was blowing into the thing like a big wet weekend. I took over from him and started blowing into this thing with great gusto. After five minutes of constant blowing I fainted, flat on my back on the ramp. I came around to find Darrel, my lovely wife Sue and Laura our head girl laughing their heads off. Janine, our trainee groom was not impressed, although nothing impressed her to be honest. It did not get any better.

We set off, after the trot up, to walk the course for the first time. The trot up is always a fashion extravaganza, never more so than at Badminton and Burghley. I always kept it simple with a pair of beige trousers and a shirt and tie and tweed jacket, usually my hacking jacket. Sue though had different thoughts and was always very glamourous.

The first look at the course left us feeling very confident. It was not big and was not trappy at all. It flowed and the water was very simple with a hanging log well before the water and a similar thing on exit. It was not very well presented and to be honest we were not very impressed. The other course, the intermediate was beautifully done.

We walked the roads and tracks, but only once. The kilometre markers were noted and we were confident with the route. Our times for dressage and jumping were only twenty and forty minutes apart so we all mucked in to get the horses ready. Dressage was in the middle of the racecourse, it was very open and very windy on the Friday. In the afternoon we had the show jumping and it was not far from the dressage. Warming up was not good as we were on a steep incline and the horses were unbalanced. I had one down, Darrel had one too but Sue was clear.

That night the party was in full swing in the big marquee not thirty yards from our box. We went and enjoyed the evening but went to bed at a reasonable time. We did not get any sleep until the early hours. It was a big lesson never to be repeated and we certainly did not park near the hospitality ever again.

The next morning and I was buzzing, I loved the endurance day and was always thrilled to be going cross country and it was heightened when the other two phases were included too. It is so sad now that these elements have been removed from the modern day sport of eventing I was sat on the ramp having five minutes looking at the programme for the event. I looked at the map of the cross country and was totally shocked. We had walked, three times, the wrong course! The yellow markers on the smaller course were not the ones we had to jump. It was the white marked Novice two day course.

Panicking, I shouted Sue and Darrel who both told me to fuck off as they thought I was on the wind up, but the look on my face told them different. We could not believe it. A visit to the Secretary and she stared at us in disbelief. Seeing our distress though She very quickly arrange the score collectors on quad bikes to jet us around the course.

They were great and the first few fences were ok, not a lot different to the yellow course. The water though was a whole different ball game, a log (big one), drop into water with a stile brush fence in the middle and then a hanging log out on not quite a full stride from the water. This was followed by a gallop down an avenue of trees which narrowed to the end where there was the biggest log pile jump out.

I said, looking at this fence that we had cocked up as this was the biggest course the three five year old babies had seen and that if Wazzy was climbing them I would suck it up and pull up. A bit further on there was a three step up combination to a very upright skinny fence at the top which again was not quite on a full stride. Finally, down a steep hill, the second to last fence was a huge trackehner …. great.

I set off on the roads and tracks, the first section went well. We trotted it at a good pace with a small bit of canter toward the end to warm up properly for the steeplechase. Counted down we set off across the racecourse, jumping the steeplechase fences used for the races. We made it in under the two minutes thirty time limit and went straight out onto the second roads and tracks. This went well and we came into the ten minute halt box. Darrel was twenty minutes behind me and then forty minutes later it would be Sue.

The vet clipped the thermometer to Wazzy's tail and pushed it up his bum. Laura was in her element here and had the horse cooled off and checked over in no time. Janine, the trainee who was about as interested as a fence post, was told to walk him round to cool and calm down. I sat down and was eating a banana when the halt box steward called me, "434 two minutes" "No I have only just come in" I shouted to him, he replied very officiously "434 two minutes"

The vet came over and removed the thermometer and said he was good to go after checking his heart rate. He also told me the steward had got all his timings wrong and it was chaos. I called Janine who was leading Wazzy around over and she could not have walked more slowly. Laura had a plastic glove on one hand and was applying event grease and was checking studs with the other, I was worried about the time and told her to get me on him, she said to wait and the steward was shouting at me to get in the start box.

Panic took over and I was screaming at her now to get me on. I had done up the girth and I was ready. The steward was shouting at the top of his voice and Laura made a lift with her hands to give me a leg up. I put my leg into her hands and she heaved me so hard and so fast I went flying over the other side of him and landed in the mud. My language was disgusting and Laura said "Well if you're going to be like that I am going" and she promptly walked off. I jumped on him and trotted off to the start box where the starter said "Hello 434, three minutes" I couldn't believe it.

I was circling around the start box and looked down at Wazzy who was chewing his flash noseband. I begged the starter to do it up for me which he did. I was all over the place by now, no serene calmness, no thrill, no adrenalin just bloody panic and anger at the bloody steward. The start man even said he was cocking everything up.

We set off and Wazzy was flying. He jumped into the water and straight over the skinny, thanks Lucinda Green for the help, he was galloping beautifully, very fit. We went down the avenue of trees to the big log pile and he pinged it like a schooling log. The steps to the skinny were no problem and he skidded to the end of the bank and drop but went straight over. Going down the hill I had to use all my determination not to take a pull or hook him. The log over the ditch was at an angle and I just simply closed my eyes and hoped for the best.

When I went over the finish line I was in tears. This horse was only five, he had done a few Novices that's all and nothing as demanding as this course. He was brave as a lion and so calm and responsive. Clear and inside the time.

In the halt box, Laura was nowhere to be seen and Darrell had managed with Janine helping. Laura did come back for Sue so that was okay. I washed him off and checked him over. Then I walked him back to the stables by which time he was cool and calm. I ran back to the halt box and passed a beaming Darrel who had gone clear and also in the time.

Sue was nowhere to be seen in the halt area and Janine and Laura were packing up the box we used and the chairs and water buckets. In the ten minute box we had spare sets of shoes for all the horses, spare breastplates and girths and a stud kit. We also had grease in there for the horses' legs, smelling salts lucosade and a banana for the riders.

I asked them where Sue was and Laura just blanked me. I tried to apologise for my language explaining the situation but she was having none of it. Sue was walking back to the stables but via the horseboxes.

I caught up with her and she told me that Tootsie had left a back leg on the last step up and had stopped at the skinny, only because she lost momentum. I was gutted for her but of course Darrel and I were on a high.

It was a long way home in that wagon, poor Sue was really down at missing the qualification, there were other ways and times within the qualifying period to get it but not in that wagon going home back to Yorkshire.

It had been a great weekend on one part, on the other it had been a bloody disaster, we had behaved like a set of amateurish muppets.

The final thing of note was that Darrel had paid for a video of his event. At £45 per horse Sue and I could not afford this facility. Total Recall were the company and they video recorded the dressage test, show jumping rounds and most of the cross country. Three weeks after the event and the much anticipated tape arrived as promised at Darrel's, he was so excited and watched it at home a few times and brought it up for us to look at. He was over the moon with it and was going on about how well it was produced and how good Mr Milligan looked.

Back at home we eagerly sat down to watch the recording. The dressage was great and looked really professional. The show jumping was clear to see and really good. At the start of the cross country Darrel looked fantastic, he left the start box and went over the first three jumps brilliantly. After the first three, the angle changed to the next camera and the horse and rider were then shown over the next five fences including the water. The problem was though that quite clearly, this rider and the rider who went onto complete the course after fence three was a girl and not Darrel.

It was quite clear to see because Darrel had on a black skull cap cover and this girl had a blue and white one on with a white pom pom on top!! I stared in disbelief, Sue wet herself laughing and we had an argument over who should call him and tell him. Sue won and called him at his restaurant that he runs in Brighouse. He flew up to our house as he was sure we were winding him up. The only thing he said after watching the video and taking it away with him was "Bastards". I still don't know if he meant Total Recall or Sue and I.

He got a new one several weeks later all done and finished but it was ages before he let us watch it.

The fabulous Blacup Connundrum (Wazzy). Skipton HT Novice

Wazzy. Just Five years old jumping the big hedge at the Marton Team Chase.

Ernie the Milkman

Bishop Burton 100.

2008

Chapter Twenty One

The National Front were quite a large organisation in the eighties. They always insisted on having marches and meeting in heavily Asian populated areas. The Anti- Nazi league were always going to march and meet in opposition.

A recipe for trouble, and the police were always of a mind to try and get the marches banned or restricted. In Dewsbury that summer, on a Saturday, there was agreement for a march by the National Front to be allowed and the police were there in great numbers. We were stood down to begin with as a secondary unit. The foot lads and dogs actually managed to police the march very well. We were bored.

We were parked outside the town centre and had converged on a garage for chocolate and sweets and drinks. It was a very hot day. The National Front had virtually dispersed with little or no trouble. The Asians who lived in Dewsbury though, were up for fun and games.

A large group of Asians, young men and women, were gathered at the bottom of a road called The Town. A car, carrying a family who were out shopping for the day, was attacked and the windows smashed and some shopping stolen. The members of the family inside the car were, of course, traumatised. It was unclear who had done this but many Asian people were around at the time. The foot units already deployed had small round shields and started walking and ushering the crowd along the road to The Town. A stand-off ensued and it was a question then of whether they would disperse or come at the police.

They came at us. Bricks and bottles were thrown and then the petrol bombs came out. This obviously was very well organised, and planned. We were called up, and mounted in sections of eight, we trotted up the road. It was mayhem, the police were stood in a line across the bottom of the road. They were taking fire from the people in front of them about twenty yards away. It was raining stones and the odd petrol bomb. Debris was everywhere. We lined up across the road a good 100 yards behind the shields. On seeing us I think it spurred them on a bit and more bricks were thrown. Some rubbish bins were set on fire and a car went up too. The fire brigade was called in but they were reluctant to go up the road under the hail of debris, and who could blame them?

Our Boss was called over to the main Commander and they had a discussion. He came back to us and took his place in the centre of the rank next to the Inspector. He came on the radio. 'Engage visors.' Thirty mounted officers clicked down their visors as one. 'Mounted branch draw truncheons.' Thirty mounted officers drew truncheons and placed them against our right shoulders. It was very impressive. I was riding Portia. The Policewomen, including Sue had all been stood down and they were absolutely furious about it. I was on the extreme right of the line and on the pavement.

'Mounted branch will advance at the walk, watch your dressing on the centre.' We all started walking in a line. The shield units all cleared away quickly leaving the road clear in front apart from debris everywhere and bins and a car on fire. We got past these as the people in front of us moved backwards. 'Mounted branch will advance at the trot, keep your dressing. Keep your dressing'.

We all began to trot and kept the whole line really well. We were quite quickly upon them and they turned tail and ran. We were ordered to halt and keep the line. We did this and as they had dispersed right up the road, quite a way from us, we turned in on the centre into twos and trotted back to the rest of the police. We were applauded back to the bottom of the road.

We thought that was it. Sadly they came back. Hundreds of them and they went into a pub called the Scarborough. They pulled all the furniture from this building out into the road and made a barrier with it. Setting it on fire, they were jeering from behind it. It was at least three hundred yards up the road and a fair way from the police units. Our boss was asked if the horses would jump the fire barrier. The fire was right across the road and there was no way the lads on foot would get over it. It was also impossible for the fire brigade to get to it safely and put it out.

We formed up again on the line and went forward. As one, in a line, truncheons drawn. The boss was shouting to keep the line. We got to within ten yards from the burning furniture and it was raining bricks and rubble. We were trotting and given the order to charge. As one, we all went forward and jumped the fire, not one horse refused and no one fell off. It was totally fabulous. The look on the faces of the people on the other side was something else.

We carried on charging them and a large group ran to the left of me into a cul de sac. A group of us broke away from the line and followed them. We were taken into a small road housing a group of garages and this was a dead end. A group of about thirty lads ran into a garden. As I was going along after them, an Asian lady ran out of a garden with a garden fork in her hands. She stabbed it towards Portia's stomach and I hit both her hands as hard as I could with my truncheon. She screamed and dropped the fork.

We got the men in the garden to put their hands on their heads and marched them out. We were escorting them back to the main road and they kicked off again trying to pull us off the horses. They got a good hiding and ran off. We went back onto the main road and joined the rest of the horses who were standing at the junction. We came under fire again and chased the lads up the road. They all ran into a mosque and over the radio the Commander was screaming at us not to go into the mosque. We went towards the gates though as our blood was up. The gates were shut in our faces to stop us going in.

We could see swords being brandished inside the mosque and were ordered to stand down straight away. Again in twos, we went back to the units and were cheered back by about three hundred policemen. It had been a great day again for the mounted branch, we had certainly saved the day.

Two weeks afterwards the air unit came to see us with a video they had taken from the helicopter. It was amazingly clear and very detailed about what had taken place. They agreed though, thankfully, to destroy it!!

Chapter Twenty Two

Back at home and things were much the same. We had full stables and were very busy teaching, riding and working full time in the mounted branch. Showing for the season was underway and we were both selected to represent the force at different shows throughout the season.

We had sold all but one of our dealing horses and so on my next day off from work I went to the Doncaster Bloodstock Sales. Sue was away on a course with work and so I had a free go at buying…. fatal.

Value was good and buying a load of horses divided into the total purchase price, they were coming home at around £600 per horse. I bought five on that day and when I told Sue she went berserk. I was confident and wanted to go back the next day too but Sue told Laura to hide the wagon keys, which she did, and would not tell me, under no amount of threats, where they were. We sold them, all five, at an average of £1500 over the next few weeks and so I was totally vindicated.

Jeanette Wheeler and her mother ran a riding school at Fagley in Bradford. She called me about a nice young horse she had called Shan. I went to have a look at him and he was a very nice 15.2 hh bay gelding of unknown breeding. He was five years old and had been placed second in his only two unaffiliated One Day Events. I liked him on sight and decided to buy him. I bid £1800 against the £2200 they asked for and they agreed. I brought him home that afternoon and turned him out. I was expecting Sue to event him but didn't get that far.

One of my liveries was a school teacher and she was looking for a horse for her daughter. Without me knowing Laura had mentioned him straight away to them. They came and had a look at him and tried him when I got back to the yard. They bought him there and then, £5000 that was a good day's work. Shan was a great horse for them for years, he showed and did workers at a local level and prolifically won classes.

A young lady called me about a big horse she had for sale as she was getting married and needed the money. A silly thing to say really, putting me in the driving seat. Bill, as he became known, was enormous, in that he was 17.3 hh. Four years old, all bay with no white markings and unbroken. I could tell straight away that he had a lovely quiet temperament. She asked £2000 for him, but being prepared to walk away I offered her £1200. As I got back into the wagon she agreed to sell him for £1200.

We had a nightmare loading him as he was just not sure how to walk up the ramp, he was not objecting he just did not know where to put his feet. He got half way up and slipped backwards, hit his head and knocked himself out. I felt so sorry for him. He did not stay out for long, maybe half a minute, and he came around. I stroked him for ages and he got up, shook himself and walked up the ramp. I was already in love with him.

Back at home and he was started and under saddle in less than two weeks. Hacking out Bill never saw a thing and was exceptional on the road. He was though, too big and gangly to ever event. South Yorkshire Police were looking for a horse and came to try him. They loved him and took him in for four weeks trial. The police had this strange system of trying them for four weeks and then vetting them, which if they failed the vetting seemed a waste of time and money.

Over the years I have sold a lot of horses to the Police forces. The Metropolitan mounted section were the best customers as they came with a wagon, a vet and a cheque book. They would try horses, vet them there and then and pay for them. It was great business when they came.

Three weeks after Bill went in and the Sergeant, Steve Thomas, called me to say he had failed the vet sadly, as he had an embryonic tumour in his eye. I was devastated because they had told me he had been to the Meadow Hall shopping centre on car park duty and never put a foot wrong. What they did not know at the South Yorkshire Mounted branch was that I knew their vet, Phil Dixon, very well from team chasing. I called him to ask him how bad the tumour was and what was the likely prognosis? He told me he had not vetted the horse and had not actually seen it.

Furious, I called Steve Thomas back and he eventually admitted that they were short of horses at a night game at Sheffield United and they had taken Bill. Nothing wrong with that I thought, but they had also taken him pitch side between the two stands where they always stood horses and watched the game. Of course though, when United scored the place suddenly erupted and poor Bill went off his head in panic. Because of this they thought he would not make it and rather than tell me, they concocted this story about the tumour. I could not believe this, talk about stupid!

I called Nottinghamshire Mounted as they were looking for a horse and they wanted 17 hh plus and all bay, no white. I told them exactly what had happened but they were happy to try him. They collected him from South Yorkshire Mounted at Ring Farm near Barnsley, vetted him, which he passed and he went on to have a very good career as a police horse in Nottingham.

A lady from Leeds came to try one of the thoroughbreds I had bought from Doncaster. He was a nice gelding at 16hh and four years old. He had never raced but had trained. She agreed to buy him for £1800 and left a deposit of £500 cash for him. She arranged to pick him up that weekend. Despite several calls and attempts to contact her we never heard from her again. The horse was sold again to a nice lady from Harrogate. Dealing horses was never easy and it never got any easier.

The rest of the season went really well with the horses. I competed Wazzy at his first Intermediate at Ivesley and he went round the course really well. We had a couple of fences in the show jumping though and that cost us a placing. The final event of the year for most people was at Bishop Burton College in October. That year though the event was cancelled due to really bad fog and Darrel called us on the phone to tell us just as we had got about six miles from home.

We settled in for the winter, which was a stinker that year. The senior event horses had a bit of time off and we had two nice babies in to bring on. We always tried to have as few horses in as possible through the winter for cost reasons of course, plus we always had a holiday during October when the event season was finished.

This year we had a cheap, all inclusive to Tunisia which was a dog of a holiday. Dead, rotting camels on the beach, poor food and when we had breakfast on the first day we were sat on a table with a young couple who told us they were only there as they had stolen a credit card from someone and used it to pay for the holiday. When they asked us what we did for a living, their faces were a picture! People never fail to amaze me.

The Bramham Moor Hunt were having trouble with antis at this time and I was rostered on duty with another officer to follow them at Harewood Park. We had fit horses and the meet was at the stud farm at the back of the estate. The Masters were grateful for our attendance and twenty to thirty antis turned up and started causing bother, although they were very surprised to see us. The police horses, never having seen hounds before, were a bit on their toes.

The field set off towards the roads round the estate and encountered the antis who were very vocal and got a bit boisterous. It was going to be mayhem and we had no way really of arresting anyone. We suggested to the Masters that they head for the centre of the park, which has thousands of acres, and we would then lose them. They took this advice and we set off into the centre of the estate. We then had a great day, jumping everything in great style, Carlton and Sultan, the horses, were brilliant and never stopped or looked at anything. I think I can safely say that day was in the top ten of my days on the mounted branch.

We had a few days out with the Rockwood and on New Year's Eve, I had a bad fall over a wall at the top of Lepton near Huddersfield. New Year's Day and Sue and I were on duty at Elland Road for the football. I was in pain with my shoulder and the day was buzzing, we had loads of arrests for fighting all around the ground and we were late off duty too, which did not help matters.

Initial preparations for the forthcoming season went well and we also managed to fit in some team chasing. I was just excited as I needed another Intermediate completion, as did Darrel and that was us qualified for a One Star International. Sue did not seem too bothered or anxious to qualify Tootsie and was content to keep her ticking over at Novice level.

We started in a very wet March at Osbaldeston and we all had good runs at Novice. I then entered Witton Castle Intermediate and Darrel went to Bold Heath in Cheshire for some reason. Witton was a good track so early on, it was not trappy, big bold and straight forward. We went clear and I was over the moon. I had such a buzz going on, I could not wait. Going to Tweseldown race course in Hampshire for the One Star was all I had an interest in. It was all consuming, planning the lead up to the event.

Darrel was qualified too and he was just as giddy as me, probably more so if that was possible. I decided that another run was needed prior to going. Much discussion took place about where to go and we sought the counsel of one or two friends about where to go for the best. Oliver Townend had qualified and he was going to Tetton, so Tetton Hall it was. Oliver was grown up now and making a name for himself, especially with difficult horses.

Tetton Hall in Cheshire was a superb venue. Caroline Pratt was based there and she was a tremendous jockey. She had real feel for a horse and rode a lot of Primitive horses. We got on really well with her, she was always very helpful, welcoming and smiling. Caroline tragically lost her life at Burghley Horse Trials some time later. I went to her funeral and it was a very sad time.

When we got there I was surprised at the size of the course, it was very big and very demanding, being on undulating ground with some steepish hills. There was also, near the end (why are they always near the end of the course?) a bloody big trackhaner for me to gulp at as I walked past it. I don't know why but I had a bit of a panic attack on this day. I did not feel confident at all as I went to the dressage. It told, the dressage was okay but I rode so fast in the show jumping we had three down. I had this mental block and went around the course like a steam train.

In the start box I was in a bit of a state, this was a serious track to me and I was following Eric Smiley, who was a serious competitor. He did not get round and that really filled me with confidence, not. I rode the first few fences terribly. The horse, if he could have spoken, would have told me to get my finger out or go home!

We went down to the water and I kicked on and rode him properly through it. From then on we went lovely. Wazzy had a lovely galloping rhythm, he never changed legs in gallop and stayed balanced and underneath himself all the time. His ears were always pricked and you knew he was looking for the next fence. Down to the trackehner and I just closed my eyes again. We finished clear but with time penalties. I did not care, I was over the moon with him.

I wanted another run though, more for me to exorcise my demons than the need for Wazzy as he was fit and jumping out of his skin. We entered Bishop Burton College in Humberside. We had a great day there, jumped around really well and especially through a brand new double of upright corners and came 9th. I was over the moon and plans were now in full force for Tweseldown.

We went down in the wagon this time and Darrel took a tent to sleep in. Sue had to work the first two days but literally just made it for my dressage test.

In those days the One Star competitions were the first steps on the road to major successes at Two and Three star. They were also classed as Internationals. The old Three Day format was very prestigious to qualify and compete in. Nowadays they have one day One, Two and Three Star events and I have to say they are de-valued in my opinion. It gives the proper amateur nothing to aspire and aim at. There are also lots of these one day events at the three levels and therefore they have become just another competition.

At Twesledown there was a proper trot up in front of the ground jury and you were announced at the beginning. There were several rider briefings and a course walk was offered with a top international rider. Darrel and I had taken our bikes and we cycled the roads and tracks which were through the forest. The ground was sandy soil and the going was great.

The course itself was big, bold and inviting. Two jumps caused me concern, the water, that came at number nine was a brush shooting butt onto a very short piece of ground and a small drop into the water. On exit you had a step up to a half stride pop out over a shooting butt type brush fence. Many riders walked this and re-walked it. Joanna Kay was there and she walked it with us and said we should show jump through it and then kick on.

The second fence was much later on in the course. It was a ramp over a log to a decent drop followed by a one stride to a very upright skinny. We talked about this jump endlessly and in the end I decided to go at it and attack it on a good strong canter. There was room to fiddle a second stride if you came off the bank slowly but that opened the door for a run out or stop as the skinny was a solid triangle and quite upright.

Darrel did his dressage test on the Thursday and he went really well. His flying change and halt to rein back was superb. He was lying tenth but ended up eighteenth by Friday evening. We were both surprised at the arena for the dressage. There were trade stands all around it. It was 60 x 20 and had judges at C and H in Range Rover cars. This is normal of course at Advanced level but there was also a very large electronic display that had your name, the name of the horse and your number on and also your nationality. It was very impressive and I had never experienced this before.

On the Friday I warmed up and Wazzy felt great. I was a bit nervous, whereas I wasn't normally. Laura came down with the grooming bag and she was nervous too as she kept fiddling with us, Wazzy's mouth and my boots. They called us in and as I entered the arena I saw my name on the electronic board. This was it, the adrenalin was pouring through me.

He started well but he objected in the rein back and threw his head up. In the extended canter he went on a bit and we lost balance in the corner as he came back to collected. I was so thrilled with him and the mere fact that I was there meant I did not really care what my score was. Darrel was eighteenth after dressage and I was twenty second. Bring on the next day.

I couldn't sleep. We had been to the cocktail party, but not for long. Up early, I was fidgeting about over all sorts of stuff. I was not due to start until 12.45 pm and it was far too long to wait. I almost set off to walk the course again but decided against it. I was sure I would see something new that would worry me. Wazzy was really calm and just ate quietly in his box which was a good sign.

Eventually, after waiting what seemed a lifetime, we were due to go. I went to the start of the roads and tracks and was buzzing. We set off at a good trot through the woods and out onto the fringe of what was firing ranges for the army. On the way back to the steeplechase I had a massive fright. A woman was trotting towards me, she came right up to me and I had a total panic. Had I gone the wrong way, had I got it all wrong? She shouted to me that she was totally lost, phew the relief was amazing. I trotted past her and left her to it. There was nothing I could do anyway.

On the steeplechase he flew, he really enjoyed it and the fences were up to height. We went round in less than the two minutes thirty allowed and straight out onto the second roads and tracks. The ten minute halt box went really well, we were, that is Laura and I, very professional. I cannot really remember the cross country course, it is in fact a blur.

I know we flew round inside the time and met every jump just right. There were a lot of people watching at the bank, drop and skinny fence which we met on a perfect stride. Coming over the finish line I was in tears. Couldn't help it, I just sobbed. Laura and Sue were too. It was very emotional. Darrel had gone clear too and we were all a very happy camp back at the wagons.

We had a funny incident later that evening. Darrel and I cycled down to the racecourse buildings for a shower. The room was enormous with a bank of 12 open showers. I was up one end and Darrel the other, as you would. There was only us two, until a man walked in for a shower and went and stood right next to Darrel. It was very uncomfortable and I left quickly. Darrel was stood on his own with twelve showers going and a man stood right next to him. I shouted from the outer room in my very best effeminate voice 'Awh Darrell, you haven't washed my back' He ran for it, out of the showers, got dressed without getting dried and got on his bike. I was pissing myself.

The next morning we were up very early, got the horses ready and went for a small hack around the grounds. I was not, to be honest, looking forward to the show jumping. I was hoping my old panic did not come back whereby I just rushed around every fence hoping for the best. After the trot up for the ground jury which went well, the warm up went well too and he was pinging off the ground. I was feeling really good. I was first to go as I was further down the order than Darrel. I went in and yep, I panicked at first. They announced me and I looked at the big electronic board. The clock was counting down to begin and I rushed through the start. I then came over all calm and the canter stride was good and the first two fences went well. Then it was Wazzy's turn, he was very distracted looking around and gawping at all the stands and people.

We actually jumped around in a good fashion. He was cantering well, in a lovely rhythm and the take-off at each fence was good, he was just not concentrating. We had three down and to be honest, initially, I was not bothered. It dropped us down to 33rd in the standings. I was very happy to have gone clear across country and within the time. The dressage I was pleased with too. Later on the journey home, the fact that we had qualified for a 2* did not quell my overriding disappointment at the show jumping which cost us. A top twenty finish would have been great but it was not to be. I knew though that my ambition to compete in an international three day event had been reached. I was giddy.

Darrel went around for one down and jumped really well. He finished 18th and was, quite rightly, over the moon. When we got home I roughed Wazzy off and turned him away for a few months' rest. He was only six and had had a fabulous season with me.

Sue had serious thoughts on selling Tootsie and sent her to Peter Mellor to sell. I don't know why she did this as we were selling horses from home ourselves really well. She went to him and came back after a few weeks, then went back again to and fro. I was very frustrated at this as it was costing us money in livery which we did not have and could have saved by marketing and selling her ourselves.

She eventually did sell, which left Sue with just Sophie, who was not really an event horse at the level we were competing. We looked at a few horses locally but nothing floated our boats. A trip to the Welton Stud was a real eye opener as we went around fields full of beautiful horses. There was nothing though that we really fancied, or that we could afford.

Fran Southgate lives in Thornton Bradford and her daughter Louise show jumped and ran a riding school in Wilsden. She called me and told me about a horse she had to sell which was Clydesdale cross thoroughbred. I went up to see her but really for a cup of tea and a chat. I did not really like the sound of this horse. After a cup or two of tea and few jammy dodgers we went out to the yard.

I looked over the stable door and saw what I thought was a common looking, big horse with big feet. I turned my nose up at him quickly and I think Fran was a bit put out but did not say anything. When I got home Sue asked me about him and I said he was common and not up to much. When she got it out of me that I had not even seen him out of the box, she called Fran and arranged to go back.

We went back that evening. Fran was laughing at me and told Sue I was nuts as the horse was really up our street. We had a few more jammy dodgers and went to see him. He looked fabulous out of the box and we could tell that he moved really well. He had a fabulous big free, languid walk and even though he had a slight dish, his trot was very elevated for a big horse. He was at least 16.3hh and still only five with growth in him. He did though, have big feet, so I was right about that at least. £2800 later and we had him home.

He was very ungainly at first and we decided to take our time with him. His stable name was Mac and he settled in really well. He was a very big horse though and we argued about who should have him. Such were the arguments, I booked him into a viewing evening to sell him at Wood Nook Arenas in Huddersfield.

Oliver Townend and his dad Alan were there and tried him for ages. They jumped him over some serious fences but we could not agree a price. On reflection, I am glad we did not sell him and I gave in to Sue for her to have a go on him.

Chapter Twenty Three

At the Imber Court Metropolitan Police horse show which was in Esher, we stabled the horses at Epsom Racecourse. We also stayed in the jockey rooms there. The RAF and Army Military Police competed too. The girls from this lot were so much fun. They would just walk into the shower block and get showered rather than wait for all the men to finish. They were always on the piss and enjoyed the social side of the scene to the full.

We had a rule that whoever got to the stables at the shows first had to set up the barbeque. On this weekend it was North Yorkshire who got there first. We sorted the stables and all the gear out. We had to put bedding down for all six horses and get their gear in place.

This took ages and it was six o clock by the time we had finished. We ate at the barbeque and started drinking. By eight thirty we were on our way. Someone came up with the idea of having a horse race. This developed into having a full race along the Derby Course on the racecourse. In drink, and being stupid, we got the horses out and went out onto the main racecourse. There was about sixteen of us.

We set off galloping on the course, left handed. We rounded Tattenham Corner and went on to the end of the course. Some were left way behind as they were big heavy horses. The rest of us finished and we trotted back to the stables. Good fun was had by all.

The next day we were getting horses loaded up and all our gear. An entourage of men and women came. The clerk of the course, head grounds man and senior Police Officers. We were all called together and given a massive telling off. The ground was ruined. The Derby course was ruined. We were to get out of the stables that day and never come back. Holy bloody hell was on.

By the end of the day it was sorted though. We all had to write a letter of apology to the racecourse. But I have ridden along the Derby course on a horse at full gallop!

Chapter Twenty Four

A lady called Sue Berry came to us on livery. She bought a lovely chestnut mare from Roger Kay and she loved her. Quite a character Sue, we are still friends. She is a lady with a tremendously good heart and a soft nature. Her husband at that time, John, was a horrible little man. He was making his money from the internet and had a firm in London. They were wealthy and John went to tremendous lengths to let us know this. They did become friends and were very prominent in our lives for some time, until John left Sue to remain in London more.

We were at a mutual friend's house, at a dinner party, and were having a lovely evening when John just laid on the carpet and went to sleep, snoring loudly. At his house one evening he brought out a very small bag of cannabis and began to roll a joint. He was making much of this but I was laughing my head off as there was not enough 'weed' to make one decent spliff let alone the three he did roll. It must have been a placebo thing because he and his mate were making out they were high after smoking them.

On another occasion, we were amongst a group at a Mexican restaurant and he became so obnoxious, talking over everyone about philosophy and quoting sayings no one understood or wanted to. Sue actually stood up against him and insisted they leave. I had all on to keep my mouth shut with this idiot but kept my peace as the 'two Sues' as they became known, were good friends.

Sue wanted to buy Mac and then sponsor my Sue to ride him. We eventually agreed this and sold him for £5000 and he became known as 'Online Experience'. His first outing was at Ivesley in the Pre-Novice and he did really well with double clear. They came 6th first time out. He continued to improve really quickly and took everything in his stride, although we were very conscious that he was a big horse and as he grew and matured we could not rush him and take him out of his comfort zone.

The new season had come around really quickly and Wazzy was back in work feeling great. I had in mind to take him to Blair Castle in Scotland for his first 2*. I was very excited about the coming year. I did not intend to team chase him but couldn't resist and took him for a jolly at Grafton in North Yorkshire.

The first run of the season was a little later than normal, in April at Witton Castle. We were double clear but the dressage was harshly marked as I thought he gave a good test. I have always held the belief that when you come out thinking 'Wow, that was a good one', the test is marked badly and does not reflect the feeling you had. When you come out thinking it was a dog of a test the marks always surprise. On this occasion I felt he was soft round and very calm and obedient. Hey ho, we did not get placed.

The next run was at Lincoln on the showground. It was always so bloody cold there, it is very open and flat and the wind, when blowing, goes through you like nothing else. We had another very good run though, not placed again but delighted with the speed, boldness and the feeling that we were a real partnership.

Two days later and he was hopping lame in his off fore. Peter Schofield came and had a look and he had to go for x rays up the road at their fabulous facility. It was discovered that he had a very large haematoma in his foot. This had also separated into several small ones. The cause was definitely a collision of some sort but I could not think of or remember him hitting anything on the cross country.

Four weeks box rest with shoes off and bute (a horse aspirin), then further x rays would tell me if my season was over before it started. I was gutted. Especially when I could not pinpoint the cause. He took to the box rest okay but once a week he was walked out around the yard in hand but was always hopping on that foot. Four weeks later and no improvement. Peter delivered the devastating news that it was going to be months before he would recover. We discussed a section operation, whereby they would take off the front of his hoof to release the damage, and that would need eighteen months minimum to recover.

His management was good in the box and I decided to go with plan A and rest him. I could not believe what had happened. One minute all was well and I was going to a 2* which meant top hat and tails. Then onwards hopefully. The next, everything is gone and blown up in the air, that's horses.

I don't know what we did especially but Sue and I had dozens and dozens of horses through our hands over the years with very little need for a vet to attend. We had a livery horse, Zico, who when we introduced sugar beet into feeds at winter time, would get colic frequently and so we stopped feeding him this. We did though have several middle of the night paraffin sessions with the vets tubing him before we realised it was in fact sugar beet he could not cope with.

Wazzy had had a problem as a youngster when he had been kicked on his hock and we had a couple of horses with locking patella's, but general day to day lameness or long term injuries, we seemed to avoid. We had a no radio blasting on the yard policy and a quiet stress free regime. Horses were always turned out daily, to be horses.

The biggest thing we did when training, which I believe helped, was going back a step. We had a knack of recognising when a horse was stressing over what we were asking it to do and we were always quick and happy to take the horse back a step, or even a few steps, if needed.

We had a great regime with thoroughbreds and many successes. In those days there was no racehorse re-training competitions or really any recognition for re-training these horses from the track and training yards. If there had been, I believe very firmly we would have had tremendous success in this field.

So four months to six months off the road, I had no chance for the season, it was over before we started. The best thing was of course that he would recover and it was not career threatening.

Mac was doing well for Sue and Darrel was still on course for a 2*. We had a couple of dealing horses in and I concentrated on them until we sold them. I saw an advert for a very nice sounding horse in the Yorkshire Post. I went to Easingwold to look at him. Paul Langrick had him, he was rising four, 16.3 hh and bright bay with four matching stockings. He was very unusual looking and very striking. He was not broken and I saw him on the lunge, by god he moved. I bought him off the lunge. Timmy was his name and he came home the next day.

Timmy did not have a recorded breeding which was a shame. He was very headstrong and if he thought he could not do something he panicked and went vertical. I mean proper vertical. I long reined him for ages and just rode him gently in the arena to let him chill and get used to basic work. We had his back, teeth and saddle checked and all was okay.

Hacking he never put a foot wrong and was very good. In the arena though he would just go up. On one of the long rein sessions in the arena he went up and came over on his side. I quickly ran and sat on his head and threw sand in his nose and on his head. I let him up and hope that his experience would put him off going up again. Fail!

Ten minutes later he was up again. I began to have serious doubts about this young man. He was silly but bordering on dangerous. All young horses will have a 'thing' that they do when they are stressed. Wazzy dropped his shoulder jumping poles and dropped me off.

Mystique would bite in the stable. We had a few horses that just dug their heels in and refused to move forward. Gentle coaxing and letting them chill and forget it always worked, but with a rearing horse you were really stuck.

Over the next couple of months he settled down and began to accept working on the flat and some basic grid work. I took him to a few shows and he did okay. Dressage, I felt, was his forte though and I registered him with British Dressage. He began at Wikefield Farm, had a little strop in the warm up but he moved so well, it was a shame he was a dickhead. He quickly started getting placed though.

Jumping wise he would be happy up a grid and a small course but anything over a meter and he threw the towel in. Cross country he enjoyed it. We took him to UK Chasers and he was jumping so well I took him towards a corner but he left a leg behind, stopping us in full flight. Such was the force, I was thrown up his neck and I knocked my front two top teeth right back against my pallet. I reach under them with my tongue and forced them back into place and promptly fainted and fell off him.

I began to seriously dislike this horse but there was definitely something about him. Laura asked if she could ride him for a while and I let her. We took him to a one day event in Harrogate, against my better judgement. He reared up in the warm up and ran off, having deposited Laura on the ground. He ran through the plastic tape that separated the dressage warmup area from the arenas. He took the whole tape with him as he galloped off around the wagons. Chaos.

That was it for me, he had to go. I sold him quickly for what I gave for him to a show jumper. They knew everything about him as I had been totally honest. They had a bit of success with him but I lost track of where he was. He did turn up though, later in my life.

After months of rest and gentle walking Wazzy was now recovered and ready to start work. The season was two thirds through and I decided I would have a couple of runs just to finish the year off at Novice. He got fit again quite quickly and he was buzzing to be back in work. We went to Bold Heath and I cantered him around really, he was clear and sound, I was delighted.

Sue was taking Mac and another dealing horse to Osbaldeston for a run. The entries had closed and I rang Norman Barge who kindly put me in the Open Novice section. I went along for a final season run out although he felt so good and right I thought I would maybe finish at Bishop Burton with an Intermediate run to end with a bang.

September 5th 1999 was the day of the competition and it is indelibly imprinted on me for life. It was a lovely crisp autumnal morning. The dressage was good, very good we were in the lead. Show jumping he was a maniac taking strides out and pinging off the ground. We were still in the lead after the first two phases. I was very happy. My intention was to just canter round the cross country to come home clear and confident.

In the warm up a friend called Natasha a La Ghaily was there, she was lying second on her dressage score to me with six marks behind. She cheekily said 'Go fast cos I am gonna beat you' I thought 'No you're not lady, bugger it, I will go for it'.

I set off with the handbrake off to be honest. He was flying and you can tell when the horse under you is loving his job and he was. At the far end of the course and the turning point for coming back up the hill homewards is a coffin fence. Single upright rail in, down a steep slope to a ditch, up the far slope to a smaller, but still quite upright skinny rail out.

We went towards it, slower than a gallop and in the right place, right speed. Wazzy took off and as he did his back legs lost their grip on the ground and he slipped, lost his back leg momentum and we hit the rail at full speed. I was shot like a cannon ball over his head and landed on all fours at the bottom of the slope. I looked at my left arm and thought 'god, that hurts'. Then I realised he was coming over the rail on top of me. He hit me full force and I was crushed. He scrambled up and ran off. I couldn't breathe at all.

I turned over onto my back and thankfully went out. I awoke to find paramedics sorting me out, my left arm was bandaged and was a big rubbery swollen mess. I couldn't breathe though and had an oxygen mask on. I was put into the ambulance and blue lights on, horns blaring. I was taken to Royal Blackburn Hospital A & E. I was unconscious for most of the journey and cannot recall any of it. Even getting into the hospital is a blur.

When I did wake up I was on a gurney outside the operating theatre. A man in a white coat said 'Stephen, can you hear me?' I nodded he said 'Your left arm has suffered a great trauma and I will do what I can to save it' I replied 'If you take my arm off, you're a dead man walking'. The look on his face was quite shocking.

Chapter Twenty Five

I awoke mid- morning the next day with tubes everywhere, especially up my nose. My left arm was suspended in a Bradford sling and I could see the top of my fingers. A nurse came over and gave me some water. I was in a lot of pain from my chest and my arm.

A couple of hours later my bed was surrounded by doctors. The main doctor was the one who had spoken to me on the gurney. He asked me if I could move my fingers and I could so I wiggled them. There was a collective gasp and he turned to the group and said 'How good am I?'

He went on to explain to me that I had hit my left hand on the ground so hard that the whole wrist had come out of the joint and was swinging freely up by my elbow. He also said I had broken my sternum, five ribs and collapsed my right lung. I was lucky to be alive and needed aid to breathe until they could re-inflate my lung.

Two days later, when Sue came to visit, she was visibly shocked at the state of me lying in the bed. I was in hospital for two weeks and then went home. Wazzy was totally fine and healthy and none the worse for the experience. I was a very lucky boy by all accounts. Three quarters of a ton of horse landing on me from ten feet or so at speed was a serious crash. I was on all fours when he hit me and if I had been laid on the floor the consensus was that I would have been crushed to death.

I had a further three operations on my arm to repair the nerve damage. It is still wonky and I don't have full rotational use of the wrist, but I am okay. The only good thing to come out of this was that I went privately for physio as the NHS provision was useless. I had quite a few sessions with a totally gorgeous blonde Australian girl called Gill and although it really was agony to begin with, it was always a pleasure, especially when she was laying all across me to get me to move my arm.

Shortly after my release from hospital I went to Halifax hospital to see the specialist. The room was packed with people waiting to be seen. I eventually got in and he did not look at my arm he just wrote on a slip 'pot off and look'. I went into the potting room and the lady just cut off the bandage and plastic plate holding my arm together. I could see the wires holding my wrist in place. The pain was excruciating and I was howling, shaking and wet through with sweat. It took them ages to get me gas and air and I was in a right old mess.

I was a frequent visitor down at the yard and as I recovered I got involved in teaching the trainee grooms and generally helping around the yard. I had no inclination to ride though. It got to Christmas Day and I still had not got on. I was on the yard and Wazzy was brought out by Laura all tacked up. I asked her what she was doing and then Sue appeared with my jods and boots. I was bullied into getting changed and we both went for a pleasant hack. I was back at it.

The first jumping session I had was a disaster. I could not do it. My heart in jumping had gone, I could not get up any enthusiasm at all. I began, over the winter months, competing in dressage and was enjoying it a lot. We also discovered a new market for good moving, thoroughbred, dressage horses. I bought a couple and sold them well and easily. Sue had finished the previous season off with Mac at Novice level. He was going great for her and we had big plans for him.

In February I was fed up of pure dressage and needed to find out if my bottle had gone. I went for a lesson with Peter Mellor at Wood Nook Arenas. He closed the doors and we were alone indoors and I told him what had happened. He just laughed at me! But within a forty five minute session I was jumping a 110 cm course with the great Wazzy. I continued to jump him a lot at home and went hunting. We had a great day with the Rockwood and jumped an awful lot of walls.

I entered a One Day Event at Tom and Helen Bell's place in North Yorkshire. This was a joint event with Ian Brown who ran Northallerton Equestrian centre. The dressage and jumping was at the centre and then you boxed up and went a few miles down the road to the Bells', for the cross country. On the cross country course, towards the end, was a very narrow, very big brush fence which was a V shaped skinny. You got 20 penalties knocked off your score if you jumped it.

I aimed Wazzy straight at it knowing he would jump it. No one else jumped it all day and as we were clear we won the competition. I was elated, very excited and couldn't wait to get going again.

His first event that year was at Witton and he went clear in the Pre-Novice to give him a run with no pressure. He was great and we were a happy team again. At home though, he did not seem the same. This lovely horse was always looking around the yard, over the door. He was a real gawper and took everything in. He seemed down though, almost a bit depressed and was always at the back of his box.

We went to Ivesely for the Novice and he stopped at a really small, innocuous ditch with a rail behind it. I was really surprised as he had never ever stopped at anything cross country. At Houghall College in Durham, the next one, I had to hit him to get him over the third fence. By the seventh fence I retired and rode him back to the wagon. I was devastated. He just did not want to know. I persevered with him at home, we went to the beach, schooling for a laugh and had him checked out with the vet. At Skipton Horse trials we did get around the course and I enjoyed the day.

I gave him a break and went back to dressage only and he got Novice points straight away. I still had massive ambitions for a 2* and could not believe that all my investment, both financial and emotional was slipping away to nothing. I entered him at Allerton Park and the bloody wagon broke down and we never got there. I then took him to Aske Hall and we got to the sixth fence and he stopped. I could tell my lovely horse had jacked it. He did not want to do it anymore.

I thought about what to do with him. I agonised about what the future held. It was so disappointing to have come so far yet at the eleventh hour all my hopes were dashed. Could it be pain memory from the haematoma in his foot? Had he just simply got stale of the pressures of eventing or did he just need a smacked bottom?

The latter was never an option and he was sound and very healthy, he looked amazing. I thought a season's hunting would maybe freshen him up. John Gill is an amateur whip with the Bramham Moor and I knew him from when Mrs Verity had bought Bonnie from me and sent her to John to hunt. He and his wife Jane farm Ducks at Aberford near Leeds.

I contacted John and we agreed a loan period for one season for him and his son Chris to hunt. I delivered him in August, full of anxiety about whether or not this was the right thing to do. John was over the moon with him and he and Chris went on to fight over Wazzy each week. They had a system as to who should ride him based on who got to the stables outside their house first on a morning.

I got weekly updates at the beginning of the season on his hunting performances. They absolutely loved him and he was proving to be a superb hunting horse. He had hounds and the whip, was a great cross country horse and would happily leave the field on his own when called on. By Christmas I was thinking I wanted him back. I decided though, to leave him with John until the end of the season as other things had come about that had totally changed my life.

Chapter Twenty Six

I think it all started when I had to retire from the Police force, and then, due to the new tenure of post policy, where you could only be in a specialist post for nine years, which meant Sue had to leave the mounted branch and go back onto the beat and shifts including nights. Also my new training business which I ran from the yard was taking a massive amount of my time up. Our marriage was seriously in trouble. We had been, first and foremost, best friends and that I felt had been disappearing.

I had been going show jumping on my own and to dressage competitions on my own for some time. Sue, Laura and Sue Berry were going off on their own frequently to show jumping and event competitions. Mac was doing really well and Sophie, who we still had, was competing at dressage and lower level show jumping. I had bought Sophie from Danute, and although Sue rode her all the time, she was technically mine.

We had a weekend together in Bruges but it was horrible. We both agreed things were not good. Other private issues arose and it looked futile. Laura, our head girl of many years, was also very naughty. She played us off against each other several times which led to massive arguments. At one point I sacked Laura on the spot for lying to us both. She had been a loyal, very hard working, at times difficult but very good at her job, head girl for some years. She just got caught up in the fallout and, I am happy to say we remained friends.

Things came to a head when, one Monday morning, Sue called me in my office and told me that she and Sue Berry were going to Australia in two days on the Wednesday to watch the Olympic horse events. I was totally devastated. That was the end though.

Whilst she was away I sold Sophie and the one dealing horse we had in. That left Mac, which was not my horse, and me with no horses. I also moved into a cottage on my own. Everything we had built, the yard, our reputation, the livery business and more importantly our marriage, friendship and partnership had gone down the plughole.

The rest of that year was a horrible time. One by one the liveries left after I decided to close the livery side of things down. Sue removed Mac to a yard nearby and by the end of February the yard was a ghost town. What had been a vibrant lively 'dispensary of equitation' as I often called it was dead empty, very quiet, and soulless. I did agree with Sue to buy her out of the yard and land, which I was very pleased about.

I got Wazzy back the following spring and he looked great. I decided to event him at Novice level and maybe if things were going well I would do an Intermediate or two to finish the year off. Joanna Kay had a lovely big horse for sale. He was a pure dressage horse called Beau Fox. He was seven years old and 17.3hh. He was in Novice classes but was working Medium at home. I tried him three times and decided to buy him. I have always enjoyed dressage, the work involved and the training.

When I tried him at Joan's I had a couple of lessons with a lady called Steph Cooper and she was a real character. Really funny and very cheeky. We got on really well, even though she thought I was gay! When I took him home I carried on training with Joanna.

Because of the business I was now running I was working very long hours and was totally immersed in it. I did not get to many events that year and although we were going well with a few double clears, the big fun element had gone out of it. It had been a major day out with friends and liveries coming with us to support and help. It was a team effort, but going on your own somehow was just not the same.

The business was doing well and growing at an alarming rate and I gave a £500 training bursary to Oliver Townend as he was really doing well and it was obvious he was going to be a major force in eventing. This bursary became an annual thing and I also went onto sponsor the top three placed horse's grooms at the Bramham International 3 day event. I also was the sole sponsor for the 2* Belton horse trials and Sue Brown the owner was a lovely lady to work with.

I had a new girl, Nicola, working for me. She was bright and bubbly and ambitious which helped. I entered a three day unaffiliated event at Milton Keynes Eventing Centre. This was a full on three day with all phases. I had heard from lots of people how good this event was so when I got there I was back in the groove and in my element. The weekend was brilliant. Entertainment every night, great friendly team and a lovely venue. In the open section there were over seventy horses entered. I came second, won a silver salver, a sash for Wazzy, polo shirts, baseball caps, a fleece and money. Oh, and a brand new bridle. I was very pleased with him. It was a great feeling to be back on top again and especially at a properly run, full on, three day event.

Fox was going well at home and we gained quite a few points at Novice level very quickly. What I did not know was that the points we gained took us out of Novice. I carried on for quite a while at that level and thought I had qualified for the regional finals, held at Aike Grange Stud near Beverley. I was gutted to be told by the dressage office that the thirty three points I had gained did not count as he was out of that class. Blonde moment.

In the September I looked at Wazzy and did not know what to do with him. I did not want to hunt him full time, hunting was a necessary evil for me most of the time. I enjoyed it most of the time and really enjoyed the social side of the sport but it was never my first love. He loved it though, he had done quite a bit of dressage with me when I had taken Fox but he was capable of much more. I contacted John and he whooped when I suggested he take him again. I also sold him another hunter for a client.

Wazzy went to him at the beginning of autumn hunting. He was a very healthy happy horse when he went for his second season with the Gills. John contacted me after Christmas and asked if it was all right for Chris, his son, to team chase him a few times. I was happy with this and they were very successful.

Competing over that winter took a backseat and Nicola rode the horses more than I did. After Christmas though, in a freak bad storm, the main block of stables blew down on top of Fox and one other horse I had bought in to sell, a Warmblood from the Zangersheid Stud. All the horses are pre-fixed with Z to signify where they have come from. The fire brigade turned up and dug them out and luckily they were unharmed, if not a bit stressed.

I was stuck now because the whole building was condemned by a building inspector. I had to move the horses up to a yard a mile up the road. The rebuild took three months but it was a state of the art building with new, beautiful, internal wooden boxes. I also had installed a four horse covered walker and had the back of the yard landscaped so it looked really smart.

The horses came back and a new girl came to work for me. She lived a long way away but was a very good jockey and came very highly recommended. She did not last two minutes though as her first Sunday when she should have been working on her own, she simply did not turn up. I just happened to call at the yard at eleven o clock to find them with no feed or haylage. I was bloody furious. I couldn't get her on the phone and called and called throughout the day.

The next day she turned up as normal. I had it out with her and she couldn't defend herself, she simply had not turned up. I told her to leave. I was amazed to find that she was very surprised to be sacked when she had just not turned up and not told me she was not coming in. If I had not gone to the yard that day those horses would have been left for over twenty four hours without feed or haylage and without being mucked out.

The dealer horse was sold to a show jumper from Hull and so I only had Fox in. I was competing him and we were making great progress. Changes were established and half pass at trot and canter. He was also getting a small amount of passage in his trot work and I was excited about him.

I got Wazzy again in the spring and he was fine. His first event though, was a disaster. He stopped at the third fence x country and refused to jump anything else. I was at a total loss about this. He was fresh from his hunting where he had jumped everything asked of him. Was it me? I dropped him down a class to Pre-Novice and we got around at Ivesley.

I had also, during this time, been back to Les Moorhouse and bought a nice big five year old called Claude. I called him Claude after Claude Greengrass from the Heartbeat TV programme. He was as green as grass when I got him and sadly he did not improve. He had no get up and go that horse, if he had had any, it had certainly got up and gone. All the preparation had gone really well although he had stopped at a pile of railway sleepers at Beckwithshaw near Harrogate, which was the unaffiliated season warm up.

I very quickly got fed up of this horse, he was very inconsistent and he was just one of those horses with a piggy attitude to everything. Even in the stable you had to push him around or else he would stand all over you and knock you about. I sold him into hunting.

Two other things happened that year. I sold Fox for an awful lot of money to a lovely lady who wanted him for a rider she was supporting. I also decided to sell the stable yard. A wheeler dealer from Halifax, called John, had been badgering me to sell up, and as an incentive he was offering way over the market value. I decided to go to North Yorkshire which is a place I had always wanted to move to. Around Thirsk and Northallerton it is wall to wall horses, good hunts and two equestrian centres which are easily reached.

It was ironic really, to think I had just got the yard rebuilt with state of the art stables and horse walker, the business was doing well so I did not need to have the yard full of liveries. It was also a place with great memories but the ghosts of bad ones too, especially relating to Sue, so it was time to move on.

Rachael Foster, who worked for me in the training company I was running, told me of a farm for lease on the Ribston Estate just outside Wetherby. Old Forrest Farm was a Georgian farm house and ancillary buildings. It came with a lovely big garden and also five acres of land. The other big selling point was that the Ribston Estate, which was over 2000 acres, had a cross country schooling course which came with it. I could ride anywhere at any time and school too.

Quite a few negotiations took place but eventually I got the lease. It was a big place and the fold yard took four lovely indoor stables and I also had a large tack room, feed room and three other stables if needed. The absence of an arena was a problem but not major. The land was clay and so it would be very wet in winter but dry and useable for schooling in the summer.

I moved up there with Wazzy in the August. I had not competed him much at all due to the business and the move. I sent him in September, back to John Gill to hunt after I had had a couple of mornings' cubbing. The new place had given me a fresh perspective and I was looking forward to the coming season.

On one of my very rare days off I went to Doncaster Bloodstock Sales. I saw a big yak of a four year old, dark bay, almost black and 17.1 hh. I bought him for £800 guineas and he was not broken. Ivor came into my life and was a breath of fresh air. He took to being broken in wonderfully, he was very laid back and easy to deal with. He moved really well and was a lovely person.

I also took a client to visit a dealer called Judy Thurloe. Judy has been selling horses for years from her yard in Coxwold in North Yorkshire. It's a beautiful yard and she has had some nice horses through her hands over the years, some not so nice too.

A few years earlier I had gone with Darrel to try a very nice 4 year old grey gelding. He was exceptional looking and moved very well As Darrel was riding him in the big back field she used to show horse, Judy and I were chatting when we heard a scream. This horse had come down on top of Darrel. It was just laid on the floor on top of him.

I ran over and the horse got up but my mate was stunned, his left leg was sore and he was not in the best of shape. We got out of there quickly. Badly bruised and more than a bit annoyed, I had not actually been back since then.

The lady I had gone with was someone I knew from Halifax and she asked me to go with her. The horse she tried, a 16.1 hh Irish bred mare was not suitable. It was a very common looking horse and a bit poor, which is why my friend was trying her as she was a cheapie. There was though, a stunning liver chestnut gelding called Cody. He was 5 years old and 16.1 hh. . He had a new English passport but was Irish bred. I really liked him and after trying him for a good hour I bought him.

Due to a business meeting the next day I could not go pick him up for two days. When I went back there was a new big black gelding in called Barry! Barry was 17.2 hh and six years old. He was very nervous of me and as Judy explained he was difficult to bridle up. He had three teeth missing from the right hand side of his mouth, all lower molars. He had obviously had a bad time of it but in his favour he was a stunner. He was dirt cheap because of his problems and he was also Polish bred. I just couldn't leave him there, and he came home with me too.

Chapter Twenty Seven

Cody was a lovely horse but he had that thing about him whereby you knew at any time he could explode. He did once have a proper hissy fit and a bronco around the field. I cubbed him out with the York and Ainsty North hunt and he was brilliant. I sold him one day in the field and he went on to hunt for years, proving to be very bold and mannerly.

I now had Barry and Ivan at home and that winter hunted them both for a few days each. The dressage was coming on very well. Barry was a pain as I had to drop the bit off the bridle and slip it into his mouth and carefully put it on over his head. There was no way at all I could put on the bridle the normal, conventional way and he also had to travel everywhere in his bridle as you had no chance of getting it on in the wagon. He was a lovely person though and easy to do.

I had to have his back done. Tim Jarman came out and sorted him in no time. Tim is a back specialist and I am very sceptical about these 'specialists'. Tim though was very honest, knew his stuff and visibly, in front of you, had results. Over the years I have seen quite a few young people who have been to college and qualified but when you see them in action, they just do not fill you with confidence about what they are doing.

Years later, when I had been to Ireland with Tom and Helen Bell, we brought fourteen horses back and Tim came to check them all. He watched them all trotting up and examined them but only treated and charged for three. Not many would do that, there is always something wrong or something that needs treating so they get their money, but not Tim. A consummate professional and nice lad to boot, it is no wonder that you can never get him to treat your horses, he is booked up months ahead.

I did not want to run three horses for the coming season and decided to leave Wazzy with John Gill. He had had a great season with him and his son Chris who had whipped in on the odd day with him. I agreed that Chris could event him lightly within the bounds of Pony Club that season and so he would, at the most only, do four small no pressure events.

I was happy with this because he was obviously unhappy with the stresses of eventing at the higher level and with two babies to bring out the logistics did not add up. I would have had to go on different days to the competitions, one day with the two young ones and the second with Wazzy, which on my own, would have been a nightmare.

I went to the York machinery sales and bought myself a small bright orange tractor that had come from a golf course. I also bought chain harrows and a pasture topper. I loved the spring evenings in the paddocks, harrowing or topping. It was really quiet and a lovely way to chill out and escape the crap of the world. It was at this time that the training company I owned and ran was at its height of activity. We had now 56 staff and five offices all over the country, distance management was a constant problem. We had 600 plus trainees in training and it was proving to be so very stressful. I was delivering on contract with the government, Modern Apprenticeships in horse care, veterinary nursing and animal care.

I would be attending meetings throughout the day, going home to ride and then be emailing and writing reports well into the night. Don't get me wrong I loved it in the main, but stress is not for me. I strive under pressure but stress is a totally different animal. It was very full on all the time.

One incident was where Manchester Learning Skills Council owed us £80,000. It was an enormous sum and try as we might they would not pay it. This is a Government quango and my sister, who was my Managing Director, had tried everything to get them to pay. I went to the office in Brighouse and picked her up, we then drove to Manchester and sat in the reception area until the Finance Director came to see us. I went mad at him about not even being offered a coffee and the poor way they had treated us, one of their main contractors. It took a loss of temper and some serious words, but we got paid there and then. A nonsense really, but typical of the day to day issues to be dealt with.

We were working now with over two hundred equestrian establishments all over the country. Sixty veterinary practices, over ninety grooming parlours, kennels and three zoos.

Sadly, over the next three years, the Government cut the funding for apprenticeships by 38% in the first wave and a further 12% in the second. They demanded though, of course, the same level of delivery within the parameters of an overall 50% cut in funding.

Chapter Twenty Eight

I started having training sessions with Ian Brown from Northallerton Equestrian Centre. He ran the centre with his wife Vicki and had a full time lady helping them, Janet Bentley. Ian had competed eventing at the same time as me and I vaguely remembered him on the circuit. Ian has a certain way of coaching, he keeps it simple and uncomplicated. What he says is measured and usually correct and he has that way of instilling confidence in you without gushing and going over the top. We got on great and I enjoyed his sessions. We are still good friends years later.

The centre was owned by a man called John Walker, he is ex-army and bought the place as an investment, knowing absolutely nothing about horses or the equestrian world or business, which I always thought was strange. Previously the centre had been run on his behalf by Robert Blane, whom I had previously met at Beverley Racecourse when on a Pony Club camp with the Rockwood. I had two trainee girls in the place when he ran it, but they never got tuition and support and I had to pull them out.

It was only forty minutes up to the centre and so I started competing there and at Richmond Equestrian Centre too, which was a further twenty minutes away. During a competition Ian told me that John was looking to sell the centre.

I hatched a plan and after a great deal of thinking and discussions with Ian and Vicki, I met with John and agreed to buy it from him. The solicitors began to sort out the legalities and three weeks later a further meeting was called by John. Now when I shake hands with someone on a deal, that is it, it's a deal.

John wanted to re-hash everything and lease me the indoor arena and toilets and let Ian have the outdoor arena and the stables. I was stunned. Firstly that he had gone back on his word, but secondly and as I pointed out to him, it would never work. I would have a jumping competition in the indoor and Ian could be having a dressage competition in the outdoor, where was everyone going to warm up? Who would have control of the café and toilets, how would the parking work for the wagons? It was a total bloody nonsense and he had no answers at all. I went onto learn that he was a bit of an idiot. So my venture into equestrian centre ownership faulted at the first fence but it had planted the seed of an idea.

I continued training and took Barry, who was going well, to the Milton Keynes Unaffiliated three day in the spring. Ivor was too young and inexperienced to go. The weekend went fabulously well, Barry took to it like a duck to water. He still had problems being bridled but he loved the attention. It had taken me some time to gain his trust but still, if you went near his right ear, he freaked. He could be clipped though and was happy to let me as near as possible to the ear as long as I did not touch it. He was a stunning horse, all over black and had a small star. He was a really friendly horse and enjoyed working.

He was lying seventh after the dressage. The roads and tracks were a doddle because it was like being at home on the estate. The gallop around the steeplechase was worrying because the ground was very hard. I took it steadier than normal and we only had a very few time penalties. Most competitors did the same and so it did not cost us a great deal. The ten minute halt box went without any problems, after the second road and tracks. On the cross country he flew around, and although it was very hot and he was very sweaty after finishing, he was in great form the next morning at the second trot up. Just before the show jumping on the Sunday, he was in third place. A clear round got us up to second, same as Wazzy a year earlier and still as many prizes. I was over the moon.

Ivesley was his first Pre-Novice and my days, it was hot. Due to the amount of entries we had to go up on the Friday to do dressage and it was a boiling hot day. I was naked in the back of the wagon prior to getting him ready, it was so hot. He did okay but I knew he would have done better if it had been cooler. The next day we went back in cooler weather and he had one down in the show jumping which I was very disappointed about. The cross country went well with a slight hesitation at the water, which we were let off for. He finished twelfth, which for his first time out, I was satisfied with.

It was obvious that he had more in him, but I doubted very much that given his start in life, and the way he moved, which was to slightly crab to the right, that he would go higher than Novice. Ivor though at home was jumping really well and moved well enough to do pure dressage. The next event was at Richmond Equestrian Centre. Barry was seventeenth but gave me a lovely ride. Ivor came out for his first event and finished second with a great dressage, clear show jumping and just a few time penalties on the cross country, mainly because of the stupid big leap he made off the bank at the top of the hill in the second field.

For coming second I won a Toggi jacket, two bags of feed and my diesel money home which was a refreshing surprise for Pre-Novice classes where you only normally got prizes in kind. I also had a very interesting chat with Judith, the owner of the centre, who had stopped me to ask what had gone wrong with the sale of Northallerton.

She and her husband Paul had bought the centre a year earlier and this was their first affiliated one day event. They had been struggling to run the place and were thinking of leasing it out to a company or an individual. Gosh, if I had known then what I know now I would have walked away very quickly. More of that later.

The next event for the boys was at Withcote in Leicestershire. I went there not knowing what to expect. Barry did well for him and was not placed but he tried his little heart out. I could not fault him really, he always gave his best within himself. Ivor was fifth and again I was over the moon. I did have a major concern though as at the far end of the course you jumped a wall into a field of recently harvested sprouts and all the large stalks were still there. Barry had some cuts on his legs and one or two other horses suffered the same fate. I spoke to the TA and steward but to be truthful, they were not interested. At Houghall College in Durham both boys went really well, Barry got himself a ninth rosette and Ivor was second again! Having looked at the Novice course I wished I had taken him in that class, I think he would have done very well.

Back at home Ivor was jumping really well around 1.05 m courses and I was very pleased with him. We went up to Richmond to compete in BSJA and dressage and he was placed a few times. Barry was doing well for himself too and in the British Novice he got the required clear rounds to qualify him for the next rounds.

I went to the Doncaster Sales and bought a lovely six year old bay gelding that had only raced three times. He was as cheap as chips and a lovely horse. Within weeks I had sold him to a surgeon form York who had recently learned to ride.

The vetting though did not go well to begin with. The vet, Nigel from Ledston Hall Equine Centre came. He walked into the stable and off the cuff, his opening remarks to me were 'Is that him?' Yes this is him' I said. 'Right, I don't think I will be passing him today.' I took off the headcollar and began to walk out of the stable. 'What are you doing?' said the vet 'I am going in for a cup of tea and some toast mate, I haven't got time to piss about vetting a horse you have already made your mind up about.' 'Ah, yes, sorry about that'. We had a brief discussion, carried on, and he passed.

I had another run in with a vet shortly after, over another horse I had sold for a lot of money. He was an Irish horse, four years old 16.1 hh and very well bred on the Clover Field lines. He was s stunning horse and I had him sent over from Ireland to sell on. I only had him a month and he was snapped up. The vet called Richard, from Knaresborough, was a nice lad but he was right up himself. He had a captive audience so went on and on.

Out on the fields we had a large strip of fallow around a big field of crop. Galloping this for interval training, it took a full three minutes to get round. Part of the five stage vetting involves stressing the horse. I galloped round this field and back to where he and the buyers were standing. He waved me round again, so I did. As I approached them the second time he waved me on again. I stopped and said to him 'No chance mate that would be nine minutes galloping. He is not going to Badminton and he is only four years old.' The buyers nodded in agreement. He was not happy but listened to his heart and wind. After a suitable break for the horse to recover I went two more times around on the other rein and the vet was happy.

Back out eventing, and a visit to Buckminster in Leicestershire for them both saw another good day for Ivor, who I then decided to upgrade to Novice. Barry was okay but he was becoming an also-ran in the dressage which always left him too much to make up on the other two elements.

Ivor had his first Novice run at Hexam in the north east. Hexham was a lovely event, run then by Trish Bracegirdle. It was set on farmland in the middle of nowhere. The parking for the wagons was always on a steep slope which did not help and the entrance way was always very tight. Other than that the course was flowing, challenging and beautifully prepared. At the far end of the course was big bank with a drop off to a skinny fence which was upright and always caused problems. He was double clear with time penalties and not placed, however I was more than pleased with his first run. I had dropped Barry off to give him a rest, I was undecided about him and there was no point in keeping him running. He was happy at home, healthy and settled.

Ivor then had a run at Aske Hall in North Yorkshire. We had a major fuck up here on the cross country. There was a large oak tree in the middle of the course around this tree was a shooting butt type jump with a one stride to a corner out into the main field again.

We were off and running really well across the top of the course when, as we were coming down hill to this tree, Ivor had taken hold a bit and was very much on the bit. We took off at the butt fence in, but got it wrong, far too close and he landed on his knees in the middle of the fences. I could see the corner fence coming at my head at speed when, from nowhere, he picked up and from a standing jump with me clinging on his back, he leapt out over the corner fence and just carried on. I was astounded but he had picked up from being on the floor and jumped the corner fence through the flags and clear.

His final event that year was at Bishop Burton. I was tempted to take him Intermediate but I just thought it was not worth the risk at the end of the season and nothing was to be gained, so I went Novice. It was absolutely freezing on the day, a really cold October day and not pleasant. The college use their students to run the event, they always have, and usually very successfully. I was warming up for the dressage and could not find the steward for my section. I was warming up for quite a while and had gone past my time.

Sat around a fallen tree were loads of young students. Amongst these was a girl wearing a bib with my section number on it. They were all messing about laughing and acting silly with the lads. I went over and asked her what was happening. She said she had been calling me and I had missed my slot. I argued that I had not seen her and had asked the chief steward a few time where she was. Other competitors from my section were also looking for her and were angry. It was freezing cold I was left with a wait now of over an hour until the next slot.

I lost my temper with this young girl because she was out of line. I withdrew there and then. Bad end to a good season really, but there you go.

I decided to sell Barry into hunting providing I got the right home. Richard Nellis, who hunted with the Cleveland Hunt bought him and he had several great seasons on him.

Chapter Twenty Nine

During the autumn, as a result of a further conversation with Judith, I entered into protracted negotiations to take over Richmond Equestrian Centre.

I felt that the training business was going well and was self- sufficient. I had become marginalised from the day to day running, such was the strength of my team. I was merely attending monthly management meetings and acting as a liaison between us and the Government. The finance was a worry though as they were actively cutting the amount of companies they were contracting with, together with a serious cut to funding streams. I was told though, that as a national provider, we were very safe.

Paul was difficult to deal with. He had an air of arrogance about him and everything was through email. I prefer a face to face relationship as things can be moved on much more quickly and you get a much better sense of who you are dealing with. I did have a meeting with him in his kitchen one evening, from which I should have learned more than I did.

I was sat in the kitchen and he came in. He had been hunting and was still dressed in riding gear. We exchanged hellos and he then spent a long time, a very long time ignoring me whilst he read his post. I was sat there like a plonker and the atmosphere was terrible. It was like waiting for the headmaster to talk to me. I just got up and walked out. He followed me and we had heated words about it.

I eventually got to the point of signing a ten year lease on Richmond and had control of the largest stable yard, the arenas, an office and three flats. I was to begin the lease on January 1st. What I did not know was, that in the background, they had been in trouble and were struggling to make the place attractive and busy. They had a party the weekend I signed the lease.

The first major issue was the diary of events put forward to me, they lied. I had been told the diary was for events that coming year arranged, agreed and firmly in place. No, the diary was a wish list for events they were wanting to run but the majority of them were certainly not finalised. I had an awful lot of work to do to fill that diary up.

The second issue was a lady called Sue who I took on to help me run the place day to day. Sue had three children who all had learning difficulties. They all helped out and were often brilliant for picking up poles, stewarding and helping out in general. The problem was that they had so many ponies on livery, they were struggling to keep them. I had an agreement with a local feed supplier and as I was spending a lot of money with them. I got a discount. Sue made full use of this discount as she worked for me and this led to problems financially between us.

The third issue was the Tuesday evening unaffiliated jumping. It was run by a girl called Donna Mews. The entries were woeful and it was a free for all, ridiculous, event. One man, who rode in jeans and a great big green moleskin jacket and no riding hat, took over the show each week and rode around the arena on a variety of horses which were generally in a very poor condition. I put a stop to it as soon as I could, without falling out with Donna.

I advertised it a lot and made it a league where people attending earned points towards an end of season big prize. I also insisted that people were dressed correctly to compete at a show. It was slow at first but did become a great success, very popular and well attended.

I moved the horses up there as it was easier, day to day, to work them, and the facilities were second to none. I also eventually moved up there. Initially into one of the flats and then into a house nearby. I introduced many innovative competitions and events to the centre. The general atmosphere and footfall of competitors and visitors rose exponentially. I was, in the first eight to ten months, very happy.

The first horse trials that I organised there for BE went well apart from one incident. We had blocked up the water fence which eventually drained it. The Technical Delegate, Janet Plant came on the Thursday prior to the event starting the next day, to inspect. Bill Watt was the course designer and builder and superb at his job, very professional and easy to deal with. He made the trials a seriously good product with his dressing of the course and the new fences I eventually introduced there.

When Janet, Bill and I got to the water fence she started 'Oh great, no water in the water jump.' I stated to explain but she talked over me. 'Come on then, back to the office, we need to call all the competitors and tell them that we are cancelling.' I was dumfounded at this outburst and walked off. She shouted after me 'Where are you going?' I said 'Back to the office, you take A to M and I will take N to Z to call everyone'. She looked at me incredulously. I then went on to explain that I had ten tons of stone on standby and asked her to examine the base of the water jump to see if she was happy. If she was I would unbung it and it would be full in a couple of hours.

She was very embarrassed at this and said it was fine. I unblocked it and the water flowed. We always got on after that On the Friday evening after the first day, we were having dinner in the café and she asked to meet the rest of my committee who had organised the event. When I explained that Sue and I had organised everything from toilet rolls to rosettes she was truly stumped and surprised. The final report we got from the steward was very good, and bearing in mind, it was my first event that I had organised, I was over the moon. It was only later that I found out that all had not been well.

Judith had been speaking to sponsors and actively discouraging them from repeat sponsorship. I also found out that Sue and her had checked thoroughly everyone's passports and that some competitors had been disqualified for minor infractions. The Steward was constantly being asked to go to the Secretaries' tent to answer queries, he got really pissed off with this and on agreement with me, on the second day we undertook to check thoroughly, one in ten passports, which is the norm. The girls were not happy about this but I put my foot down and insisted. On the last day Judith had words with the Steward too about how 'bad it had been', thankfully he did not agree.

I just could not understand this behaviour. I could not work out why they would have this attitude, surely the idea behind leasing me the centre was to drive it forward without the pressure of running it day to day, so why discourage and not encourage? It was, sadly to get worse.

During the event I met a woman who was fence judging for us. I was very attracted to this lady, she looked like Goldie Hawn, and was very enigmatic. She was a friend of Judith's and, I found out later, was called Pam. She came back on the Monday, as hundreds of others did too, to school around the cross country courses. I went to take her money for the schooling round and she refused to pay, stating she was a friend of Judith's. I was not happy but let it go. I asked Judith about her and was told firmly that I had no chance, she was out of my league and to forget it. Charming!

I had not competed Ivor as, being the organiser, it was very much frowned upon and that is understandable. What did become clear was the amount of work and attention to detail needed to run a BE One Day Event over a weekend. It should be mandatory that all members give up a day to assist and realise just what is involved. It would also help for them to understand the actual costs involved. I had previously helped out at the Bretton trials as the Health & Safety officer but that was nothing compared to organising.

I took him a couple of weeks later to a new event in the Lake District called Cumwhinton. It was a beautiful event and the fences were very well built and presented. I got some great ideas from there for future fences. In the water jump was a half- submerged wooden crocodile. The horses, of course, did not know it was wooden. We jumped in over a dinosaur egg and when Ivor saw the crocodile he performed airs above the ground by jumping so big out of the water, I did well to stay on.

Double clear and time faults let me think he was ready for Intermediate. Aske Hall was the chosen event. We had a disaster in the show jumping with, I think, five down. Gutted, I went cross country for the education. Good lad, he flew it. Back to the drawing board with some sessions with Ian Brown, who was very honest and told me straight he was not athletic enough to cope with the show jumping phase. Gutted, but realistic, I took him back to Novice level. Due to commitments at Richmond we only had one more run that year. We ended the season at Bishop Burton, not placed in the top ten, but we finished strong and I was fairly happy.

Back at the centre, and not long after the one day event I had the Festival of Dressage to organise and run. I was delighted to have been awarded this event, but my days, I was like a lamb to the slaughter with organising it.

We basically ran Preliminary tests right through to PSG (Prix St Georges) and PSG freestyle to music. Over three hundred tests with mounted prize giving's over two days. It was so intense I could not sleep. On the first day my team of voluntary scorers were swamped. I had an ambition that by the time competitors had got back to their wagons and sorted their horses out, got changed and come up to the café, their score would be on the board. We quickly fell behind to about 50 minutes, and then over an hour.

I was panicking. The café was swamped too and I was constantly going to Tesco's for food, especially chips. We totally fucked up with the Preliminary Restricted section. The girl awarded first prize was in fact second by 0.3%. I spoke to her and there was no way, no chance whatsoever that she would give up her sash and first place rosette. The girl placed second who was actually first was great, she understood and was amenable to my profound apologies. She was though, incredulous that the other girl would not give up her sash and rosette. I made sure she got a duplicate through two weeks later. I still cannot get my head around the girl who kept the first place sash and rosette. It was just false, she never won it.

I heard, from the café, a very loud female voice shouting the odds about me and the scores. I went down from the office to find a large, very scruffy lady with the hugest boobs I have ever seen shouting about how badly run the event was and that the scores were all wrong. I invited her into the office for a chat to sort it out but she was having none of it. She had an audience and was going to have her moment. I established she had no connection to any competitor or horse competing there and was actually from the yard that had previously held the festival. She was therefore, just making big mischief. I invited her on the strongest terms to leave, which she did.

The second day was much better and all was well. The feedback was good and the scores were up within twenty minutes of the completion of a test. The only blot was Paul Hodgson who turned up and was complaining all day that the tables and chairs around the arenas were not in the right place. He was a right pain in the arse making the smallest thing seem like a major catastrophe.

Dressage judges are also a law unto themselves. They can be right divas. Most of them are okay but the odd one leaves a great deal to the imagination. One lady would not start judging until she had had a very large piece of cake and a latte. Another, if we asked her to judge on a Saturday before 10.00 am, gave me a runners list and her money and I had to go to the bookies to put on her bets for her for the racing. Payment was made in cash and I also always offered them a bottle of red or white wine as a sweetener. They all, nearly always, took both. One doyen of the dressage world, was just impossible to work with. She was rude and condescending to everyone and everything. Nothing was good enough for her and I quickly dropped her off our preferred list.

On one occasion we put on judges' training. This is where the normal competition takes place and alongside the judge's car are sat other judges in training, on seats. The appointed judge was provided with coffee and food as she required. There were fifteen judges on this occasion and they all expected teas and coffee and food. They were not happy when I refused. Very few of the judges brought a writer along and so I used my Livery customers who got free entries in lieu. Some of the lady judges were just horrible to them and it was very difficult at times to keep the peace.

Chapter Thirty

I was schooling in the indoor arena one afternoon when I saw this apparition appear at the side of the arena. She was tall with very long blonde hair and totally gorgeous. Marsha, was looking for livery for one horse and of course, I had a spare stable.

She moved in at the end of the next week, she was very flirtatious and I was very attracted to her. She lived in Catterick Garrison but was very hesitant about her home life. Oh well, that did not bother me too much. She did not wear any rings and had an awful lot of free time. We started a relationship and were getting on very well until she dropped the bombshell that she had a son and was married to a soldier!

I was having none of this and ended it. She went to great lengths to tell me that although she lived with her husband they were apart. Her friends conformed this and I was actually invited out in the company of her best friends and spent time with her son. We decided to go into partnership buying and producing horses for sale. We went to the Doncaster Sales as she had never been. Initially we went to have a look, but we bought three horses and brought them home.

The first one had been point to pointing. I was doubtful about him as he had a piggy eye, there was something about him I did not like. The first time I rode him a few days later was in the indoor school, he bucked me off properly. Putting me down, I was unconscious for about two minutes. We took him back to the next sale and lost money. A new one for me losing money on a horse. The second one was a four year old, well put together, bay gelding. We kept him for about three months. Marsha and I, by now, were over for good and she did not have anything to do with him. I competed him in dressage and unaffiliated jumping. I had a phone call one day from a family who were on holiday in York. They had seen the advert for him and wanted to try him on their way home. Later that day they came to the centre, fell in love with him and bought him there and then. They also bought a trailer, from a livery, that was for sale on the car park, and drove him home that evening having paid for him in cash. I love those deals when they just turn up, try and buy.

The third horse was a stallion called Brutus. I would never normally buy a stallion but he was gorgeous, a totally gorgeous horse. He was four years old, 16.1 hh and had amazing presence. He also moved really well. He came home with the others and settled very well. The day after he arrived I went to Holland so Marsha had him to deal with. She was taking him off the walker and he turned around and kicked her in the stomach which did not exactly endear him to her. The rest of the weekend he was looked after by Val who was a Latvian man working for me as an odd job man. He dealt with him really well for a man who had not got a clue about horses.

I had been invited to go to Holland by a hunting man called Peter who was also a potato farmer. He and three pals had formed together to start a stud farm near Helmsley in North Yorkshire. They already had a couple of mares in foal that they had bought in Germany.

He invited me to go to the Elite sales just outside Amsterdam, to give them advice on potential mares from a stud. We met early in the morning and went to Robin Hood airport for the flight. Another chap came along for the ride, he was a young lad who ran an equestrian centre near York called the GG centre. He had never flown before so his face was a picture on the plane.

We got to Schipol airport and hired a minibus to take us all. Driving through the countryside it became apparent just how many horses were kept and bred in Holland. Every place had fields full of horses. We got to the stud and to be honest, I was awestruck. There were barns after barns of young horses all running together in pens. They had bars alongside the central concrete track and hay was put out for them to feed through the bars. They were in effect, farming horses. It was amazing to see.

The stallion house was even more impressive. Beautifully apportioned and immaculately clean. It was like a show house on a new housing estate. There was an enormous indoor arena with a massive viewing gallery that was used for open days. Jeanette, who owned the stud, was more than happy to show us around and she was rightly very proud of her amazing place.

We went into the 3 year old pen and I was asked to choose a likely mare for breeding. I looked inside and went in. I pointed out a stunning big black mare that to me just stood out from the rest. They agreed with my choice as they had already bought her and were waiting for her to be covered by Heartbreaker, one of the standing stallions. I was secretly very pleased with myself as I could have chosen anyone of those mares. There were at least twenty in the big pen, so to choose the one they had already bought was good.

We got to the sales in the late afternoon and after walking through the temporary stables to look at all the horses we were invited, by Jeanette, into the VIP area of the arena. We were given supper and some drinks and the sale started. Horse after horse came in, ridden on the flat by riders in top hats and tails. Then they were loose schooled or jumped. I would have bought anything, they all looked fabulous. The prices amazed me as they ranged for 2000 euros to 40,000. The boys bought another mare in the sale that was guaranteed in foal to Ladykiller. It was a fabulous evening and I thoroughly enjoyed it.

Later that evening and we went into Amsterdam for a 'boys' night out. We parked up and walked down the road into the red light area. We had not gone forty yards when the lad who had never flown before was in. He went into the first window parlour he saw, a big black lady. The rest of us did not want to wait around for him to have fun so we went into a bar leaving Peter to babysit. A bit later and they reappeared. He was smiling big time. We were drinking and having a laugh with some girls who were offering us anything we wanted for 150 euros. This lad left to go with two. He came back later, into another bar we had gone to and said he had had a great time with two. Much later and he was off again for, as he put it 'pudding'. The thing was he never came back and we could not find him. We were very worried about him and seeing as Peter had his passport for safe keeping, he was in trouble. We had had enough of him to be honest. At five thirty we drove to the airport to hand in the minibus and catch our plane home. We had been looking for him a while but gave up when we realised he had done one.

He was asleep on a bench in the airport so panic over although to be really honest I was pissed off with him. The rest of us had had a lovely night in the bars and a lovely meal in the early hours, a great day out and I was very impressed with the sales and stud farm we had visited. It also had sown the seed of an idea for home.

Brutus was castrated and recovered well. He still, now and then, bit you and he just had to be respected and watched. He moved really well and in two or three competitions went from Preliminary to Novice level in dressage. I enjoyed riding him and decided, as Marsha and I had split, to keep him. Ivor was also doing well in dressage and was at Medium level.

I had also been to Brian Smart, a racehorse trainer just outside Thirsk, and bought a very nice chestnut gelding for one of the staff at the yard to ride and produce. He was a lovely chap and had a sweet nature. He was slow to lose the racehorse build though and always looked like he was, a flat horse, 16.hh and a bit scrawny. He jumped well and was an easy sell to a lady from York. The vet came though, even at £1800, for a five stage vetting which was ridiculous. He passed which was a relief.

Later that summer Judith came to see me in the office. Things were very tense between the owners and I but this was a good deed. She gave me Pam's number and told me to call her and take her on a fun date, nothing heavy like a romantic restaurant. She had been having a bad time and needed cheering up. I called her and she agreed to go out. I told her to bring her passport, clothes for really cold weather, and smart clothes for a meal. She was very intrigued, as was Judith.

I picked her, up from her house, it was a lovely summers evening. I took her into South Yorkshire (The people's republic of South Yorkshire) hence the need for a passport! We went to Escape and we went sledging for an hour, which is why she needed warm clothes, which she loved. We got changed and I took her to Harrogate to the Tepanyaki restaurant. The chef there cooked some lovely food and throughout juggled knives and made smoking mountains out of onions.

Sat at our table was Bill Nelson from a group called Be Bop Deluxe, who had hits in the seventies, and I had a good conversation with him too.

We got on really well, Pam and I, and over the next three months or so we became an item. She introduced me to a lot of people, especially in the Bedale Hunt, many of them have remained friends. Hunting with the Bedale was very different from the hunting I had experienced with the Rockwood Harriers.

This hunt had access to a lot more open land, mainly on privately owned estates. The etiquette of hunting was observed in greater detail and the dress code and behaviour in the field were strictly observed. Along with this though there was big clique, if your face fitted you were okay, if it did not you were largely ignored. Some lovely, genuine, down to earth people hunted with the Bedale, but sadly there were also a lot of complete tossers who thought they were much better people than they actually were.

I had some great days hunting in those early days. The huntsman, Andrew Osborne was, quite honestly, mad, but in a good way. He was passionate about his hounds to the extreme. On one occasion, on a freezing cold cubbing morning, hounds crossed a swollen and very fast River Swale. Andrew simply took off his coat and dived in, against many protests, including my own. The hounds lost scent on the other side and came back across followed again by Andrew, who was struggling on the way back. Thankfully he was a good swimmer and eventually made it. He was offered several flasks and was clearly a bit distressed.

His hollering was legendary and the whoop of the man would break decibel levels. He did a great deal to improve the hounds and he was great company at social events. Another big character was a man called Ronnie. I used to play rugby with Ronnie back in Bradford, which is where he is from.

Ronnie had a legendary horse called Trigger and he could be heard several fields away shouting 'Whoa whoa Trigger, stop you fucker.' On one occasion, a senior member of the field, Willy White, had fallen off under a bridge! Don't ask. We all got off to help him and Ronnie could not get back on Trigger. Victoria Lumley held him against a gate but Ronnie was still struggling to get on him. Victoria said 'Can't you just jump on him Ronnie?' to which he calmly replied 'Who do you think, I am Frankie fucking Dettori?' We all just fell about laughing.

I had a mare in called Cilla to sell for a lady from Derby. I don't know how she found me, but she contacted me and I took this horse in commission and livery basis to sell. Cilla was a superb mare, she was 16.2 hh, seven years old and Irish bred. A bit cobby, I hogged her mane and she looked the part, being a big, solid built mare. She was impeccable in the field and had a serious jump.

Pam wanted to hire her out as she did hirelings, but I was against this. She was not actually my mare and hiring her out was fraught with danger. My friend Craig Chambers had just started to ride and hunt and he borrowed her a couple of times while I took Ivor. She would have been superb for him as his first horse, but he was talked out of it. After Xmas though, he was struggling to find a horse big enough to carry him and quiet enough for his level of riding at that time. After a lot of negotiation and trying him, he bought Ivor from me.

It was the right thing to do with Ivor, he had a superb home and had, with me, reached his peak in eventing. Melba, Craig's girlfriend, is a consummate horsewoman and she took on Ivor to event too. I also sold Cilla to Tim Easby who was then the Master of the Bedale West of Yore Hunt. She had a successful and lengthy career with them.

The social side of the hunt was exceptional. Once every two years they put on a pantomime at the Masham Town hall and it was always superb. There was a fair amount of talent about, especially those who could sing really well, and the dancing which was very well done too.

The point to point at Hornby Castle was a great day out and I sponsored it every year. Racing was always good and the ground was usually superb. At most of the social events Craig, Mike Lumley and I ran the bar for the hunt supporters. We had a couple of incidents of note. One couple, who were particularly obnoxious, were always very rude. The chap would hold his glass up in the air and shout 'Wine.' I just ignored him every time but he never got the message, he was a prat. We also had a bloke who, for some reason, thought the drinks were free and would buy huge rounds and always try and get out of paying. He was funny really as we could never believe his attitude and we had fun getting his money from him. Andrew Osborne always bought us a drink as a 'thank you' for manning the bar.

The lady Field Master at that time was Mary Tweddle. She was very quiet, held a great deal of authority in her aura, and was very well respected by everyone. She is the mother of Olympic Silver eventing rider Nicola Wilson. Always very well mounted, she had no fear and jumped some amazing hedges. She led by example and was a great loss to the hunt when she eventually called it a day as Field Master.

All in all they were a great bunch of people and I had seven good seasons with them. Great country, very good terrier men, and every day was well organised.

Chapter Thirty One

Back at the centre, the relationship between Paul, Judith and me was getting much worse. Just before Xmas I put on a Xmas jumping extravaganza based on Olympia. It culminated in a Puissance with a £50 to the winner takes all prize. Sue's husband Mike and I had done a dry run practice on setting the wall jump up and increasing its height by 5cm each round. There were two wall jumps but one of them had blocks missing, so we used the right one which was a traditional red brick wall.

Half way through, Paul and a man called Robert Shields, who was going out with Judith's daughter Chloe, came into the arena and started saying we were doing the wall wrong and that it was not going up by enough height each time. You have to remember this was unaffiliated and the people taking part would have been easily put off if we went too high too quickly. They came out of the jump store with blocks from the other wall. These did not fit and were a different colour too. I took great pleasure in telling them this and telling them to get lost and stop interfering.

I had managed, after a great deal of argument with British Eventing, to get a JAS (jump and style) competition on. This national competition is run indoors, it's a mixture of show jumps and cross country fences. There is a national final and it is quite a prestigious and lucrative event. Prior to me getting this event based at Richmond, the nearest one was in Lancashire or Birmingham.

We were packed out with entries and on the Friday eventing the team from BE came up and put up the track. They brought all their own jumps and they were very spectacular. It was very impressive and I took lots of pictures for future advertising.

The next morning was a very early start and I walked in to find the course had been jumped around and altered a great deal. I was so angry, it was embarrassing and the BE team were, quite rightly, furious.

It came out eventually that the people who had schooled round the track were friends of Judith's and they had come late at night at her invitation.

When I first started running the dressage competitions, Judith would assist with stewarding. I was happy about this, of course, as she was a great help. I was getting people coming back to me though, telling me she was bad mouthing me all the time and saying how badly the competitions were being run and how slack the organisation was. I decided to confront her about all this and went to see her in her office.

We ended up having a row and she told me she would not steward anymore. I was glad about this to be truthful, and for ages she stayed away.

Paul was a nightmare with the parking on the car park. True, it was tight on busy big days but Mick did it for me and always did a great job. Paul could not help interfering and running round the car park like a loony, shouting at people and contributing nothing.

He came to see me one day and dropped the bombshell that we, yes that was we, owed Npower over £6,000 in unpaid electricity bills. He demanded £2,000 there and then. I told him no chance and that I wanted to see copies of the bills. He was obviously shocked that I would want to see the bills. He did eventually give me copies, but these proved that the £6,000 owed was for the whole place, including his house, buildings, stables and other cottages he rented out. My contribution was, in fact, just less than £1,200

The café was proving difficult too as members of their family, on a competition day, were coming up and taking food and drink and putting everything on a tab. The amount of money owed at the end of every month was always questioned and argued about. Simple, I introduced a system in a book where they signed for food and drink as they took it, but they flatly refused to do this. We had a big argument about this as they were claiming it was their café and that they should be able to use it when they wanted. This of course was wrong and very unfair.

We then started having members of their staff coming up for tab food and drink. I stopped this straight away. It was getting impossible. The atmosphere was also bad on a day to day basis, especially when one day I pointed out to Paul, very strongly, that it was not his café and not his arenas as he had leased them to me for ten years. It seemed to have the desired effect as they stayed away for a while.

In the spring we were full on in preparation for the first of two BE events. I had that year, with the sponsorship of Camerons Brewery, bought seven new fences for the cross country course. Their daughter Libby was the pony eventing European champion and rightly so, we were all very proud of her. Sue and David Soley are lovely people and they went to great efforts to support the event.

I also had made signs to be put into the ground in front of every fence on the course. Each fence had a unique name on these signs and it just added to the spectacular dressing of the course. It looked amazing when we started. I had put into the programme, a pony trials at Novice level. There was a big gap in the area as nearly all the trials for pony riders were held down south. The kids riding these ponies are amazing and the competition was fabulous.

The whole weekend went without a hitch and it was, for once, a great pleasure to organise it and be the host. Of course I had the usual operational tiny minor issues and these were built up by the Hodgsons to be enormous, earth shattering problems that only the United Nations and European court of human rights could sort out. The generator that powered the scorer's caravan ran out of petrol, which was sorted out in ten minutes. The rider rep notice was not posted in the secretary's tent until the afternoon of the first day.

Over six hundred entries all turned up, competed dressage, show jumping and cross country without a hitch. The prizes for each section were fabulous because I bought them and so ensured they were of a high level. The feedback on the new fences and the whole venue was great too. Sponsors were happy. All my volunteers got a goody bag with vouchers, sweets, key rings and other gifts. They had regular refreshments brought to them and at the end of the day they were also given a bottle of wine. More importantly, the BE people were very happy.

But of course it was an unmitigated disaster of huge proportions, due to the lack of petrol and the omission of a notice in the tent. This ruined the reputation of the centre and our ability to put on events. I was furious and also gutted at their attitude.

Other issues were bubbling between myself and a lady called Janice Mews. Janice is actually a lovely lady and works tirelessly for jumping in the north of England. She runs most of the BS (British Show Jumping) competitions. To do this she hired the centre from me to run competitions there.

Janice was approached, behind my back, by Judith, to take over the centre. This was common knowledge and went a long way again to undermine my business and my standing at the centre. Instead of saying 'No', Janice tried to engage Ian Brown, my coach and friend to come on board with her to take it over. I think what they all fundamentally failed to grasp was that I had a legal 10 year lease. Ian for his part, being a friend told me straight away, and of course turned her down.

The arrangement Janice and I had was that she hired the arenas on a Wednesday to put on affiliated show jumping competitions. She had the arena hired from 12pm until 6pm which was classed as a half day hire for £150. I had the café and it was always busy so I usually made a good day's money. The problem was though, that Alan her husband, built the courses himself and needed to start at ten thirty am to be ready for 12pm. Many a day she was that busy she didn't finish until past six pm and this restricted my liveries from using the arenas.

Things came to a head shortly after the attempted coup. They started building the course at 11 am and used Val, my handyman, to help them. They did not finish until after 8pm as they were so busy, which was actually a good thing. However, there was a broken fence filler which was going to cost £80 to replace and Janice left me a cheque for £150. It was just simply not enough to cover the cost of the full day hire and the new filler. I spoke to Janice about this and she was not happy at all. I got quite a snotty letter from her which, given she had also tried to oust me not long before, resolved me to end the agreement forthwith.

I was confident I could run the shows myself, though given that you have to submit proposed competition days to the British Show Jumping Association months in advance, it was some time before I could put on shows under my auspices. The fallout from this decision was immense. Firstly, people thought it was payback for the attempted coup, which if I am honest, had something to do with it, but mainly it was a business decision, you cannot keep on making a loss.

The Hodgsons were incandescent with rage about this. Chloe, their daughter was doing fabulously well show jumping with her boyfriend Robert Shields and they needed the competitions to help them. It was said that that was the end for me and they were determined to get me out. I think that had started much earlier.

The other competitions were going really well and I had introduced some innovative events to bolster the footfall through the centre. Dressage to music and tests at the higher level such as PSG and Intermediaire were never catered for and although they were loss leaders for me, I ran them to uplift the competitions we were offering.

I also put on two viewing evening, where people brought their horses, displayed them in the arena for potential buyers and I gave a running commentary about the horses. These were by and large successful and well received and supported. The pre-event show jumping that I put on every Tuesday morning was very popular with both show jumpers and event riders. Scott Smith was a show jumper of some note. He had jumped on Nations Cups and was regarded as an International rider. He came one morning with six young horses to jump.

The first one was young and did not jump well. He set about it with a long schooling whip and beat the devil out of it. I had a stand up row with him about this and told him to leave. He got very angry and aggressive but I was not having any of this beating horses for no reason and I made him leave

Based on the sales in Holland, I organised a Sport Horse sale. We had thirty three really good quality horses brought forward. Andrew Spalding was the auctioneer and a great job he made of it too. The indoor arena was dressed with flowers and looked amazing. The horses had been available the day before for viewing and trying. They had all been vetted prior to the sale too. I spent over £500 advertising the sale and simply no one turned up! I was devastated, but hardly anyone came. Two horses were sold out of the whole thirty three.

I ran one more, later on in the year and Timmy turned up, the horse I had sold four years earlier. He had been hunting with Phillip Watt, Huntsman with the York and Ainsty North. He was sold to Ronnie Dobson for his daughter Erica to ride. I had a problem now and thought I should tell them about this horse and especially his propensity to rear vertically.

I told Sue about my worries and, unbeknown to me, she told Judith who turned it into a problem. She told Erica that I had said she would not be able to ride one side of it and I found myself having to explain to her that I had not said any such thing. These sales cost me money and were going nowhere. I decided not to run another.

Just after the sales I had arranged for British Dressage to come up on a Sunday and have use of the indoor arena as a star spotting day. They had invited junior riders from all over the North of England to come along for assessment to be considered for the star spotter's programme. I levelled and set the indoor 60 x20 m arena and dressed it. We closed off the arena and went home.

Next day, and an early start shocked me to the roots. The indoor arena had been flooded in one corner. The dressage arena had been moved and the actual surface was cut up and had been ridden on. I had a great deal of work to do to recover the use of the corner, I had to literally bucket scoop water out of there before I could re-level and set the arena. We were an hour late starting and although they were understanding, the British Dressage people were clearly not impressed.

It all came out later through Sue. Robert and Chloe had qualified horses for the Scope show jumping festival and in the corner of that arena there was always a big fountain. To get the horses used to this they had gone into the arena and set the hose pipe running on a garden sprinkler system to assimilate the fountain, whilst they schooled around the arena. They knew what I had going on the next day, but did not give a shit.

I had a very big row with Judith over this because, as usual, Paul was nowhere to be seen. It was the beginning of the end for me. I had had enough of this rubbish. The situation was impossible and untenable. I carried on though as I am, if nothing else, stubborn.

Liveries in the stables had got to a point where I had some vacancies. I did not detect that anything was particularly wrong with the service I was offering but it was quiet. Deidre Johnston, wife of the race horse trainer Mark was always very kind to me and supportive. She had bought an Intermediate eventer for her son but had no room at home for him. I happily agreed to take him on livery for a while until they could sort him out a space.

He arrived and had had a terrible accident in the horsebox on route to us. He had torn his head open all around his ear and had lacerations down his forehead. He was frankly, a mess. The Johnston's vets attended straight away and we had six or so weeks of nursing him back to health. It was a great shame really because he was a lovely horse and a good patient. I had several other horses from Deidre as she was competing eventing and did really well. She is a good rider and, to be honest, a superwoman. How on earth she fits in riding out lots in a morning, running the yard, attending races and riding and competing her own, I just do not know.

Sue Soley also sent me a lovely bay gelding by Primitive Rising that had raced. He was very slightly built for a tall horse and was tricky. Angus Smales tried him and I thought I had a sale but he was expensive and the deal did not go ahead. Eventually he was taken back from me for Sue to ride. I still had Brutus and really only had the time for one horse at that time. He was now competing at Novice dressage and jumping unaffiliated tracks at 90 cm and 1 metre.

A young lad called Mathew Fox sent me a horse to sell for him. It was a big grey gelding, 16.3hh and seven years old. He originally had bought it from Pam Ashworth for a fortune. He had done nothing with it.

I sold it three times for him to three different people, including Deidre and a girl who was on livery with me called Mel Chapman, she went onto become a very talented and exceptional dressage rider. Each time though, this horse failed the vet. I ended up just before the vetting for Mel, at ten pm at night, tubbing his foot and having him re-shod. He still failed the vet. Nothing was diagnosed, he was just short on that front foot on the flexion test.

Darrel came up and tried him as we was actually a lovely horse, he moved well and had a huge, scopey jump. Darrel took him down to Hirds vets to have him looked at as we were sure Peter Schofield would find out what was wrong. It was a negative though, he was just not quite sound which was a great shame.

I told Mathew and he did not believe me. We had a man to man about it because he was calling me a liar. He ended up taking the horse away and loaning him.

The relationship between Pam and I was very up and down. She was not as committed as I was that was for sure. Pam is very tricky to deal with and at times I would say High Maintenance. That spring we had been with a few friends to Badminton Horse Trials and had a very pleasant weekend. Craig Chambers, who had tried Cilla and bought Ivor from me, had never been before and he wanted the whole experience. He could not believe the size of the fences and the speed at which the horses flew by and the shopping. He reminded me of myself years and years earlier when I first went.

That evening on the Saturday Craig and I were in the mood for a drink. The rest had gone to bed. We asked the landlord for his best port and he came up with a bottle of 1975 vintage. £80 and the deal was done, he de-canted it and it was like nectar, we had already had a bottle of wine with supper but we were on it. We asked him if he had another and I don't think he could believe his luck. He came up with a bottle of 1987 which, he thought was corked when he tested it. Neither, Craig or I thought there was anything wrong but we protested most strongly in a jocular way and he let us have it for £30.

The next day and even though he was dying Craig wanted to make the trot up. So 8.30 am and we were stood in front of the big house surrounded by people. Such was the crush we couldn't move and had no chance of getting out.

We were seriously dehydrated. Anyone coming to the crowd drinking water and we were bidding against each other in a mock auction to buy their water from them. One girl came with a big hot dog I offered her a tenner for it but she refused. I badgered her and she kept refusing. Trying to shut me up she licked it from one end to the other at which I immediately offered her £20.

The trot up started and some of the girls were playing fast and loose with the amount of boob jiggle going on. Craig had a horse at home called Murphy or Murph, he was a big 17hh bay gelding, very common but a diamond. One girl presented a big bay gelding and started her run in front of the crowd and the ground jury, it went very quiet and Craig shouted out 'Its Murph, I told you we could do this eventing lark' I said equally as loud 'Yes well we can all trot up and down Craig it's the other three elements that would fuck you up'.

It was a good time that weekend. It was however marred for me by Pam. We were in a pub, whilst having some supper, she was asked by one of the group we were with if she had been to Badminton before and competed there. She said she had. I was so surprised at this because I knew for a fact she had not. It was quite disturbing to be honest. I did not want to embarrass her in front of all our friends so I kept quiet, but I made it right later.

She had a lovely horse she had bred called Jolly Java Jack who was by Java Tiger, a famous stallion who produced many a good eventer and sport horse. Jack was three and she sent him to me for breaking, which I did slowly, over a three month period. He turned out to be a superb horse. She did start to event Jack and did quite well at 90 cm and 1 metre, which was the old Pre-Novice. The first Novice she did was at Aske Hall and when walking the course she was not for listening to any advice, and certainly not from me. At an offset double which had a really short one stride in it, I suggested she went the long route. Nah, she wanted to go straight and did, but Jack bless him, just could not make it and stopped. Pam did go onto have good success with Jack and other horses, especially in the Burghley Young Event horse classes.

Darrel had tried the grey horse I was trying to sell for Mathew and it failed the vet. He was definitely looking though and Pam said she had a suitable horse in to sell at her place. She ran the equestrian centre attached to Queen Mary's private girls school at Baldeston. I told her that Darrel had torn his cruciate ligament in his groin and could not try or buy any horses that bucked or that was too narrow in build.

He arranged to go try this horse, having been assured it was straight and okay. He got there early, not really to catch anyone out, he just got his timing wrong. It was a good job really as Pam was riding this horse in the arena and it had obviously been worked for a while. He was not happy at all but liked the look of him. He got on and it promptly bucked like stink and put him down heavily. He was absolutely furious as well as being in agony.

He came up to Richmond and he was clearly in great pain. What could I say? He was one of my best mates and my so called girlfriend dealer had fucked him up good and proper. We had an almighty row about it and I fell out with her big time when she said it was Darrel's fault as he was not a good rider. Just to set the record straight, he did buy a horse called Caruso which he took to 2* level.

The second Horse Trials that year went really well. I felt that I had got right on top of it. Sue was an immense help in the organisation too. I was quite happy. The Festival of Dressage was two weeks later, which logistically was a nightmare again with so many tests to get through in such a short time. I also introduced music classes for the first time at PSG.

On the Tuesday before the start of the weekend it was suggested to me, by a couple of liveries, that as the previous one last year had been 'such a disaster', maybe I ought to get some more help. I did increase the scoring team to six, and purely by way of self-protection, I devised a form on which we recorded feedback from as many competitors as possible.

Pam kindly did this for me, stopping riders and getting their opinions. This was going really well and the feedback on the first day was excellent. The second day was the same. On the Sunday it was a lovely summer's day and in the evening, under the spotlights of the main big outdoor arena, we had the PSG to music.

Loads of people had stayed behind to watch this. Each rider submits a CD with their music on it and I spoke to them all individually to find out at what point they wanted me to start the music. All sorted, we started. I sent out jugs of Pimms to the spectators which was warmly received. Paul though, kept coming to the commentary box and interfering. He wanted to know if I was ready for each rider and had the music started on cue. I politely told him to get lost, but he just couldn't resist coming up. I had a very strong word with him and ended up telling him to fuck off out of it.

Two days later and the feedback analysis showed a really strong positive. I was really pleased. Paul came to see me and demanded that I gave up one of the flats I had within my lease for a reduction in the rent. The need for him to have a flat stemmed from the fact that two months earlier he and Judith had actively poached Emma Gordon, my head girl, to work for them. On leaving the position with me she also vacated the flat that came with it. My new head girl was moving in that week.

Emma had been staying with Chloe, their daughter, since leaving and they wanted the flat for her. I flatly refused. A week later and Paul asked for a meeting in my office, on a Sunday morning when we did not have anything on. I turned up and found that my key did not fit the office door lock. I could not get into my office. Paul came round and I saw, skulking around the arena, Sue and her husband Mick. I knew something was afoot. The meeting began with Paul stating he wanted the centre back in house, under his management. I refused straight out but asked for half an hour to think about it.

I had had enough of this horrible man and the centre as a whole. It was going okay but never was it going to make me a decent living as the overheads were far too high. The atmosphere was untenable and the future was bleak. If you get up every morning and go to do something you are not looking forward to and you are not happy doing, it's a time to change. I was at that point.

When he came back in I asked him if he had changed the locks on the office, café and office within the indoor arena, which he had no right to. He confirmed that using Sue's keys he had gained access the previous evening and changed them all. I was stupefied. I wanted a bit longer to think and he agreed. I shot up to catch Sue and she told me an awful lot.

She had been reporting back to them since the day I took over. She had been photocopying my bank statements and handing them over, the reports from my sage accounting records were also made available to Judith and Paul.

Because I owned the website within the lease agreement, I had been trying to re-register the domain name into my name. As I had it for at least ten years, I wanted to change the website when I needed to and upgrade and improve it. I had sent two written copies of the transfer through the post, or I thought I had. Each one had been thrown in the bin by Sue at the behest of the Hodgson's. This was total treachery from a lady who was supposed to be my friend and who worked for me and a rotten thing to do to anyone.

I went down to the office and took the computers, printer and as many of the files I could get in my car, before Paul came back. When I spoke to him again in his office I asked him if it would be better for me to have a staged exit for the good of the centre and then we could nip any rumours in the bud. No, he wanted me out there and then. 'Okay I am going' I said.

I left and he called me later screaming about the computers which were mine. They had everything on them, as you can imagine. The show details, timing templates for dressage and all the details pertaining to the horse trials. The following Tuesday I saw my solicitor and she served notice that the changing of locks were an absolute prohibition on my enjoyment of my lease and that they had to respond within seven days. They did.

The following day and I went to see my mother for the day. On return home, I was confronted with outside my house, dozens of boxes of frozen food, chips, salmon en croute, cakes, pies and other stuff. Paul had just emptied the freezers from the café and dumped it all outside my house. There was stacks of it. He had not, of course, dumped the Pimms and wine and other expensive things.

Another very strongly worded letter from my Solicitor ended up with me finding him on my doorstep. It took me all of my resolve, and I mean all of my resolve, not to kick him all the way back up to the centre.

My financial agreement with this arrogant, rude, immature individual is subject to a privacy clause, safe to say, I was satisfied.

My biggest regret was losing Val back to Latvia and then poor Katie, my new head girl had lost her job before it started, which was a horrible to have to tell her. Sue took over the running of the centre calling herself REC events. She has lasted six years into a twenty year lease and is still seeking redress through the courts. The people that took over the livery yard from me lasted no time at all, having invested a fair amount of money in improvements.

Chapter Thirty Two

Thankfully, when I left there, I only had Brutus. Pam agreed I could take him to her yard and I moved there with little trouble. I actually took two stables as I had decided to start dealing full-time. The market was good and there was a fair bit if trade. It was not long before Pam was saying she needed all her boxes for hunter liveries, and the school horses came first and it was always a temporary arrangement. I got the message although it had been kind of her to allow me to go there in the first place of course and started looking around for a livery yard.

Melba Reed, Craig's girlfriend offered, me some boxes at her yard. The problem was that they were very run down, at the back of the farm and quite small for the big horses I would be buying in. She offered to do them up of course, which was very nice of her, but it was a shame and I always regret not going there. As a temporary measure I moved Brutus up to Gwenda Lupton. She has the most fabulous place, lovely boxes and big arena and very good grazing land. A horsewalker and lunging pen was also a great bonus.

I moved up there and felt right at home. Richard Howard, whom I have known for years, was there with his partner, John Guy. I got on great with the lads and we had some good laughs. Another stable came free and I bagged it.

There was not though a great deal of quality horseflesh to be found locally. I went to Andrew Cawlwood's yard in Cheshire and bought a nice 16.2 hh, 6 year old hunter type. Irish bred, I paid £2000 for him. Back at the yard he was settled very well. I advertised him straight away as he was made and would suit the hunting market.

A lady from Harrogate came along and tried him and decided to buy him subject to vetting and him travelling in a trailer. He passed the vet a few days later and she came with a trailer to put him in and hopefully take him home. She had been tricky to deal with as she was very suspicious of dealers. On the way to the trailer she asked me if I had doped him or drugged him. I took him back to his stable, I was so angry with her. She knew she had pissed me off and apologised. He went into the trailer without a hesitation and that was that, he was sold.

A lady contacted me as she had a grey gelding to sell. I took him in and he was gone within a few weeks of Christmas. He was a lovely horse and the girl that bought him went on to have good success with him and they were very happy.

On Christmas day I was doing the horses and, as my family were so far away in Bradford, I was spending the day on my own. For reasons best be known to Pam I was not invited to her house. After mucking out, Gwenda insisted on me joining her family for lunch which I thought was a wonderful thing to do and I will never forget her generosity. I did not go hunting on Boxing Day as really I only had Brutus, who was a dressage horse.

In February I still only had Brutus who I was enjoying, but it was a struggle financially. At a party, where I went with Pam, I was talking to Tom Bell, He straight away offered me the use of a yard at his place near Thirsk. With the yard were seven boxes, use of their arena and extensive cross country course. It was an opportunity too good to miss.

I have known Tom and Helen Bell as people to nod to and say hello to in passing at events. They had supported the sales events I had put on at Richmond with their horses. Helen was an international rider competing at Badminton, Burghley and the European championships. Some years earlier she had had Andrew Nicholson and Andrew Hoy up to her place conducting a training clinic. Sue, my ex-wife, had attended and had a very rare fall which resulted in a broken collar bone. They were great, stabling the horse and sorting her out until I could get there.

Just before I was due to move, Tom got planning permission on the block of stables I was going to take and therefore I couldn't go. They ensured though that their old yard, which now belonged to a doctor and her husband was made available. They did not need to do this for me at all and I can only put it down to their genuine kindness.

The yard had seven boxes and a store area for hay and straw. There were two fields with it which amounted to about 4 acres. I could not turn out all year round but that was fine. Sam who owned it was lovely, she never bothered me and left me to my own devices. I moved in with Brutus and made one of the stables into a tack room and somewhere to have a cup of tea.

I had stored all my spare tack and equipment in my large garage at home. I had so much collected over the years in my dad's old tack trunks and boxes. When I started unloading it I was missing some things; leather headcollars and a couple of 'Winergy' labelled dressage squares. These squares were prizes won from the Burghley young event horse classes I had competed horses in. I loved this competition and always had horses trying to qualify for the finals at Burghley in the September.

A week or so afterwards I was at the riding school Pam ran and I saw a 'Winergy' dressage square on her horse Jack. Some careful questioning of her girls resulted in me finding out that, when earlier she had borrowed a saddle from me, and had later returned it to my garage, which I knew she had done, she had helped herself to some of my things. The irony is I would have given her anything at that time. I got it all back and ended the relationship. That did not last long though and she was soon back in my life.

At the end of March Tom and Helen were going to Ireland to the sales at Gorsebridge. I was short of horses and they invited me to go with them. It was a great trip and I really enjoyed myself. Guinness was consumed and we stopped in a wonderful hotel which I love and still visit, the Langton in Kilkenny. I worked with them checking and looking at horses and we soon got a system going. I would watch the horses jumping in the indoor school and make notes about them. Helen would be outside watching them on the flat and Tom was floating from the stables to the lunge area. We used to share our thoughts on any horses we fancied.

Of course everyone knows that Ireland is a major source of horses and when you are there it is like being a kid in a sweetie shop. I could have bought hundreds of horses in the times I went there, but have to confess at always being frustrated at never having enough money.

On that first trip with the Bells we were there for one day only, for the ponies. We then went to Athlone to see Jim Derwin. Jim and his brother Francis are big hitters in Irish dealing. They will have upwards of 300 horses at any one time. I have, over the years, seen Jim buy over 100 horses at a sale. A quiet man giving the impression he is a deep thinker, Jim could really, really ride a horse and was very impressive. On that first visit Tom bought three horses. I asked if he had any cheapies and he sold me a very nice five year old gelding. Bay, 16.2 hh, he had a green passport which meant his breeding was recorded and he was fully registered.

I had him vetted and he came home five days later. He was called Guinness which was very apt. I sold him four weeks later to a livery of Pam`s, Jean McQuarrie. Jean had several great seasons on him with the Bedale and he was a triumph of a horse for her.

Dealing has its ups and downs and can be very rewarding but also very frustrating, and in some cases downright lousy. The biggest drawback apart from timewasters proved to be veterinary inspections. I had words with so many vets over the years it became a constant problem to me. I have never ever put in front of a vet, a horse that I knew to be wrong.

I have never ever doped a horse prior to vetting. I would even point out things to a vet in order that they build trust in me and we could foster a relationship, but it was not always appreciated. The biggest bone of contention was the flexion tests. Different vets did it in different ways, some would do all the four legs, and some though would do front only or back legs only. Some would lift the leg up so high the poor horse had no option but to hop away. One vet held up the legs for up to four minutes and another for less than thirty seconds.

A vet, one day, was over three hours vetting a horse for a farmer to hunt. It was ridiculous that vetting. I had an occasion where the vet told the client that, in her opinion, the horse was not suitable for her due to the horse's age and experience. That had nothing to do with her she did not know if or how the client rode and what she was looking for. That was my job.

Later, when they introduced to the five stage vetting the lunge section on hard ground, I thought this was totally overboard, ridiculous and a step too far. Lunging a young horse, on concrete, in a ten to fifteen metre circle is a total folly. I have known and seen horses come down doing this and in one case a horse seriously injured its knee. For what the vet can see and ascertain from this task, is most certainly not worth the risk.

I had a reputation for not selling a horse to someone if I did not think the match was right. It was stupid selling the wrong horse to the wrong person. It only resulted in them causing you trouble and grief. Of course some dealers would sell anything to anyone and that is why people are naturally suspicious of dealers. However, they are protected by the Sale of Goods Act. Dealers who follow this philosophy, that any sale is a good sale, are idiots and reap what they sow.

I had a lovely five year old in called Mr Magee He was from Jim, was 16.1 hh and jet black. A girl called Sophie came to try him. As soon as she walked into the wash box she was kissing him and had fallen in love with him. She had told me on the phone that her Granny had died and left her £6000. She wanted to buy a horse and a trailer with this money. Mr Magee was for sale for £5000. Sophie was a novice rider and quite unbalanced in the saddle. There was no way I was going to sell her a 5 year old sport horse.

When I told her the bad news she was in tears. I had just got back to the yard with him and I heard her father stomping his way around. He came charging in shouting 'My daughter's fucking money not good enough for you, what the fuck you doing?' I shook his hand and explained to him that I would sell the horse, no problem, but that I would insist on writing on my receipt that in my professional opinion, the horse was unsuitable. I went onto tell him that I would find her a suitable horse, given a couple of weeks.

Three weeks later I bought a horse from Pam for £3500. He was a cobby type but had a lovely conformation and attitude. She loved him and was kissing him in the wash box as soon as she saw him. £4800 and he was hers. Her Dad shook my hand because, as he said, I knew they had £6000 to spend and I was being straight with them.

Another occasion when I ended my relationship with Pam was because of a grey Connemara she had in to sell. I had a client for it, she was fourteen, had outgrown her first pony and was looking for the next step up. Pam was gushing about this horse and how good it was. She told me it was eminently suitable for a fourteen year old. I arranged a viewing on Saturday morning. I turned up in riding gear and a flat cap.

The pony was saddled and there was only Becky who was a groom there. I called Pam and she said she had something on at home and could not come down. Smelling a rat, I spoke to Becky, the girl who worked for her. She was very vague and noncommittal. When I asked her to ride him she refused, blaming her need to get finished on the yard.

I got him out and got on him myself. A typical Connie gelding, he was about 15.3 hh He was quiet in walk, trot and canter and I did not jump him because the young lady client was desperate to get on. She only managed to get down one long side of the arena before he went nuts. He did the wall of death, round and round getting faster. I was in the middle of the arena trying to talk her into turning him into a smaller circle. She was, by now, screaming at the top of her voice, making things worse. The horse ran straight for the gate at the end of the arena. My immediate thought was 'Oh god don't jump it'.

It didn't but it just hit it full on. The young girl went straight over his head, did a triple salco with toe loop, and hit the deck on her back. She was out cold when I got to her. An ambulance was called and she was taken to hospital. I did not have words for her mum, what could I say? She said, to me just before they left, 'The only reason I have not slapped you is because you got on that horse with a flat cap on and no helmet, so you obviously did not know the horse'.

I called Pam and told her urgently and hysterically that the girl was dead and the police were here demanding to see her straight away. I was having a cup of tea in the tea room when she came down. She looked suitably frightened. We had serious words and I walked off. I never had any more horse dealings with her after that. Another fall out came as the result of me buying a lovely horse by Carrabawn View from Ireland. He was called Cliff and was a superb hunter. A big, strapping, 17 hh gelding, he was well made and certainly had a leg at each corner.

Matt Penrose, who whips in for the Bedale, tried him and wanted him subject to vet. I had a five stage vetting certificate from Ireland but he wanted him looked at. The vet came and Mathew's mum Judy came. He could not pass him, but he could not say why, he just 'couldn't put his finger on it'. Brilliant, that left me nowhere. Judy was furious and being blunt, she thought the vet was a right idiot. I was gutted obviously. I had missed a sale but also having a horse of mine whipping in with the Bedale would have been good advertising.

A couple of hours later, Pam called me and very condescendingly, told me not to offer dodgy horses to the hunt. It would not do my reputation any good, and as Mathew now thought I was a dodgy dealer, it would have repercussions. She told me that he had told one of the lady Masters about this and she had called Pam to ask her what on earth I was thinking about.

I called Mathew straight away and we had a conversation where he told me he had not said any such thing to the lady Master and that he was gutted about the horse. He then told me to find him another. We left it at that and then Pam called a little later, screaming at me for going behind her back. When I explained calmly that she had lied and that she was just causing mischief, she hung up.

Back in Ireland, on one trip, we were very late leaving for the airport. I drove like a loony back to Dublin. We normally got back to the airport in time to fill the car, call at a hotel nearby and have a Thai meal, then hand the car back and get the plane. We were pushing it because Helen had made us late waiting for a horse to go through, which she did not buy. Tom was not a happy man. At the airport he was directing me through traffic. He told me, forcefully, to pull in behind a queue of cars. I did and we stood still for five minutes. 'We are not going anywhere Tom.' He got out to have a look and got back in shouting that we were 'In the fucking taxi queue.' He was apoplectic, but we just laughed.

At the sales Tom had a knack of finding superb horses. He could just spot them a mile off and bought some excellent horseflesh, not really a horseman, but he could find them.

Helen did them at home, brought them on and sold them. They did sell them well. He wanted to go out hunting on one of his purchases but he did not have any jodhpurs and borrowed a pair form me. He kept them for nearly three years and then the cheeky bugger gave me them back when they moved.

In the hunting field he was very brave and would jump some serious fences but falls and injuries followed. Helen, for all she went around Badminton and Burghley, was frightened to death half the time and regularly was white as a sheet out hunting.

That first summer being down there and they had a holiday in America with Helen's mum in tow. I was asked if I would house sit and look after the dogs for them, which I agreed to do. They had only been gone a day and Tom's mum Anne came around. I had met her before a few times and got on well with her. She was a horsewoman and had been Yorkshire women's point to point champion in her youth. She was not happy at all about me house sitting and made it quite clear.

When I went to pick them up from the airport and brought them home, they had already spoken to her a few times on holiday, and she had been telling tales which were unfounded. When we got back to the house she had been in and thrown all my food I had left in the fridge, in the bin. As she walked around the back of me, when no one could see, she hit me. They had bought me a lovely camera and some ranch gloves for house sitting. Hazel, Helens mum, gave me some money for looking after her dog and Anne went mad at her.

I was shocked actually at her venom, but she hated my guts with a vengeance. She told a few people that she had found a dirty magazine under the bed I had been using and that I was a dirty man. Not a chance, I never had such a thing. Helen, to her credit, tried to diffuse this with her and said it was Tom's. That caused them to have a fall out. It was a silly and funny situation, but it took a turn for the worse.

The drive to the farm was about two miles long and a straight road with crops on either side. I hacked out my horses two or three times a week to relieve the boredom of them being in the school all the time. Anne, if she was driving along the drive at the same time, would just drive straight at me, Tom knew this and spoke to her about it but it was clear she was going to kill me if she could. One day I was hacking out with a friend of mine, Liz Morgan, and Anne was coming along the drive. Undeterred, she sped up and came for us. We got out of the way but Liz, bless her was really shocked.

One day I set off out on a hack and I woke up in a puddle, on my back, wet through. I had been out cold and had wet myself. I was disorientated and a lady from the next door farm picked me up and took me home. The horse was back at the stables and Helen was just setting off to find me. We still do not know to this day what happened to me, but Tom and Helen are convinced it was Anne.

One other occasion, a photograph of me jumping a horse, was on the front page of the programme for the Thornton Watless Horse Trials. At the event Anne was sat with Richard and John, and Richard being naughty, pointed it out to her and she was furious. 'How did that man get on the front of that?' Richard offered to frame the picture so she could have it at the side of her bed!

Tom and Helen insisted that I went to them for Christmas dinner rather than being on my own that year, but I had to wait until Anne had been and gone. I had a lovely afternoon with them and it was just so kind of them to have asked me.

Colin Leggot was a livery customer of Pam's and he was quite a character. He lived in the borders and hunted throughout the season with a horse called Pukka. One Saturday morning and I took Jean and my horse to the meet, together with Pukka for Pam, who was ill.

We parked at the Wyville Arms car park and were awaiting the arrival of Colin. It was getting very near the time to get up and go to the meet and he still had not arrived. I got Jean mounted and then I saw him walking down the car park. I shouted him to tell him where we were. He turned on me 'I know you're there Stephen. I will be along in a few minutes, get my horse ready.' He said this very angrily and other people stopped and looked, such was his venom.

I turned to Jean and rolled my eyes. I got my horse, Henry, who I had got from Jim, out and got on. We then trotted off. A few minutes later I had an irate Pam on the phone begging me to go back and get him on his horse. He was her client and she needed me to get him on. I very reluctantly trotted back and he was there, very angry. I said 'Say one word Colin and you can get stuffed and get on your bloody horse yourself'. I got him on, which is always a struggle, as he cannot open his legs he is that stiff. On the way to the meet he meekly apologised. I just told him that no one speaks to me like that and that he was lucky I had not slapped him.

I had several more fall outs with dear Colin and it was more to do with him being in love with Pam than anything else. He bought a horse a few years later from a dealer called Phillip Macateer. He bought it off the phone and went to see it alone. He left a deposit on the understanding that Pam would approve it.

She would not even go to look at it as she had a horse herself she wanted to sell him. Phillip, of course, would not refund the money and called me to complain. It was nothing to do with me at all and I told him this. Colin called me and had a go, saying he was a mate of mine and we had stitched him up. I was not in any way involved in this sale of this horse. By then Pam and I were over and had been for a number of years. I knew Phillip because he used to come jumping at Richmond, but that is it.

Later, when it was the time for Pukka to go to kennels, Colin had owned and hunted him for over nine years. Pam asked him to go catch Pukka and bring him in so he could be taken. Very sadly, Colin went to catch his horse and was walking back down the field with him telling him what a lovely wonderful horse he had been, what great days they had out in the hunting field and how grateful he was to this horse. He put Pukka on the wagon to go to the kennels. When Pam came out to take him, thankfully, she checked the back of the wagon and asked Colin why Bailey was in the wagon and not Pukka.

Pukka was still in the field and he had been and caught the wrong horse!

Later that year I got a call from John Gill. Wazzy was now seventeen, he had had the summer in the field but his arthritic hock was so bad he was very lame on it. I went straight down on the Sunday to see him and he looked aged. He still had a twinkle in his eye but John was right it was time. I agreed and the following Tuesday he went the journey.

The following Sunday I went down to the Gill's with a load of photographs of him. We all sat around the kitchen table looking at the pictures. Jayne got the wine out and we drank a toast to him. Chris got up quickly and left the room. Jayne was crying I am not sure who went first between John and me but safe to say we all had a good cry at the loss of this amazing fantastic horse that had given so much pleasure to so many people in his life.

Chapter Thirty Three

Brutus was sold to a lovely lady from Ripon and she had great success with him in dressage competitions. I had been back to Ireland numerous times and had a great time buying some horses. I also had an arrangement with Jim, whereby he sent me two horses at a time, for which I paid for one and then the other when it was sold.

I had some lovely horses through, but sadly some wrong ones too, and they had to go back. The return was free but getting them over was £200 per time. It worked out that I spent £1400 in returns and this was daft and a waste of money. I was out and about competing at unaffiliated eventing and dressage and decided I wanted to go back to proper eventing. I bought a lovely horse from the sales called Diamond Lad and he went up to Pre-Novice quickly. He was a bit quirky in the show jumping, choosing to rush his way around. It was just lack of confidence, but even with help from Ian Brown, we couldn't change him.

He was a brilliant hunter and I sold him to Charlie Kirk to hunt with the Bedale. This was the horse I was on the front of the programme, that Anne loved so much. He went on to Mat Penrose eventually and he is still hunting him now.

By now all my horses were pre-fixed with Manor House and I had become known for my daft names. I could only call them a name of my making of they were not already named on their passports. Each horse though, had its own stable name. One such horse came from Jim and he was a lovely old fashioned type of hunter. I called him Bernard the Butler. He was a big brute of a horse but in a nice way. Hell of a jump, brave and very bold.

I had a call from a man called Reg Hopkins. He hunts with his sons who are all over 6'2" tall and need fitting up with suitable horses. Reg hunts with the Berkley and was up in Yorkshire for a joint meet with the Sinnington, but the day had been cancelled due to the weather and could he come and see Bernard? I explained that the weather was so bad he had not been ridden for three days and that the roads and fields were iced over. Undeterred, he arrived with his lovely wife. He had on a flat cap, white jeans and dealer boots. He loved the look of him and, much against my better judgement, I tacked him up and put him on. He shot off up the road and disappeared into the gloom. I was quite worried and proper scared when he returned at full speed and went into the field and jumped him over a few jumps.

He came back to me, shook my hand and said 'Sold mate'. He came back the next day with cash and a wagon. I love those sales. Bernard, now renamed Yorkie Boy, has been great servant to Reg and his sons. I later sold him an enormous chestnut gelding which he took straight out hunting. I got a very quiet, whispering call from him a few weeks later. He was in hospital having taken a bad tumble of this horse and had all sorts of injuries. I was really worried about him but he is fine and still hunting into his seventies.

A big grey horse was bought at the sales, he was seven years old and a really nice dapple grey. I took him to a local hunter trials for a spin and a lady in her sixties came to try him. She took him around again and bought him there and then. He was a lovely horse and I was pleased to find him a great home for life.

Jimmy Cricket was a bay gelding I bought from Jim and he was 16.1hh. I took him straight into Pre-Novice at Northallerton Equestrian Centre and he went really well. At Beckwithshaw Horse Trials near Harrogate, the week after, and a lady called Jane Dracup, who had worked for me in the training company came up to me after I had finished. I was sat on the ramp and he was just grazing having been washed off. She gave me a blank cheque and told me to fill it in as she was buying him. I didn't do this of course but she came back and tried him and bought him the week after. Fergus, as she re-named him went up to One

Star level before striking into himself and damaging his leg which meant he had to have a year off.

On a trip to see Jim, I took my friends Craig and Melba to shop for a horse. We looked at several horses for Craig as a hunter and walked straight passed a fairly common looking liver chestnut. We tried greys and bays but nothing was suitable. I suggested, before going home empty handed, that he look at this chestnut. We got him out and he was a big horse. Called Romeo, he had a full book and looked well. Jess, who rides for Jim, jumped on him and took him into a field full of horses. She just galloped him around jumping all sorts of stuff.

On the way back up the field there was a five bar high post and rail fence leaning in towards the field we were in. Undeterred she just jumped him over it. I was very impressed but not as much as Craig and Melba. The finish was when Jim picked up a strand of plastic electric fence tape held it at a metre plus high and this wonderful horse just leapt it. Safe to say Craig couldn't get his money out quick enough. A couple of seasons later and Craig was invited to carry the whip for the Hurworth Hunt. He had come on so much from the early days with the Bedale. He is totally hooked on hunting and all it has to offer. Romeo carried him in the early days of his new position and he is a brilliant hunting horse.

At the same time I bought a big skewbald horse who I saw at the last minute. Jim asked me to take him and he was £2500. I only saw him in the stable and I liked him. I have always liked big coloured horses as they stand out. He was 17.1 hh and four years old. When he arrived I was even more impressed until I realised he was a shiverer. I did not want to keep him but other things took over.

This horse had a lovely eye and was a good looking lad. He was though, absolutely frightened to death of me and any other man. He had obviously had a bad time with some fella. When I went into the stable to be with him he tried his best to climb over the back wall to get away from me. I was used to horses like him though, having had Barry and others with a similar disposition. I spent hours with him in the stable just playing with his ears and talking to him, to make friends. In the wash box he was fine and settled in quite well. Clipping him was a doddle and he was a very slight shiverer. He also shod easily.

I schooled him all winter and he improved a great deal. He jumped, competed in dressage and hacked out with no problem in heavy traffic. I took him hunting and at the meet Pam asked, with scorn, what he was and what I was doing on a gypsy horse? Defending him to the hilt I said he was lovely. She said he should be pulling a milk cart and that was it. I named him Ernie the Milkman.

That day, his first, he was brilliant and he had obviously hunted before. I had a great day out on him and I was genuinely falling for this horse. I also had in a big grey called Oscar to sell and hunted him too, but now and then he would bronco like nothing else.

Mike Raper was a guy that hunted and was known by a lot of people. I did not know him very well at that point, but he was without a horse. He had been asking people for rides and had no luck. On Boxing Day he was at the meet on foot and looked fed up. He was asking people if anyone had a spare horse. I felt sorry for him. I called him later in the week and offered him Ernie to ride on New Year's Day.

He jumped at it. I told him the meet was at twelve and that I would be leaving the yard at eleven. I was up early and getting the yard done, washing the horses down as I had a skewbald and a dapple grey to do. At 10.30 he still had not appeared and so I called him. He said he was on his way as he had just got up. I was quietly furious. He turned up after I had boxed them. We set off to the meet and I got on the grey that bucked and he got on my lovely coloured horse.

An hour or so into the meet and Pam came to find me and asked me why I had lent him my horse. I explained that I felt sorry for him. She told me he was up front slagging the horse off and me too. I was incredulous. I went further up the field and someone else told me the same thing. I confronted him straight away and he blustered his way through some sort of answer. Later we were crossing a big open field, flat out, and the grey went on a spree. He was bucking like mad and for only the second time in the hunting field I hit the shit. I was okay but had to walk across the field to catch him. I was covered in mud and wet through. Thankfully, not long after, they blew for home.

Back in the wagon going home and I wanted to know why Mike had been slagging my horse off, saying it was a typical Steve Place horse and no good, why he had said it was as green as grass and he shouldn't be out on it.? He couldn't answer. I wanted to hit him. When we got back to the yard they were un-boxed into the stables and I got changed quickly from my wet muddy riding gear so I could wash them off and sort them out. He excused himself and fucked off, leaving me with two wet and muddy tacked up horses to sort out.

That was the start of a very poor friendship between Mike and me. A few years later I was asked to go onto the committee of the Northallerton Riding Club and I accepted. He was chairman and we often fell out. At almost every meeting he was critical of my input and I eventually after two years walked out. I had arranged various things for them in the two years I was on the committee. One was a lecture demonstration by Oliver who came up with Alan his dad. It was sold out more or less and we made good money for the club. It was great evening, he was very entertaining and great with the kids. I was the organiser of the annual horse trials we ran at Helen and Tom's and this took a lot of work.

The final straw was at a meeting when he was at it again criticising my arrangements for a coming series of competitions which I had organised. He went onto say that if I organised my business and private life like this, then he did not hold out much hope for me.

This from a shepherd, who lived in a caravan.

Chapter Thirty Four

I took Oscar, the bucking grey, to the team chase at Marton Cum Grafton and he flew round in good form. A lady spotted him and he was sold through that competition. Ernie was taken to Frickley to do the team chase there. I was in a team with Helen, Pam and Lucy Morgan. Lucy is a good friend, she started helping Helen out when she was younger and was very successful. She is a very talented young lady on a horse and it is a pity she has not had chance to further this into eventing at a higher level.

Helen wanted to go steady and use it as a schooling round. She also wanted to swap lead horses as we went around. Not a chance, I was there to win or else what was the point? I insisted on going first and we set off like stink. We were going great with Helen hollering at me to slow down.

I was laughing my head off to be honest, and Pam, who was behind me was laughing too. Sadly we lost Lucy as she fell off. Now in team chasing, you just carry on no matter what but Helen went back to make sure Lucy was okay, which she was. Only the two of us finished and the time was brilliant so we could have won. We had a great afternoon out and a good laugh. I had picked Pam up and taken one of Helen's other horses, and as a result, Pam and I sort of got back together again although it was very on and off and not really a proper relationship.

Ernie was brilliant at the team chase and I intended to register him for eventing. I took him to the Hornby Castle hunt meet with Lucy who was on a pony of Helen's. We had a great day but by 2pm I had had enough and so had the horses. We had jumped a lot of hedges and post and rails and I bid goodnight and went back to the wagon. I got off him and put my left arm through the reins. I was trying to loosen his girth and other horses were whizzing up and down. He panicked a bit and tried to run off. I was shouting at him when he ran away from me and I still had hold of his reins. He doubled barrelled me with his back legs. One in the face and one in the chest. I just sat down on the floor instantly out cold. Ernie ran off. He jumped two cattle grids, ran straight across both lanes of the A1 and was found in a field next to the A1 without a scratch and his tack was perfectly intact too.

I kept coming in and out of consciousness and an ambulance came. I was laid now on a horsebox ramp with Pam laid over me holding my hand. I couldn't breathe though, and had to shout at her to get her off my chest. She was very worried and upset and came to the hospital with me in the ambulance which was a blue light journey to hospital. I had been lucky as he had hit me in the face on the right hand side and missed my nose by a whisker. I had broken four ribs though and boy, that was painful. I was let out the next day and struggled for weeks mucking out and dealing with the horses I had in. Lucy and her mum Liz were fabulous and helped me out every day.

It's funny how rumours spread and it was thought by many that I was in a coma and seriously injured. I had lots of lovely messages and best wishes which was fabulous.

I later took two, lovely young horses off Jim and two sisters from Aberdeen came and bought the big chestnut who went on to represent Scotland at Preliminary Dressage at the Home Internationals. He also won many working hunter classes. The bay horse that came with him was called on his passport, 'The Perfect Jumper. ' Now who would have ever called a horse this? Someone not in their right mind! I did sell him to a girl from Pontefract as a hack and light competition horse.

Ernie's first event was at Richmond. I entered not knowing if my entry would be accepted, but it was. I was later told that this was an oversight and if they had known I would have been balloted. I went back the next day and fence judged with Pam for the day and had lunch in the sponsors' tent as Pam was sponsoring a section. I was told later that when Judith found out she was turning over tables in her temper. I do know that when I went back on the Monday to help Helen video some of her horses as they jumped round on the schooling day, Judith called Helen and told her I was most certainly not welcome.

Ernie was double clear so I was happy about that but the dressage was not that good. He did two more and was average. I liked him though so was not that bothered. At the area Riding Club competition he was in the Pre-Novice level section and did really well.

The lady that had bought the grey horse, after the hunter trial, came to see me at Bishop Burton. They were looking for a sensible horse for her husband and he had fallen for Ernie. They bought him and later, with a friend of theirs riding him, he qualified for the Grassroots Championship at Badminton Horse Trials.

I bought another coloured horse soon after selling Ernie. He was 17.2 hh and piebald I hunted him in the autumn and he stood like a stallion. I loved him he was a gorgeous' look at me' horse with a superior, big presence. I was not going to sell this one quickly, not a chance. NO way was this beauty going anywhere However, he did.

A girl came to look at a bay horse I had in but did not like him. She saw the piebald's head over the door, and that was it. I told her he was not for sale, and even an outrageous price for him did not deter her, so he went. I told myself that, at the end of the day, I was in the business of making a living by selling, but it was cold comfort.

We went to Cavan sales in Northern Ireland. This was a funny sales and I don't know why, but I detected an atmosphere which I felt uncomfortable in. We had to drive through Belfast to get there from the airport and it was an eerie drive. Anyway, at the sales there was some real crap, proper rubbish, which I was surprised about. Two girls were there with a really nice bay horse, they were kissing him and being very attentive. I saw them ride him and they were not very good but he moved really well. He was 16.2 hh and five years old.

I spoke to them and unless they were very good actresses they were genuine about him. He had hunted lightly that autumn and was ready to go. He was a Warmblood but bred in Ireland. He was a proper sweetie and I thought he would make silly money. Far from it, he was knocked down to me for £1800 and I was very happy. The man with him and the two girls was not happy about the price though and would not make him lucky.

The other horses in the sale were fetching really daft money and I did not buy anything else although I wanted two. Helen only managed two smaller ones, so all in all it was disappointing. We always used Eddie McMahon to travel them home for us, he was very good and looked after them well. We never got them back with rubbed bottoms as we did with others on a regular basis. They had rugs on if they needed them and he gave them a bit if ACP if they were not travelling well.

Back home and this gelding was a lovely horse. A family came from the Brocklesby hunt and the wife tried him first. It was very frosty again and slippery. I had just clipped him too and he was very fresh. When I got off he would not stand still for her to get on, but she managed. The first jump he took, he bucked afterwards and I thought right, that's that then.

No she loved him. Her hubby had on green overalls and those cheap green wellies that dairy men wear and a flat cap. He leapt on and took off. I was cringing but he was a good jockey. He jumped him around the whole course and two of the jumps were of advanced proportions. Sold, subject to him going well on Boxing Day out hunting. He did go well, he was so well behaved and a good one that one. Good profit made, it was a good trade, that horse.

Back in Ireland a couple of weeks later, at Gorsebridge, I bought a great big bay horse. He was six years old and 17.3 hh but he was also very well built. My days, he moved and as he was an Irish Warmblood he had great presence. I got him home and took him hunting straight away. We met at Langton Hall which was always a good jumping day.

I never got near a jump. He was good at the meet and stood well. When they moved off though, he went berserk. He blew his head and I could not hold one side of him. I had to go home after half an hour. He was going to hurt himself, someone else or worse, me. It took him two days to settle down again. I started schooling him though and it was a pleasure. It felt like you were sat on a Rolls Royce. I advertised him as a dressage horse and took him unaffiliated and he won his first two classes. He was sold to a lovely girl from York. Actually she was gorgeous, so the selling process was a pleasure.

It was the latter end of the hunting season and trade was very good so Jim sent me two more horses. A black thoroughbred looking Irish bred sport horse that was weak and not totally level behind. He had a wonky back leg and I should have sent him back really. Pam told me I could turn him out at her place as she needed company for one of hers. The other horse was special, he was a great big bay horse called Buster.

He had a phenomenal jump and out hunting he was amazing. I wanted a lot of money for him and missed the last bit of the season so I was stuck with him. I took him jumping and to a couple of hunt organised hedge hops but he was an out and out hunter. I turned him out too, just up the road at a farm.

I had always had thoroughbreds passing through and was contacted by a lady called Fiona Scott as she had some horses in to sell. I went to have a look and bought from her a very nice bay gelding. He was 16 hh and a chunky horse which is the type I preferred. I only had him a couple of weeks and sold him. I went back to Fiona and bought another from her and sold that quickly too. Fiona was surprised at my turnover and asked me to take one on her behalf and sell it to make her some profit as she was struggling.

I agreed to help her and she brought me a black mare. This horse had a serious problem. You could not put a bridle on. She shook her head violently when you did manage to get one on. I got the vet as I felt so sorry for her. When he came she was tied up in the wash box and when he went to her she went up vertical, tearing her headcollar in bits and she fell over backwards onto the floor. I was shocked and so was the vet. We couldn't do anything with her and I called Fiona and explained the problem. She was not a happy girl and even though I asked her to bring me another she refused.

When she came to pick her up she was shouting the odds about the state of the horse and that it had lost loads of weight and was in a terrible state. I have to say I lost my temper with this lady. The mare was fine and had not lost any weight in a week. I stood the cost of the vet myself. I was only trying to help her after all.

I went back to Ireland to see Jim and bought a nice event type gelding, he was five years old and a real stunning looking little horse. I made a big mistake though as the flight over on Ryan Air was £1.99 and the return that day was £170 so if I waited until six a.m. the next morning the flight back was £12. I decided to sleep in the airport and went through security and waited at the Ryan Air gates in the terminal.

A Garda came to find me and told me I was airside and therefore could not be there until the gates opened next day. I was escorted through the terminal back to the shops and restaurant area where I had to wait. It was packed with other people sleeping and waiting. I did not get a wink of sleep on the couches and chairs. It was so warm and noisy. I was knackered when I did get home and it was a lesson learned, never to be repeated.

Chapter Thirty Five

The rest of that summer flew by very quickly but some major changes were taking place. Tom and Helen had bought a new place called The Paddocks at Breckenbrough, which was a few miles away in a village called Sandhutton. It had been racehorse training centre and had all weather gallops, a swimming pool and about 100 acres of land. They have now turned it into a very successful events centre and hold BE affiliated events. The cross country courses Tom has built are extensive and superb.

They asked me to go with them and rent a yard from them as there were fifty five boxes. I thought about it for ages but politely declined and decided to look for a place of my own. It was going to take ages to sort out the move so I was okay for the foreseeable future. They put their property up for sale straightaway but it was not selling.

The bay horse with the wonky leg was still turned out at Pam's yard and she called me about him asking what I was going to do with him. I said I would come and get him, but she stunned me by saying she was wanting to buy him from me. I was very surprised. I went down to the yard, and only by a fluke, arrived just as a vet was vetting him. Stuart from Stirks vets was there looking him over. I asked what the hell was going on and very sheepishly, she told me her next door neighbour had fallen in love with the horse and wanted to buy him.

I asked her how much she had asked the neighbour and she said £500. I told her no chance, I had paid £1800 for the horse and £200 to get him home. She did her best to deride him and the vet, surprise, surprise, failed him on a flexion test. When he understood that the horse was actually mine and that I did not know anything about the vetting, he was very embarrassed but also quite annoyed. It also turned out that she had promised the neighbour the horse for £500. I said I would pick the horse up after Burghley, in a fortnight.

Burghley Horse Trials were two weeks away and as we always had gone together, I had asked a few times if we were going. She was very non-committal about it, saying she could not afford the time off and she was not sure about going. This had been going on for a while and I was getting fed up with it. On the Sunday before Burghley she would still not say if we were going or not. I picked up her daughter Amelia from a garage where she had dropped her car off for a service. The plan was to go back to Pam's house for Sunday lunch.

On the way back I asked Amelia about Burghley and why her mum was being difficult about it. Amelia told me they were both going for the whole weekend and had got tickets and were staying with a friend of hers, and what was worse was, that they had planned it weeks ago. I dropped her at home and went on my way home.

I had been in an on/off relationship with Pam for three years and had had enough. The next day I went to the school took my horse and that was it. The horse sold within two months of me getting him back. As I had to get him back into work and produce him a bit, I was pleased to have him away.

In the autumn I brought Buster back into work and got him fit and looking well. I advertised him on Horse and Hound online at ten a.m. on a Friday morning. At 10.30 I had a call from a lady called Jane. She was the Field Master for the Grafton. After some very direct questioning about him she said she would be at the yard at 5p.m.

She arrived with her husband, Stuart Hastie, who is a renowned vet and had been the equestrian team vet for GB, he has also written many books. He was on a walking stick now though. I got the horse out and ready and started riding him. After a few minutes, Jane asked me if he would jump the five foot high post and rail fence that was around the edge of the field. I asked her if he did, was she going to buy him, and she said yes. I took him into the next field and jumped him back over the rails. He soared it and I think she was quite impressed. She rode him for little more than five minutes and agreed to buy him.

They both then went on to vet him and had so many arguments it became funny. But I was wide awake and realised quickly that this was a strategy to point out technical things wrong with him to get the purchase price down. They eventually finished, after several cups of tea. They made an offer which was low, based on the fact that he had a slight slip in his stifle. I was not having this of course, and even though she was a tough negotiator, the price came up much more towards my original asking price.

I was impressed with this lady, she knew her stuff, could sit a horse and was very forthright. I was even more impressed when she rang Coutts Bank at seven thirty in the evening and had the money transferred into my account.

The next day I was judging the hunter classes at Osmotherley show near Thirsk and her groom turned up to pick Buster up. I was not expecting her so soon, but it proved that she is a lady that gets things done.

A lady called me about a bay horse I had for sale. He was a hunter type I had bought from a lady near York. He had hunted and whipped in. She was very posh and spoke with a right mouth full of marbles. The horse was intended for her son who was going to whip in for the Bedale West of Yore.

They came to try him and the lad was a good rider. He jumped him all around the cross country field and came back with a big smile. The mother then dropped the bombshell that her daughter Pandy, (short for Pandora), would have to try the horse before they could buy it. I explained that it was for her son and he was happy with him. She was not having this though, and she insisted that Pandy simply must come and approve the horse too. The problem was, that Pandy was down with the Fox Pitts, and would not be back for two weeks. She asked me did I know the Fox Pitts? 'No' said I. I can't stand name droppers. Fair enough, off they went. Although she wanted me to keep him for them without a deposit, I refused of course and said they would run the danger of missing him, but she was adamant that I should not sell him in the coming two weeks before Pandy returned.

I had the enormous pleasure, when she did call, of telling her he was gone and had been sold. She just would not believe me, and to be honest, I felt really sorry for her son as he would have been well mounted.

In the spring a friend of mine called and asked me to go to the Malvern horse sales in Worcestershire. I did not really want to go but she had seen a nice horse she wanted to buy and she wanted me to go help her have a look. It had to go to the sales to dissolve a partnership of ownership.

She offered to buy me a full English breakfast and so I said 'yes'. We got there and the horse she wanted was bloody awful and I talked her out of it. I found her another though and she was very happy. Whilst I was there, I was watching the horses parading outside, waiting to go into the sales ring. A big giant of a horse was playing up and he eventually got away from his handler and skipped across the grass area with this tail aloft, snorting. He seriously moved and had a hell of moment of suspension in the trot.

I groaned because I did not really want another horse, but I sought out the seller who, it turned out, had bred him. He was by Maximillian Saluut and was out of an Irish bred mare. He was three, rising four and 17hh, broken, but he had not done a great deal. He was there to be sold as he had grown so big and she wanted shut because as she said to me 'I can't keep them all'.

Twenty minutes later and he was mine... bugger. I really did not want another but he moved so well I could not resist him. I shared the costs of the transport home with my friend.

Three weeks later and I rode Max (as he was now known) into the International Arena at Bramham Horse Trials to compete in the Burghley young event horse 4 year old class. He performed a fabulous test and in the jumping he had a really naughty, sneaky baby boy run out at the second part of the double. The conformation test did not go well and that was understandable as he was a really big, gangly, youth and looked weak. He did get the second best dressage mark out of 49 entries with Caroline Powell the only one to beat us. I was a happy boy.

In view of Tom and Helen moving to their new place, I was looking for somewhere to base myself. I had looked at a couple of stable yards but none were suitable. Ian Anderson, Master of the Hurworth Hunt, offered me his place as he was giving it up. Haggit Hill was a Georgian farmhouse with eleven stables and good pasture grazing. It was very big the house but enchanting. I negotiated for months with Savilles Estate Agents but they were very difficult and very unhelpful and it did not come off.

I was desperate to find somewhere, especially when I found out that Pam and her new boyfriend, John Chadwick, were moving into Tom and Helen's old house and therefore would have control of the arena and cross country course. I have nothing against John, I have known him since we were kids back in Bradford and he competed at Aire Valley on his pony, Bomber.

She though, was like a an itch I could not scratch, Tom and Helen both apologised profusely to me, but as they explained, they couldn't sell the property so the next best thing was to rent it out, which I understood fully.

The first thing they did was put up my contribution toward the cost of the arena and cross country course. I used to pay Tom and Helen £120 per month to use both and Pam put it up to £200! Sod that I was off. I eventually managed to rent four large fields in a nearby village and moved out. The horses I had were off for six months whilst I secured a place of my own.

It is a typical thing that when you are looking for somewhere or something you can never find what you need. When you are not looking of course, five come at the same time. I had to wait an awful long time that early spring to find somewhere, and in between, all I could do was keep the three horses I had ticking over. Lucy Morgan was a brilliant help to me, coming to hack out and helping me with them in general. It was a dire time for me really. I did a small amount of competing with them but I cannot say I enjoyed it.

Chapter Thirty Six

Leases Hall was built in 1704 it was originally a coaching inn for the Great North Road. Next to the now A1, it is ideally placed for transport to and from equestrian centres and the local hunts. It came available after the Highways authority had purchased it from the owner when they began to upgrade the road. They then found out that they did not need the land so the property was up for rent.

I first went to see it in the previous November and it was in a right old state, they had had water leaks all over the house but it was salvageable. The land extended to 38 acres of post and rail fencing grazing land and it had a 60x25 arena and 23 stables. Perfect. The house is a mansion and has eight bedrooms five bathrooms and two kitchens! I did not want this but it came as a complete package. I submitted an application for a five year lease, which was turned down.

It was January when they called me asking if I was still interested. The situation at the yard was getting worse with Pam there and I jumped at it. Further negotiations took place whilst my horses were moved and turned out. I actually signed up for it in August but moved the horses there in the June. I loved it from the outset and felt right at home. I quickly filled up with liveries. I was at Bramham HorseTrials, helping Rupert Cox with his horse as he was in the working hunter class which was a qualifier for HOYS, when I got the call to say it was mine.

I had some more horses sent over from Jim. One was a 17hh coloured gelding called Woody and a bay horse, 16.2 hh, called Lost in the Fog (Foggy). Foggy was superb. He was a fabulous hunter and jumped a 1.05m track with ease. I had him quickly sold for a lot of money, but the vet said he had a serious heart murmur. I was furious, a good sale down the tubes and especially, when I had him checked by two other vets for clarification, neither could find anything wrong with him.

Woody was a lovely horse too. I kept him to run alongside Max who I was going to event during the next season. Max was slow to furnish himself and I knew it was going to be a long term project. He did really well at dressage though and he enjoyed cross country schooling. His problem was jumping over the coloured poles. He was just so big he found it very difficult to shorten up and regularly had one or more down. I was convinced, that with grid work, he would get better, and as he got stronger he would get more athletic.

I started hunting Woody but this time with the Hurworth hunt, as they were less inclined to set off like stink from the outset, and my young horses lasted a little longer than one hour before they blew up. Craig, my friend, was now whipping in for them and they were a very pleasant group of people.

Evelyn (Tad) Beeney asked if she could borrow Woody for a day with the Bedale, as they were hunting over her boyfriend's land, and she had a free day. Tad used to be a Whip with the Hurworth and is a very stylish, careful and brave jockey. My only worry though, was that she was three months pregnant. I reluctantly agreed as, knowing her, she would have got a horse from somewhere and better the devil you know. She had a fantastic day on him, jumping everything direct and thrusted up the front all day.

I competed him in dressage and he was always placed. He was a fabulous allrounder. One Sunday, on a day off, I was bored and I knew there was a coloured horse show on at the local centre, Northallerton. I caught him, washed him off plaited him and set off.

When I got there it was bedlam. Coloured horses everywhere. I went to see the entries lady who was very surprised to see me. I entered the Novice Ridden Horse class as it was really only what I could do. I had not got a clue what to do as I had never been showing in my life. I asked about and found out the rudimentary rules of the class. I went in the arena and there were a lot of horses in the class. I positioned myself right in the middle so I would not have to go first at anything.

After the first bit I was pulled in second, I couldn't believe it. We did a show, of sorts, then everyone took off their saddles. "What was that about?" I asked myself. I trotted him up for the judges and saddled him up again. The final walk, trot and canter around brought me into second. I was happy and the prizes we won were fabulous. I also had a certificate saying Woody had qualified for the World of Colour at Peterborough later in the year.

I decided to sell him and offered him for sale at a whopping price. He sold very quickly although we had a laugh along the way. Lord and Lady Middleton had been earlier and bought a lovely big bay horse from me for Lady Middleton. Pauline was over the moon with him.

They were now looking for a horse for her husband. They came to try Woody but had not told him he was a piebald horse. He was not amused, although he liked him. He took him for a gallop in my big back field and when he came back his groom, Karen, asked him what he thought. His reply was, 'He wouldn't win a race'. I knew then he wouldn't buy him.

Merry Mate Boy is a 16.1 hh 5year old I got from Jim. He is a lovely horse and moved, jumped and had it all. The first lady to try him came all the way up from Northampton, one Sunday, with her hubby. She had called a few times to make sure he was not gone and tell me how much she loved the look of him on his video and photographs.

She also told me that she had looked at dozens of horses. Now this, for any dealer, is usually the seal of doom in that people that look at dozens of horses are usually time wasters and end up buying a totally unsuitable horse for them that is very talented and ends up in a field for most of its life.

They arrived at eleven a.m. and the husband, as soon as he saw him, was enthused. He was saying how much the horse was the best by far they had seen. She was gushing too. We took him into the arena and Sam, who worked for me, rode him, jumped him and showed him off. The sun was out too, which always helps. She couldn't wait to get on him and so we got her on board and did the stirrups adjustment and everything else she needed.

She rode him away from us, down the long side of the school and across the diagonal, straight back toward us. She stopped and said 'He is perfect, a lovely horse and everything you said he was.' There was a slight silence, and then she said 'But he is not for me'. Her husband shouted 'What?' She went on to explain that she thought he was wonderful but she just knew he wasn't for her.

Nothing surprises me about people buying horses nowadays, I just find it soul destroying at times how some people behave. Her husband apologised and was clearly angry. She was apologising too but I did not care. I just said to her, 'Don't worry love, it's not a problem but I am glad I am not in that car with your hubby for the next four hours'.

I sold Merry Mate Boy to a lady called Jackie Tait and she loves him. He has gone Novice level eventing and has proved to be a fabulous horse for her. She keeps me informed all the time about how he is doing and it is lovely to hear how horses are doing.

That first winter at Leases was fabulous. The liveries were happy and proved to be a good secondary income stream from dealing. I had a great house warming party and took different horses hunting out with the Hurworth. Max was getting stronger and I could not wait to event him.

A friend of mine introduced me to a man who brought me some really nice Dutch Warmblood dressage horses. The first one was a big bay gelding, 6 years old and 16.3hh. He was beautiful and although I competed him and got placed every time out including a few wins, he had to go. I was very tempted to keep him though. He of course sold straight away and even though I made a very good profit on him, I was sorry to see him go.

Dressage had grown exponentially over the last few decades and is now a massive sport. Ladies mainly were embracing it and spending good money on horses that moved well. I had always enjoyed competing and the people involved were very nice on the whole.

I bought two more horses from this fella and they were mares, something I normally stay clear of. A bay mare, by For Pleasure, who had won an Olympic gold with Marcus Henning in show jumping. She sold eventually into show jumping but we had problems with her as she was quite temperamental. The other mare a bright chestnut called Beaudine with matching stockings and was by Good Times, another jumping stallion. Much more straightforward, she moved beautifully and was much more bent towards dressage.

I had to pay a further £75 on top of the registration fee to British Dressage to get her down-graded, as on importation she was automatically awarded 250 points. I competed her and a very good friend of mine, Elaine Wombwell, rode her for me too. Elaine is an excellent rider and has two fabulous horses she is progressing up the ranks. He friend Debby Dunleavy used to be a nightclub singer, she is very funny and down to earth. She has a fabulous horse that just wins everything for her. These two girls have had more column space in the Horse and Hound than Carl Hester and that is saying something. They have just had so much success. Beaudine was always placed and got points straight away, just missing out on the Regional Final qualifications.

The first lady to view her came from Scotland. Her friend came too as she was trying a horse belonging to a friend of mine that I had advertised on my website. I had her advertised at £10,000. They arrived on time from Central Scotland and they were in a small old Peugeot 106 that had the back wing and wheel arch missing.

I showed her Beaudine in my wash box and she seemed to like her. She asked if she could see her trotted up. Sam took her out and walked her away. The lady said, completely out of the blue, 'Oh no, the Selector's won't like her walk.' I was startled and said 'Selectors, what do you mean?' She came straight back with 'Yep, GB Dressage Selectors.' So I asked her if she was on the Olympic pathway or the star spotters programme and she said no she wasn't. I asked her 'So are you hoping to get on a GB Dressage team?' She said she was.

Now any team horse, prospective or established, is not going to be £10,000, competing at Novice level but working at Elementary. I was astounded. I said to her, 'If you ever get selected for the GB team or the training squad, the selectors will have changed by then so how do you know what they are looking for in a walk?' She did not reply.

I was fed up with this girl and what she had said. It was insulting to my horse, and to me. I said 'Do you know who the selectors are at the moment, and do you know the horses chosen have to be Grand Prix?' She said she did. I asked her if she had ever ridden at Grand Prix, and she hadn't.

She went on to tell me though, very seriously, that she had taken her friend's horse from Medium level dressage to Prix St George in three months. I just said 'You have as much chance of getting selected for the GB Dressage team as my car love'. Thankfully, her friend bought the other horse and I got commission on that sale to make it worth my while. People honestly are so trying at times. They have ideas way above their ability or pocket.

Beaudine was later sold to a glamour model who turned up for her in a bright pink horsebox, tried her, paid for her there and then via her mobile phone, and took her away. Best sales, those.

I had a call from a lady looking for dressage horses. She had seen my website and was interested in them all. She turned up and being a big built lady, not fat, just an amazon type of lady, I was not sure I had anything in big enough. She had qualified horses for HOYS although she had not ridden them herself. I showed her all my horses but she did not like any of them.

She asked me for a cup of tea and use of the loo which I agreed to. She went to her car for her ipad and when we were in the kitchen, she opened it at pictures of the horse she owned. I was flicking the screen through these pictures and she said 'Oh don't go too far.' I flicked on and then was presented with pictures of her lying legs akimbo, naked on her bed! I was shocked, flicked again and another picture came up with her naked. A few weeks later, a fella I know who sells horses, called me and told me about a woman that had been to look at his horses and who had insisted on showing him pictures of her horse, which were not just pictures of her horse. We had a laugh, but it makes you wonder about people.

In the spring I took Max to four BE events. He always did a lovely test and was clear across country. The first three were at 90cm level and the last one was at BE 100. The problem with him was, that he could not cope with the show jumping. He had three or more down at each event, and to be frank, it was a waste of money and my time taking him to any more. I knew that my serious eventing days were over, and although I had always struggled with my weight I had managed, when younger, to keep it in check with fasting and cycling an awful lot. It was much more difficult now though, and the incentive was not there.

I was gutted really as I was hoping he, Max, was going to be my swan song. I was also privately fed up but took it in good part when, at Bishop Burton, the commentator described me as one of the 'elder statesmen of eventing'.

The rest of that year I competed in dressage. I had some success and at unaffiliated level I had a good deal of success. The want to get up and go competing, two or three days per week though, was waning. I hit a big stone wall when Sam, who had been living in the flat with her boyfriend, walked out on me over something and nothing.

I had been and bought wormers for all the horses. I asked her to worm them before their tea time feeds. A week later I found the wormers in the vet cupboard. I did not shout at her, that has never been my style, but I did remonstrate with her about not worming them. She left the next day and took her horse with her. I was totally dumbstruck, but that's people.

I then had a succession of girls come to work for a week on trial, that were totally not suitable. They were either inexperienced, lazy, or their attitude stank. I managed to get Debs Collinson to come part-time and she was very good, knew her stuff and was funny and a pleasure to work with. The problem was she could not school, she hacked out brilliantly, but could not school.

Things came to a head one Monday morning in October. Debs was pulling manes and I had nothing to do, so I decided to go to the garage and fill my car with diesel and get some coffees. On the way back a car came flying out of a gateway and broadsided my car, bent it in two and knocked me out. I came round in the ambulance and was okay. My left knee though was not, I was in a lot of pain and it swelled up like a football.

I went to the Festival of British Dressage the following Sunday but could not ride properly. Max came 10th in the Open Novice section but we should have done much better. I could not ride and all three horses were roughed off to be turned out. Just before Christmas I was walking down the steps into the stables with feed buckets in my arm, my knee locked and I fell. I broke a rib.

I was in trouble now. Debbie had left as I had no work for her. I could not ride and eventually had to have two MRI scans to find out the damage to my knee.

My decision to retire form horses full time was taken on Christmas day. My eldest son rang me to wish me Happy Christmas. I was out in the yard, struggling to muck out three and was having trouble breathing. My son calmly but firmly told me off and suggested that enough was enough.

I sat down when he rang off, and had a good long think. I was not enjoying competing. I was not making a great living from dealing as, due to the recession, horses were difficult to sell in the numbers I had been. I realistically was not going to event again and certainly not at the level I wanted to, and this had always been my first love. I managed to sell the two dealing horses just after Christmas, leaving me with Max. I then sold all my tack, saddles, horsebox and other stuff that you collect over the years. People were coming and making ridiculous offers for the things I was offering at knock down prices. I told more than one where to go and asked them to leave.

So that was it, a lifetime of horses and competing. Seven days a week 365 days a year, for 45 or so years, working with horses, living with them, looking after their every need, competing them, buying them, producing them, selling them and loving them all.

I have many wonderful memories and some not so wonderful. I have met some wonderful people and have made many lifelong friends. Funny encounters keep me chuckling, as I recall them. I have the constant reminder in my left arm of just how difficult and dangerous it can be.

My final thought on this religion that has been horses, comes from my dad, Raymond. He always use to say the same thing and we often told him to shut up going on about it, but on reflection he was dead right:

'Horses are the most wonderful creatures, what a shame they bring out the worse in people'.

Other books from SAP Books

All rights reserved.

DODGE CITY (A Coppers tale)

The rollercoaster tale of a young Bradford lad who joins the police force as a Cadet. The story takes you through his initial training and on into the world of policing a large city centre and all that that brings. It was a strange and difficult time dealing with the Yorkshire Ripper, the inner city riots and the miners' strike. It also deals with the tragedy of the Bradford City Football fire where 56 people lost their lives.

Funny, tragic and sad, it is a real journey through policing a varied urban city. Honest and real it pulls no punches and gives a true insight into what goes on.

DONKEY WALLOPER (A Coppers tale part II)

The second part of the story of a young Bradford lad working as an experienced constable on the streets of Bradford. This story takes you through his time as a detective, his ups and downs and flirtations with undercover work. The vice squad, dealing with rapes, child abuse and shoplifting, and eventually his transfer from mainstream policing to the highly specialised Mounted Branch are covered.

An honest account of the day to day life of a copper. Pulling no punches and being a real inward look at the police at that time, it is eye opening account of a young lad's journey.

Available from the author direct, Kindle and Kindle Direct and Amazon Books

Printed in Great Britain
by Amazon.co.uk, Ltd.,
Marston Gate.